DAILY LIFE OF

THE
ANCIENT
GREEKS

DAILY LIFE OF
THE
ANCIENT
GREEKS

ROBERT GARLAND

The Greenwood Press "Daily Life Through History" Series

GREENWOOD PRESS
Westport, Connecticut • London

Library of Congress Cataloging-in-Publication Data

Garland, Robert.
    Daily life of the Ancient Greeks / Robert Garland.
       p. cm.—(The Greenwood Press "Daily life through history"
series, ISSN 1080–4749)
    Includes bibliographical references and index.
    ISBN 0–313–30383–5 (alk. paper)
    1. Greece—Social life and customs. 2. Greece—Civilization—To
146 B.C. I. Title. II. Series.
DF78.G276   1998
938—DC21   97–53109

British Library Cataloguing in Publication Data is available.

Library of Congress Catalog Card Number: 97–53109
ISBN: 0–313–30383–5
ISSN: 1080–4749

First published in 1998

Greenwood Press, 88 Post Road West, Westport, CT 06881
An imprint of Greenwood Publishing Group, Inc.

Printed in the United States of America

The paper used in this book complies with the
Permanent Paper Standard issued by the National
Information Standards Organization (Z39.48–1984).

10 9 8 7 6 5 4 3 2 1

For my mother, who never ceases to look forward

Contents

Chronology

All dates are B.C.

The conventional divisions:

c. 1600–c. 1100	Mycenaean Period
c. 1100–c. 900	Dark Age
c. 900–c. 725	Geometric Period
c. 725–c. 630	Orientalizing Period
c. 630–480	Archaic Period
480–323	Classical Period
323–31	Hellenistic Period
c. 1600	Mycenaeans come into contact with Minoan civilization based on Crete
c. 1500	Shaft graves built at Mycenae
c. 1150	Approximate date for destruction of Troy
c. 1100	Collapse of Mycenaean civilization
c. 800	Earliest evidence of writing in Greece
776	Traditional date for the first celebration of the Olympic Games

c. 735–715	First Messenian War
c. 730	Colonization movement begins
c. 700	Homer composes the *Iliad* and *Odyssey*
c. 700	Hoplite armor invented
669	Spartans defeated by Argives at Hysiai
c. 660	Sparta crushes Messenian Revolt
c. 650	Formation of Peloponnesian League
594–593	Solon introduces economic and constitutional reforms in Athens
546	Peisistratos establishes tyranny in Athens
508–507	Kleisthenes introduces constitutional reforms
499–496	Ionian cities revolt from Persia
490	Athens defeats a Persian invasion force at Marathon
487	Athens' magistrates are henceforth elected by lot
482	Athens builds a fleet
480	Persian invasion of Greece launched by Xerxes; victory of Greek fleet over Persians at Salamis
479	Defeat of Persian army at Plataiai and of Persian fleet at Mykale
478	Formation of Delian Confederacy under Athenian leadership
464	Earthquake in Sparta; helot revolt in Messenia
461	Peaceful democratic revolution takes place in Athens
460–450	Payment introduced for Athenian jurors
458	Aeschylus produces his trilogy *Oresteia*
447	Athens begins extensive building program under supervision of Perikles
443	Beginning of Perikles' political ascendancy
431	Outbreak of Peloponnesian War
429	Death of Perikles
421	Peace of Nikias brokered between Athens and Sparta
415	Athens sends out expedition to conquer Sicily

413	Athenian disaster in Sicily Sparta resumes hostilities against Athens
404	Surrender of Athens
404–403	Spartan-backed oligarchy, known as the Thirty Tyrants, rules Athens
399	Execution of Sokrates
338	Philip II of Macedon defeats a coalition of Greek states at Chaironeia, thereby putting an end to Greek freedom
336	Death of Philip II of Macedon and accession of Alexander the Great
334	Alexander crosses into Asia
331	Foundation of Alexandria in Egypt
323	Death of Alexander at Babylon
146	Romans sack Corinth
31	Octavian defeats Mark Antony at Actium

Maps

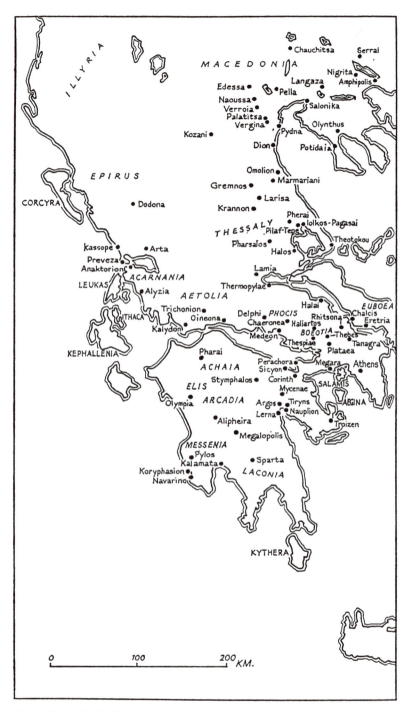

Map of mainland Greece. From D. Kurtz and J. Boardman, *Greek Burial Customs* (London: Thames and Hudson, 1971). Courtesy of University of Oxford.

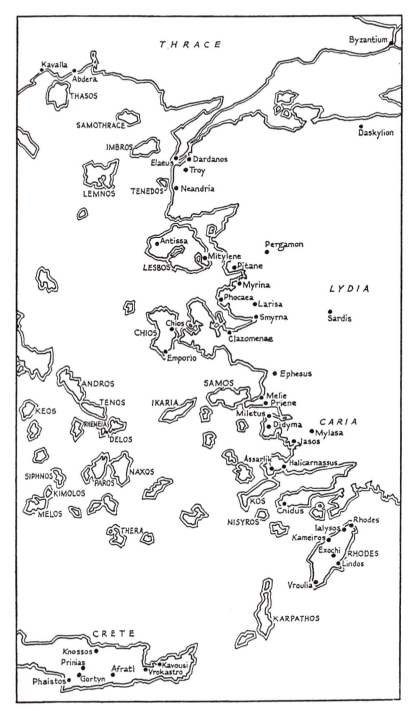

Map of eastern Greece. From D. Kurtz and J. Boardman, *Greek Burial Customs* (London: Thames and Hudson, 1971). Courtesy of University of Oxford.

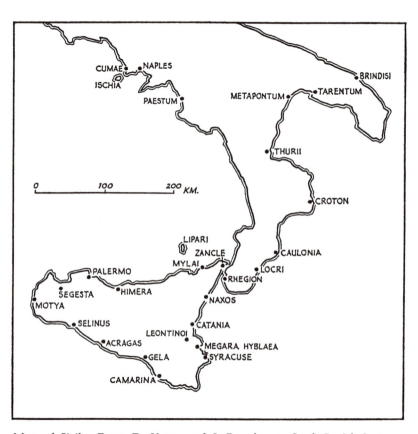

Map of Sicily. From D. Kurtz and J. Boardman, *Greek Burial Customs* (London: Thames and Hudson, 1971). Courtesy of University of Oxford.

Author's Note

All translations of Greek text included in this book have been made by the author. Bibliographic references that are provided refer to any standard edition of Greek texts, not to specific copyrighted translations. Students can refer to any English translation of the works cited. Translations of inscriptions that appear in Greek epigraphical works are also included, but no sources are provided for these as they can be consulted easily only by those who read Greek. In other instances, the author has noted "in fragment from a lost work" because the fragments in question appear only in scholarly Greek anthologies. Finally, the author has used standard Greek notation for those Greek authors who wrote only one work: that is, only the section of the work is noted, and no title is given.

Finally, I would like to thank Roger Just and Pavlos Sfyroeras for teaching me so much about Greekness, ancient and modern.

Introduction

There are serious limitations to any book that calls itself *Daily Life of the Ancient Greeks*. To begin with, it is impossible to confine our description of daily life to a single chronological period. The evidence is far too fragmented and disjointed. Similarly we cannot assume that the picture which we build up incorporates more than a small part of the geographical whole that we identify as the Greek world. There are vast areas about which we know very little because the people who inhabited them, though essentially Greek, have left few traces of their way of life. In the Classical era we know most about Athens and its surrounding countryside. This is due not only to the fact that Athens' population has bequeathed to us a wealth of archaeological data in the form of household objects, remains of buildings, depictions on vases, and so forth, but also because Athens was an extremely literate society whose literature contains plentiful allusions to daily life. After Athens, we probably know most about Sparta. This is not because Sparta possessed any of the attributes that I have just ascribed to Athens—Sparta was in many ways the exact antithesis of Athens—but because historians and philosophers were fascinated by Spartan society and wrote a great deal about it. We know relatively little about other major centers, such as Corinth, Thebes, and Megara, on the Greek mainland. And when we move outside the world of the city-states or *poleis*, as these communities were called, the picture becomes extremely hazy. Even though Macedon became the dominant Greek power from the 330s B.C. onward and conquered virtually the whole known world, we know next to nothing about the daily life of the Macedonians and can say little about its distinguishing characteristics. For the Hellenistic era (i.e., post-323 B.C.), we have abundant evidence about the Greeks living in Egypt in the form of letters and other personal documents that have not survived anywhere else in the Greek-speaking world.

There are other limitations to our study. The literary evidence that has survived from ancient Greece does not represent Greek society as a whole. Most of it is the product of well-to-do, leisured, adult male citizens. Virtually none of it focuses on women, adolescents, metics (immigrants), slaves, the disabled, or those living in the countryside. Furthermore, the Greeks were almost wholly incapable of identifying a social trend, formulating a social theory, or implementing a social policy. What the modern world therefore identifies as "social evils," such as vagrancy, homelessness, divorce, illegitimacy, and juvenile delinquency, for instance, could be observed and discussed only on the individual level as constituting so many separate and unrelated personal tragedies. They could not be perceived as phenomena that were embedded in society as a whole, nor could they be discussed within a conceptual framework. This was due in large measure to the self-evident fact that the Greeks did not keep statistics.

It is important to emphasize that the tenor of Greek society was predominately shaped by the aristocrats, or *aristoi*, who, as this word implies, considered themselves to be the very best. Their social inferiors were known as "the bad" (*kakoi*). Athenian society remained elitist even after radical democratic reforms were carried out by Perikles and Ephialtes toward the middle of the fifth century B.C.; even though Perikles claimed that poverty was no bar to advancement, aristocrats continued to exploit their economic, political, and social status.

Many scholars regard the investigation of such questions as "What did the Greeks eat for breakfast?" as irrelevant to the serious study of history. They have a point. Viewed in a vacuum, many questions having to do with daily life do not help us to come to terms with what makes the Greeks so different from (and in some ways so similar to) ourselves. It is all too easy to depict the Greeks as nineteenth-century gentlemen of refined artistic taste who had a regrettable penchant for homosexuality, waxed philosophical all hours of the day, and seriously mistreated their wives. I have tried to do better than that. What I have attempted here under the general heading of daily life is to investigate what the French call the *mentalité* of the Greeks.

Some of the questions I do consider important are the following: What did the Greeks do with their income? How did they treat their slaves? How did they treat their wives? How did wives treat their husbands? How stable was the family? How were old people treated? How did the young treat the elderly? Were the Greeks afraid of death? Did they share our notion of romantic love? What did they think of foreigners? Did they indulge in premarital sex? Did they use contraception? Did they perform abortions? Did they practice euthanasia? Did they believe in progress? How did they relax? Were they all highly cultivated? Were they intensely patriotic? Questions like these are inherently worth asking, regardless of whether we consider the Greeks our spiritual, cultural, or intellectual ancestors.

Investigating the daily life of the ancient Greeks can be as exciting as any other branch of inquiry conducted in the social sciences. Ancient history is not locked in a time warp. On the contrary, few branches of learning have proved to be so receptive to new modes of critical thinking, including Marxism, feminism, structuralism, and deconstruction. To be an accomplished ancient historian today requires not only a knowledge of the literary sources, the archaeology, the inscriptions, and the papyri, but also an understanding of such disciplines as anthropology, sociology, economics, and psychology.

Though our knowledge of the ancient world is always expanding, what we can know will only ever be a fraction of what we would like to know. This must not, however, stop us from asking impertinent questions. As Jacob Bronowski (*The Ascent of Man*, p. 153) once remarked about science, "Ask an impertinent question, and you are on the way to the pertinent answer." This is no less true of historical inquiry.

DAILY LIFE OF

THE
ANCIENT
GREEKS

1

Historical Outline

THE BRONZE AGE AND THE MYCENAEANS

The beginnings of Greek civilization are shrouded in mystery but since the Greeks looked back fondly to the Bronze Age as constituting an era when they were united under a single king called Agamemnon, it seems appropriate to begin this historical overview there. This was the period of Mycenaean culture, so named after the hilltop fortress at Mycenae in the northeast Peloponnese. Other important Mycenaean fortifications include Tiryns, which lies a few miles south of Mycenae, Pylos on the west coast of the Peloponnese, Thebes in central Greece, Iolkos in Thessaly, and the Acropolis at Athens. Several Aegean islands, the most important of which was Crete, also came under the influence of Mycenae. The Mycenaeans traded extensively in the Mediterranean, notably with the peoples of Egypt, Syria, Sicily, and southern Italy. On the basis of the profile of a Mycenaean-style sword engraved into one of the stones at Stonehenge, it has even been fancifully suggested that they traded with Britain.

The most striking evidence for the early phase of Mycenaean culture is the so-called shaft graves at Mycenae. These graves, which are dated to the sixteenth century B.C., are cut into the living rock to a depth of several meters. They were excavated in the nineteenth century by the German archaeologist Heinrich Schliemann. The shaft graves, which have yielded some of the richest finds ever discovered on the Greek mainland, provide confirmation for Homer's description of Mycenae as "rich in gold." In the fifteenth century B.C., a different style of burial was introduced in the form of beehive tombs, so named because of their domed appearance. The most impressive of these is the Treasury of Atreus, incorrectly named after Agamemnon's father. In the following century the fortification walls of Mycenae were rebuilt. They were now provided with an ornamental gateway surmounted by a relief depicting two lions flanking a pillar. The Mycenaeans were literate, though their script, which is known as Linear B, was used merely for inventories and other bureaucratic purposes. It was never put in the service of literature, which says much about their priorities. Without literature, we cannot investigate thoughts and feelings. In short, we cannot know what kind of people the Mycenaeans were.

The Trojan War
Later Greeks preserved the memory of a major expedition undertaken by the Mycenaeans against a town called Ilion or Troy. The Trojan War and its aftermath were commemorated in two epic poems ascribed to Homer, the *Iliad* and the *Odyssey*, both composed around 700 B.C., though whether they were the work of the same poet continues to be a subject of debate. Once again it was Schliemann who excavated the site claimed to be Troy, which he identified with a mound called Hissarlik, situated a few miles from the coast in northwest Turkey. However, doubts remain as to whether the site that he excavated really is Troy. As Moses Finley pointed out in *The World*

Gold cup from Shaft Grave IV at Mycenae.

of Odysseus (1978), the sole piece of archaeological evidence that connects its destruction to a coalition of Greeks is a single bronze arrowhead of Greek design, which was found among the debris in one of the streets of the city known as Troy VIIA (p. 160). Even so, most scholars concede that Homer's legend contains at least a kernel of historical truth. The Trojan War, which is perhaps dated around 1150 B.C., is said to have lasted ten years. It ended in the total destruction of Troy. Shortly afterward the entire Mycenaean world collapsed. It seems that the war represented the dying gasps of Bronze Age civilization.

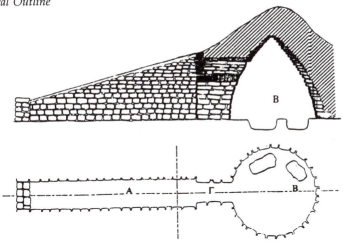

Plan and section of beehive tomb. From *Religion and the Greeks* by Robert Garland (Bristol, U.K.: Bristol Classical Press, 1994). Reprinted by permission of Duckworth Publishers.

In the period from c. 1300 to 1100 B.C., almost every Mycenaean site was plundered and burnt. Thebes was destroyed in c. 1300 B.C., Pylos in c. 1200, and Mycenae in c. 1150. Of the mainland sites Athens alone provides evidence of cultural continuity. The cause of the collapse of the Mycenaean world **The Dorian Invasion** is not fully understood. Later Greeks attributed it to an invasion by a people who swept in from the north. They called this people the Dorians. Those Greeks who traced themselves back to the Dorians were subsequently organized into three tribes known as Hylleis, Dymanes, and Pamphyloi. The original leaders of these tribes were said to be the sons of Herakles, the greatest of the Greek heroes. The archaeological evidence for the invasion is, however, negligible. No distinctively Dorian pottery has come to light, and the only artifacts that may be attributed to an invader are the iron sword and the long bronze dress pin. In light of such scant evidence some scholars have doubted the existence of a Dorian invasion altogether. However, a majority favors an invasion or successive waves of invasions as the most likely explanation for such widespread destruction. It has been suggested that the Dorians were a pastoral people whose lifestyle did not encourage the production of pottery and other artifacts.

THE DARK AGE

The collapse of the Mycenaean world ushered in the so-called Dark Age, which lasted several hundred years. The art of writing was lost, poverty became widespread, communications ceased, and the arts declined. The period for which there is least archaeological data lasted from 1025 to 950 B.C. The pace of recovery varied from region to region. Until recently it was believed that the Dark Age enveloped the whole of mainland Greece. However, we now have evidence of an important tenth-century B.C. settlement at a site called Lefkandi on the island of Euboia, just opposite Attica.

Excavations conducted by the British School at Athens have brought to light a long apsidal-ended building, the finest of its age to be found anywhere in Greece. No less sensational is the discovery of the burial of a wealthy warrior, who has been dubbed by archaeologists the "Hero of Lefkandi." Beside his bones, which were interred in a bronze amphora with an iron spear and sword, lay the skeleton of a young woman. In an adjacent pit were the bones of four horses. Both the woman and the horses had been ritually slaughtered, presumably so that they could accompany the "hero" to the underworld.

THE GREEK RENAISSANCE

The period from 900 to 725 B.C., conventionally known as the Geometric Period, is named for the profusion of geometric motifs that adorn the painted pottery of this era. In around 800 B.C. there occurred a resurgence in cultural activity of such intensity that it is appropriate to speak of a renaissance. One of the most important developments was the adaptation of the consonantal Phoenician alphabet to the Greek language. It is not known where this adaptation first took place but a likely candidate is Al Mina, a mixed Phoenician and Greek community situated at the head of the Orontes River on the present-day borders between Turkey and Syria. This invention conventionally marks the division between prehistory and history. In the century from c. 750 to 650, writing became widespread throughout the Greek world. Written records indicate that the first occasion when the Olympic Games were celebrated was in 776 B.C., which is also the earliest date in Greek history. From 683 B.C. onward, the Athenians began to keep a list of their magistrates inscribed on stone.

One of the principal reasons for the Greek renaissance was a vast increase in the size of the population. From an analysis of graves, archaeologists have calculated that in the first half of the eighth century B.C. the population of Attica quadrupled and that in the next half-century it almost doubled again.

Restoration of Grave Circle B (drawing by A. Voyatzis).

The *Iliad* and the *Odyssey* are among the greatest achievements of the Greek renaissance. Though their origins as oral poems—poems handed down by word of mouth—probably lie in the Dark Age, they were brought to completion in around 700 B.C. The world described by these poems is that of an imaginary Mycenaean past as envisioned by an impoverished and vastly reduced society that is looking back nostalgically to an epoch of military power and material prosperity. The poems also provide us with our most important source of evidence for the social institutions of the eighth century B.C. Many of the institutions that they describe, including marriage, slavery, warfare, hospitality, trade, and religion, are more likely to reflect eighth-century Greece than the long-forgotten Mycenaean past. They also reveal the beginnings of an instinct for democracy that is a central feature of the Greek character. Though the *Iliad* and the *Odyssey* are the earliest surviving examples of epic poetry relating to the Trojan War, they come at the end of a long tradition. Paradoxically, it was their success that killed off this flourishing genre. Other epic poems on the same subject have survived only in fragments.

The Homeric Poems

Homer depicts a world in which monarchy prevails, though it
Social is possible to glimpse a power struggle between kings and re-
Unrest bellious aristocrats. Probably about a century before Homer,
however, aristocratic rule had replaced monarchic rule in most
parts of Greece. The poems of Hesiod, a peasant farmer from Boiotia
who was perhaps a younger contemporary of Homer, testify to a new
power struggle, this time between the aristocrats and the common people, or *dêmos*. In *Works and Days*, Hesiod warns aristocrats who pervert
justice that they will not escape the "all-seeing eye of Zeus."

The challenge to aristocratic authority at the beginning of the seventh
century B.C. was caused by many factors. One of the most important of
these was writing, which makes it possible to codify laws and establish
a constitution. Writing also makes it easier to detect evasion and mal-
practice on the part of those in power. The first written laws date to the
seventh century B.C. Literacy in the Greek world was not confined to a
particular social group, as it was in Egypt, for instance, where only members of the priesthood were literate. This made for far greater openness
in all aspects of Greek life—civic, political, and religious.

THE RISE OF THE CITY-STATE

The most distinctive political unit in the Greek world was the polis or
city-state, from which our word "politics" is derived. Though no two
poleis were identical in physical layout, all by definition possessed an
urbanized center and surrounding territory. Each polis formulated its
own law code, kept its own army, developed its own system of government, and recognized its own set of gods. The polis system prevailed in
the heartland of the Greek world. Around its fringes lived peoples such
as the Ambraciots, Thessalians, and Macedonians, who had no urban
center and were organized, much more loosely, into tribes or *ethnê*, from
which our word "ethnic" derives. Since, however, *ethnê* have left no
literature and few artifacts, it is virtually impossible to investigate the
lives of their peoples. So when we come to investigate the daily life of
the Greeks, it is the lives of the *politai*, or citizens of the city-states, that
will be our primary focus.

The polis system proved to be remarkably resilient. Even after the
Greeks had lost their independence, first to Macedon and later to Rome,
it continued to flourish. Its success over such a long period of time was
due in part to the inherent particularism of the Greeks—their preference,
that is, for living in politically independent communities. It is for this
reason that the notion of "Greekness" was largely confined to the lin-
guistic, religious, and social spheres. As a political concept it amounted
to very little.

COLONIZATION

The period from c. 730 to 580 B.C. witnessed an enormous expansion of Greek civilization through the medium of colonization. This was made possible by a power vacuum in the Mediterranean, since the two most important states in the previous era, Egypt and Phoenicia, were both in decline and no other state presented a serious obstacle to Greek enterprise. The influence of the Near East on Greek culture, which came about as a direct consequence of this movement, was so strong that historians have dubbed the century from c. 725 to 630 B.C. as the Orientalizing Period. Visual evidence for Near Eastern influence is provided by the profusion of Oriental motifs that now begin to replace the geometric designs of the preceding era.

The primary motivation behind colonization was to resolve the twin problems of land shortage and population expansion. The depth of the crisis is indicated by an anecdote told by the historian Herodotos concerning the plight of the citizens of the island of Thera (4. 156). The Therans were so badly afflicted by famine that they exiled some of their fellow citizens. When the exiles attempted to return after failing in their initial bid to find a suitable location for a colony, they were showered with arrows and forced to sail off again. Eventually they succeeded in establishing a colony at Cyrene in modern Libya.

Initial bands of colonists probably averaged no more than about two hundred and were drawn from all levels of society. Very likely women arrived only after a colony had been securely established. Given the fact that those who embarked on this kind of adventure were facing a common challenge and a common danger, some loosening of the divisions between social groups was inevitable. The colonization movement thus further weakened the power of the aristocracy. The chief colonizing cities were Chalkis and Eretria on the island of Euboia, Corinth and Megara in central Greece, and Phokaia and Miletos on the coast of Turkey. Notable absentees included Athens, which had sufficient fertile land not to need to send out any colonies, and Sparta, which took the alternative course of expanding into her neighboring territory. When the colonizing movement ended, the number of Greek cities had probably doubled. Southern Italy was so densely colonized that it came to be called *Magna Graecia*, or "Great Greece." It was at the Greek colony of Kumai (Roman "Cumae"), just north of Naples, that the Etruscans and Romans first came into contact with Greek civilization. Here, too, the Greeks, who called themselves *Hellênes*, first acquired the name *Graeci* in the Latin language, which they have retained ever since. (Both *Graeci* and *Hellênes* were originally the names of obscure Greek tribes.)

Though colonists brought with them sacred fire from the civic hearth of their mother city, the tie between a colony and its mother city was not a particularly close one. Corinth alone established something resembling a colonial empire. Far from serving to forge links between various parts of the Greek world, therefore, colonization further contributed to its disunity and particularism. It is important to appreciate that the limits of Greek colonization did not define the limits of Greek influence. Greek artifacts have been found as far afield as northern France, Switzerland, Germany, and Sweden.

ARCHAIC GREECE

The period from c. 630 to 480 B.C. is called the Archaic Period. This name, which derives from the Greek word *archaios* meaning "ancient," was originally coined by the eighteenth-century German archaeologist Johann Winckelmann to identify a period of Greek history whose artistic productions were regarded as crude compared with those of its successor. It thus constitutes a value judgement on the achievements of a whole era to which many contemporary scholars, who now judge Archaic art much more favorably, would not subscribe.

Solon We know little about Athenian history until the beginning of the sixth century B.C. when a lawgiver called Solon came to power.

At the time, Athens was experiencing economic hardship and agrarian distress, probably aggravated by drought and famine. The crisis had become so severe that indebted Athenians were becoming enslaved to their fellow citizens. Solon solved this problem by adopting the radical step of canceling all debts. In addition, he legislated that no Athenian was permitted to incur a debt on condition that if he failed to repay it he would become the slave of his creditor. If a father omitted to teach his son a profession, the son was released from the obligation of having to support his father in old age. Solon also forbade the export of corn and other agricultural products, with the single exception of olive oil, of which Athens had a surplus. Finally, he introduced measures that set Athens on the road to democracy. An assembly of citizens now met on a regular basis, and a court of appeal was established to check the abuse of power by magistrates.

The Tyrants From the mid-seventh to the mid-sixth century B.C., though rather later in the case of Athens, many Greek states were ruled by tyrants. The majority of tyrants were disaffected aristocrats, who nursed a grudge against their peers. Their rise depended upon the support of the common people, with whom they allied themselves against aristocratic power and privilege. This coalition of interests typically lasted for two or three generations, after which the ruling tyrant, having lost popular support, found himself isolated and beleaguered.

Though the Greeks vilified their tyrants in later times because of their detestation of unconstitutional power, tyrants played an important part in the progress toward democracy by serving as a catalyst at the point of transition from aristocratic to popular rule. This was particularly true in the case of the Athenian tyrant Peisistratos, who came to power in 546 B.C. and gave Athens a stable period of government which lasted until his death in 528 B.C. It was under his rule that Athens took the first steps to becoming a major military power. Though Peisistratos safeguarded his position by ensuring that prominent magistracies were filled by his own supporters, he left the constitution essentially intact. In the words of the historian Thukydides, "The Peisistratids observed the existing laws. They merely saw to it that the highest offices were always held by their friends" (6.54).

The somewhat unfortunate title "father of democracy" is most appropriately applied to the politician Kleisthenes, who, in 507 B.C., devised a way of undermining the grip over the Athenian constitution that was being exer- **The Father of Democracy** cised by powerful aristocratic kin groups known as *genê* (singular, *genos*). Kleisthenes, who was himself an aristocrat, made each citizen's political identity dependent upon the Attic deme or village to which he belonged. Henceforth each citizen was required to identify himself as "X, son of Y, of the deme Z." Kleisthenes then assigned each of the one hundred and thirty-nine demes to one of ten new tribes. In this way he broke the stranglehold previously held by the *genê* since regions that had previously been dominated by a single *genos* were now divided among several tribes. Aristocrats could no longer manipulate or intimidate ordinary citizens as they had done in the past. The new Kleisthenic system was complicated and artificial, but it was wholly successful in making the Athenian political system more representative.

SPARTA

Sparta, which is situated in south central Peloponnese, was a highly distinctive city-state that never succumbed to tyranny. It flourished in the Mycenaean period but experienced an eclipse, like most other Mycenaean centers, around 1200 B.C. We know very little about Sparta's history over the next two hundred years. In the ninth century, however, she began to expand into her surrounding territory, first northward and later to the south. In the second half of the eighth century B.C., she made further territorial gains to the west by conquering Messenia, one of the most fertile regions in mainland Greece. The outcome of this event for the future course of her history was decisive, since overnight it made Sparta prosperous and agriculturally self-sufficient. No less crucial was her treatment of the inhabitants of Messenia, whom she reduced to the level of helots or slaves. She henceforth became extremely conservative, wary of both political change and foreign ventures, and incapable of taking any decision without considering its consequences for her control over the helots.

Some time after the conquest of Messenia, Sparta acquired a new constitution, which she ascribed to a legendary lawgiver called Lykourgos. Even assuming that Lykourgos was a historical figure, this new constitution probably evolved over a period of many years. The bulk of it, nonetheless, was probably introduced around 700 B.C. Some of the enactments were enshrined in a document called the Great Rhetra (*Rhêtra* means "the thing said"), which established a compromise between aristocrats and commoners (Plutarch, *Life of Lykourgos*, 6).

The Spartan constitution was greatly admired in antiquity because it was thought to exhibit a harmonious balance between three systems of government: monarchy, aristocracy, and democracy. At the head of the Spartan state was a dual kingship. The kings, who had equal power, could campaign either together or separately. Aside from their military role, however, their powers were strictly curtailed. They were subject to constant scrutiny by five magistrates known as ephors, who were elected annually. If found guilty of impropriety, they could be deposed or exiled. The aristocratic feature of the constitution was the *gerousia* or council of elders. This consisted of the kings plus twenty-eight citizens over the age of sixty chosen from the aristocracy. Finally, there was the *apella*, or assembly, which all citizens, who were known as *homoioi*, or "peers," attended.

In 669 B.C., following the introduction of the reforms ascribed to Lykourgos, the Spartan army was decisively defeated by the Argives at Hysiai in the northeast Peloponnese. The effect of this defeat upon Spartan morale was considerable. Within a decade, and presumably as a direct consequence, the helots revolted. A protracted war ensued, which Sparta eventually won. It was during this war that Sparta developed her celebrated ethic of *eunomia*, or "obedience to the law," which was destined to become the hallmark of her culture for centuries to come.

In the second half of the seventh century B.C., Sparta continued to import luxuries from abroad, her potters and painters developed a lively and original style, and her poetry and music were second to none. Foreigners, too, were welcome. Around 600 B.C., however, a shadow fell over Spartan society, and her citizens became increasingly isolated from the mainstream Greek culture. This is symbolized by Sparta's refusal to mint coins, which placed her outside the nexus of trade in which most other Greek states participated. Her overriding purpose henceforth seems to have been to acquire military control over the Peloponnese. This she did very successfully at the head of the Peloponnesian League, which pursued a single foreign policy under her leadership. By the end of the sixth century B.C., Sparta had become the dominant power in the Greek world.

In the second half of the sixth century B.C., the Greek cities of Asia Minor on the western coast of Turkey fell under the control of the rapidly expanding Persian empire. In 499 B.C. they revolted and appealed to the mainland Greeks for help in a war of liberation. Only Athens and Eretria responded. Such **The Persian Wars** was the might of Persia that the revolt was doomed from the start. After it had been quashed, the Persians launched a retaliatory expedition in order to punish those who had assisted their subjects in their revolt. Having razed Eretria, they landed on the Attic coast close to the plain of Marathon in northeast Attica. In view of their huge numerical superiority, they confidently expected to achieve an easy victory. Instead the Athenians, aided only by a small contingent from a neighboring polis called Plataiai, achieved one of the most stunning military successes in history. The losses on the Persian side were reportedly 6,400; those on the Athenian side numbered only 192.

Ten years later the Persian king Xerxes returned with a much larger expeditionary force intent on conquering the whole mainland. The Greeks declared a general truce and formed an alliance under the leadership of Sparta. Their resistance, however, proved to be ill-organized and *post eventum*. Such was their disorder that there was no force waiting to oppose the enemy when they invaded Thessaly in 480 B.C. Shortly afterward, a contingent of 300 Spartiates, under the command of the Spartan king Leonidas, took up a position guarding the narrow pass at Thermopylai, which provided entry into central Greece. Although the contingent was wiped out, the prestige won by the Spartans on account of their bravery was enormous. On the same day a naval battle took place off the coast at Artemision, close to Thermopylai. Both sides suffered heavy casualties, but the Greeks did not succeed in halting the Persian advance.

Shortly before the Persians invaded Attica, the Athenians consulted the Delphic Oracle and were told to "trust in the wooden wall" (Herodotos 7.141). The meaning of this puzzling phrase was hotly debated in the assembly. Eventually a politician called Themistokles persuaded his fellow countrymen to interpret it as an allusion to Athens' newly built fleet. A few Athenians interpreted the words literally, however, and took refuge behind a wooden palisade surrounding the Acropolis, the highest defensible spot in Athens. The Persians began devastating the Attic countryside, sparing neither sanctuaries nor grave monuments. They easily overwhelmed those who were trying to safeguard the Acropolis. The Greek alliance was now in real danger of breaking up, but Themistokles managed to persuade his allies to engage the Persian navy in the straits of Salamis, a small island off the southern coast of Attica. As Themistokles had predicted, the enemies were unable to maneuver their ships and suffered a major defeat. A year later the Persian army was defeated at Plataiai, just north of Attica. The expedition was abandoned and the Persians retreated in disarray.

CLASSICAL GREECE

The beginning of the Classical Period is conventionally put at 480 B.C. It is so dated on the grounds that the defeat of the Persians ushered in a new era of self-confidence. This self-confidence is allegedly demonstrated by the artistic achievements of the age and by the move to full democracy that followed soon afterward. The most remarkable features of Greek culture, however, including democratic representation, artistic innovation, scientific speculation, and drama, had taken root before the Persian invasion. Like "Archaic," the term "Classical" is laden with artistic prejudice, since it implies that the era so named represents a peak of unequaled cultural achievement.

The Athenian Empire Immediately after the defeat of the Persians, the Greeks went onto the offensive by forming a voluntary confederacy under the leadership of Athens. This confederacy had the twofold objective of providing protection against the Persians and ravaging Persian territory. It is not altogether clear why Athens rather than Sparta took the lead, but the reason probably had as much to do with Spartan inertia as it did with Athenian enterprise. What the situation clearly called for was a maritime power to hold Persian expansion in check. Sparta was ill-equipped to take a leading role in such a venture both because her economy was wholly based on agriculture and because she was reluctant to commit her forces abroad for fear of a revolt among her helots.

We do not know the names of all the signatories to the confederacy, but it is estimated that about 150 states initially joined. The principal requirement was that each member had to contribute ships to a common fleet; however, the smaller states were permitted to pay an annual tribute to a common fund instead. This annual tribute amounted to 460 talents in the first year of the confederacy's existence. Within a short space of time, however, larger cities also found it more convenient to pay tribute rather than provide ships. Eventually only the islands of Lesbos, Chios, and Samos, situated off the Turkish coast, continued to provide ships. Though this development came about as the result of voluntary decisions on the part of member states, it had the inevitable consequence of converting Athens into an imperial power.

The council for the confederacy met on the tiny island of Delos in the Cyclades. Though each state exercised only one vote, it soon came to be dominated by Athens, since she could influence the votes of the smaller states. It did not take long for Athens to reveal her hand. When the island of Naxos tried to secede in 470 B.C., Athens forced her back into membership. Four years later a similar fate befell the island of Thasos, after her inhabitants had appealed in vain to Sparta for help. By now it was evident that the confederacy had become an instrument of Athenian policy.

In the late 460s and early 450s B.C., Athens took the final steps along the road to becoming what is known as a radical or participatory democracy. It was a political system for which there exists no modern parallel. The Greek notion of *dēmokratia*, or "power in the hands of the people," was very different from our system of democracy. In the Greek world there was no menacing equivalent of Big Government. Nor were policy decisions taken by faceless bureaucrats accountable only to their immediate superiors. On the contrary, the Athenian citizenry or *dēmos*, which consisted of all adult males over the age of twenty-one, was completely sovereign. The *dēmos* wielded its formidable power through a voting assembly known as the *ekklēsia*, which met approximately four times a month, although extraordinary meetings could be called at times of emergency. Each citizen exercised one vote and had the right to speak on whatever issue was under debate. Magistrates and junior officials were in the strictest sense its servants, since they were subject to investigation both before taking up office and on laying it down. It was also the *dēmos*, sitting in court as the *hēliaia*, who constituted the supreme judicial authority.

Radical Athenian Democracy

THE AGE OF PERIKLES

In the late 450s B.C., Athens sent out an expedition to assist the Egyptians in their revolt against Persia. However, she suffered a major defeat and the expedition ended in disaster. As a result of this setback, Athens transferred the league treasury on Delos to the Acropolis for safekeeping. Five years later she concluded a peace with Persia, which meant that there was now no compelling reason for the Delian Confederacy to continue to exist. Not surprisingly there were signs of unrest among her allies, initially in the form of nonpayments. Shortly afterward several members tried to secede. Athens also suffered a defeat at the hands of the Peloponnesian League at Koroneia, which lies to the north of Athens. When Megara, Athens' nearest neighbor, also revolted, the Peloponnesians invaded Attica.

Largely due to diplomatic initiatives on the part of a rising politician called Perikles, however, a full-scale war was averted, and a peace was concluded that was intended to last for thirty years. This peace acknowledged Athenian supremacy in the Aegean and Spartan supremacy on the Greek mainland. The entire Greek world now became increasingly divided into two camps. Less and less was it possible for any state, however small, backward, and insignificant, to remain unaffected by this central polarity. The Greek world was destined to become as divided as Europe on the eve of the outbreak of World War I.

It is against this background of growing tension that the so-called Age of Perikles must be set. It began in 447 B.C. when work commenced on the Parthenon, a temple erected in honor of Athens' patron deity Athena. The Parthenon is the symbol par excellence of the Periklean Age. Perikles held no executive position other than that of general, to which he was reelected on an annual basis. The immense authority that he wielded over the assembly was thus mainly a result of his charismatic personality. The Periklean Age was one in which man's reliance upon his unaided intellectual capacity has rarely, if ever, been so paramount. "Man is the measure of all things. Of the being of things that are, of the non-being of things that are not," wrote Perikles' contemporary, Protagoras of Abdera, in a lost work.

Not all Athenians were prepared to tolerate this attack on conventional morality, however. Many, moreover, were deeply offended when Anaxagoras, a friend of Perikles, pronounced that the moon was not a god, as was popularly believed, but merely a lump of earth. Many, too, who were not genuinely offended, found it convenient to capitalize on the popular sense of outrage to make a veiled political attack on Perikles. Though he survived the attack, several of his closest friends were prosecuted. The Age of Periklean rationalism did not win universal approval.

The Peloponnesian War

The Thirty Years' Peace with Sparta lasted no more than fifteen years. The reasons for the outbreak of war are highly complex. The Spartans placed the blame on Perikles, claiming that he had encouraged his countrymen to go to war in order to distract their attention from domestic affairs. However, it is difficult to see what advantage Perikles could hope to gain from war in view of the fact that Athens' power was steadily increasing. It is far easier to make out a case in support of the theory that it was the Spartans and their allies who engineered the war. As G.E.M. de Ste. Croix points out in his definitive study *The Origins of the Peloponnesian War* (1972), it was they who voted for war, they who committed the first warlike act, and they who launched the first major offensive.

The aims of the two protagonists were not identical: that of the Peloponnesians was to bring about the destruction of Athens; that of the Athenians was to convince the enemy that they were unbeatable. The Peloponnesians had the more powerful army, whereas the Athenians held undisputed mastery of the sea. On Perikles' recommendation, the Athenians abandoned their farms and took shelter within the walls that surrounded the city and the port of Piraeus. By turning their state into an island, the Athenians therefore nullified Peloponnesian superiority by land. Perikles was convinced that they could not be forced into submission if they adhered to this policy rigidly. What he failed to allow for, however, was the effect upon Athenian morale of having to watch the

Attic countryside being devastated. In addition, and as a direct result of this strategy, there was a severe outbreak of plague, which is estimated to have carried off about one third of the population. Among the plague's victims was Perikles himself.

The first part of the war ended in stalemate in 421 B.C. Then in 415 B.C. Athens launched an expedition to conquer the island of Sicily. It was the failure of this expedition that led to the resumption of hostilities in 413 B.C. Athens' final defeat came about in 404 B.C. Her citizens expected that their city would be totally destroyed, as many of Sparta's allies urged. The historian Xenophon tells us that the Spartans did not adopt this course, however, because "they did not wish to destroy a city that had done so much for Greece when she was facing her greatest dangers" (2.2.20). The more cynical might argue that Sparta wanted Athens to continue to exist as a counterweight to the growing power of her own allies.

The course and outcome of the Peloponnesian War inevitably fills the student of history with a sense of tragedy. When it breaks out, Athens, the city-state par excellence, is at the height of her powers. Her final defeat, which followed after a bitter period of civil war, provided the Greek world with no lasting peace but merely led to further attrition and fragmentation. And yet the war, though it solved nothing, had been inevitable, since Athens' empire had represented a challenge to the autonomy of the Greek city-states.

THE RISE OF MACEDON

The early fourth century saw the rise of Thebes at the expense of Sparta, who squandered her position of dominance by causing resentment among her allies. When Philip II came to the throne of Macedon in 359 B.C., the focus suddenly switched to northern Greece. Previously Macedon had played no significant part in Greek history. Situated north of Thessaly, her fortunes had been determined mainly by her neighbors. From this date onward, however, Macedon was destined to dominate Greek affairs until the Roman conquest.

Philip gained control of mainland Greece not by embarking on an all-out war of aggression but by exploiting the preexisting rivalries between the city-states. When a dispute broke out over the control of the sanctuary of Delphi, Philip marched south at the invitation of the Thessalians. Some years later he made peace with Athens, his main rival, and then again marched south to take over control of Delphi, celebrating the Pythian Games under his presidency. The final showdown between Macedon and Athens took place in 338 B.C., when Athens, in alliance with Thebes, was overwhelmingly defeated at Chaironeia in central Greece. This year also marks the terminal point for the political freedom of the Greek city-states, which were henceforth destined never to regain their independence.

Philip did not destroy Athens as the orator Demosthenes had often predicted. Instead he returned the prisoners whom he had captured without demanding any ransom. Several months later he summoned representatives from all the Greek states to meet in a council known as the *synhedrion*. Each member had to swear to uphold the common peace. It was Philip's intention to create a federation, rather than to impose direct rule. However, he also set up military garrisons in the hope of deterring any uprising. Despite the leniency of his settlement, however, the Greek cities continued to agitate for their freedom with all possible energy. It was at the second meeting of the newly formed council that Philip announced his intention to conduct an expedition against Persia. Each member state was required to contribute forces. Before the expedition departed, however, Philip was murdered at his court in Pella in 336 B.C. by an unknown assassin.

Hitherto a backward and insignificant region situated on the fringes of the Greek world, under Philip's leadership Macedon came to dominate mainland Greece as no other state had previously done. A speech attributed to his son Alexander by the second century A.D. historian Arrian serves as a fitting obituary to his reign:

> Philip found you helpless vagabonds, mostly clothed in sheepskins, pasturing a few sheep on the mountains and putting up a poor fight against the Illyrians, Triballians, and neighboring Thracians. He gave you cloaks to wear instead of sheepskins and brought you down from the mountains to the plains. . . . He turned you into city-dwellers and civilized you by means of laws and customs. (*Anabasis of Alexander* 7.9)

The discovery in 1977 of a magnificent tomb at Vergina in Macedonia by the Greek archaeologist Manolis Andronikos provides clear evidence of the extraordinarily high degree of Macedon's technical and artistic accomplishment at this time. A reconstruction of the skull that was found in the tomb has led many historians to believe that it belongs to Philip himself, on the grounds that it provides evidence of an injury that caused him the loss of his right eye.

THE EMPIRE OF ALEXANDER THE GREAT

When Philip died, his son Alexander by his wife Olympias became king. He was just twenty. With his accession, the Greek world underwent enormous changes. Few Greeks seriously believed that the Persian empire could be destroyed, and yet this is precisely what Alexander accomplished. To finance the invasion of Persia, he relied heavily on plunder. His main striking force was the cavalry. This represented a new departure in Greek warfare, which until now had been waged primarily by infantry.

Alexander won three major victories against the Persians. After his second victory at the River Issos in 333 B.C., the Persian king Dareios offered to share his empire by ceding all his territory west of the River Halys. Alexander rejected the offer and pressed on south into Syria. He besieged Tyre for seven months before eventually taking it. Dareios now made a new offer, surrendering the whole of his empire west of the Euphrates and offering him the hand of his daughter in marriage. This offer was also rejected. Alexander continued south, capturing other cities and visiting Jerusalem. He then invaded Egypt, which fell to him without a struggle. Since the Egyptian pharaoh was regarded as the incarnation of Horus, the son of Ra and beloved of Ammon, Alexander now became a god in the eyes of the Egyptians, though there is no evidence of his deification elsewhere at this date. It was in Egypt that he founded the first and most magnificent of his cities, Alexandria, at the mouth of the Nile, which he filled largely with his own veterans. By the first century A.D. its population would reach nearly 300,000. Alexander is credited with founding some seventy cities in the course of his travels, many of which he called Alexandria.

During his stay in Egypt Alexander was filled with a longing, as Arrian (*Anabasis* 3.3) tells us, to consult the oracle of Zeus Ammon in the Libyan desert. This episode is one of the most remarkable in his career, since it served no strategic purpose whatsoever. Dareios was raising a fresh army, and Alexander's first priority should have been to prepare himself for this decisive encounter. The purpose of his pilgrimage remains a complete mystery. On being questioned about his encounter with the god afterward, Alexander merely replied that he had heard "what was according to his wish."

In 331 B.C. he won the last of his great victories at Guagamela on the River Tigris. He followed it up by burning down Persepolis, the palace that had been built by King Xerxes, leader of the expedition against Greece in 480 B.C. Shortly afterward Dareios was murdered and Alexander was able to proclaim himself king of Persia. Following the final defeat of Persia, he undertook two further expeditions, the first to Bactria and the second to India. On his return to Susa, the Persian capital, in 324 B.C., he held a great banquet at which he married Dareios' daughter, insisting at the same time that his Macedonian officers should marry Persian women. Not surprisingly his policy caused bitter resentment, particularly among the Macedonians who considered themselves racially superior to the Persians. He pressed on eastward as far as the River Ganges in India before his troops refused to go any further.

Alexander died at Babylon in the spring of 323 B.C. after a short illness

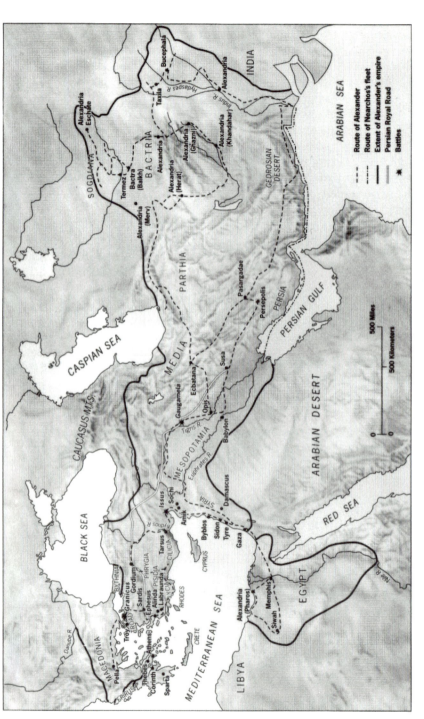

Empire of Alexander the Great. From N. Demand, *A History of Ancient Greece* (New York: McGraw-Hill, 1996). Reprinted with permission of McGraw-Hill.

following a prolonged banquet and drinking bout. He left behind him an empire that stretched from the Adriatic in the west to the Punjab in the east, from southern Russia in the north to Ethiopia in the south. He was thirty-two.

THE HELLENISTIC WORLD

The period from the death of Alexander until the Roman conquest is called the Hellenistic Period. It takes its name from the fact that Hellenic or Greek culture was now disseminated over a very wide geographical area. Greek culture did not, however, obliterate local traditions. On the contrary, for the most part it coexisted peacefully with them. On Alexander's death, each of his generals tried to seize as much of his empire as he could. It took nearly half a century before three stable kingdoms finally emerged: Macedonia, ruled by the Antigonid dynasty; southern Turkey, Babylonia, Syria, Iran, and central Asia, ruled by the Seleucids; and Egypt, ruled by the Ptolemies. Henceforth all the Greek city-states were subject to these three competing monarchies.

Rome first came into contact with Greece in 280 B.C. when Pyrrhos, king of Epiros in northwest Greece, an- **The Roman** swered an appeal from the town of Tarentum in southern **Conquest** Italy for help against the Romans. In 168 B.C. the Macedonian king Perseus was defeated by the Romans at Pydna in southern Macedonia. In 149 B.C. Macedonia was reduced to the status of a Roman province. Three years later a doomed Macedonian revolt took place, which the Romans ruthlessly suppressed. The Seleucid dynasty in Syria surrendered to Rome in 69 B.C. The Ptolemies were Roman vassals until the death of Cleopatra in 31 B.C., when Egypt became a Roman province.

Sadly, one of the most enduring legacies of Roman rule in mainland Greece would prove to be depopulation and economic decline. The following observation by a friend of the Roman orator Cicero made one hundred years later in 45 B.C. says it all:

> At sea . . . on my way back from Asia I was looking at the shores round about. Astern lay Aegina, before me lay Megara, on my right the Piraeus, and on my left Corinth—all once teeming cities, which now lie ruined and wrecked before our eyes. (*Letters to Friends* 4.5.4)

Greece's economic and political decline notwithstanding, her people and her culture were to exercise a profound influence upon the Romans. As the Roman poet Horace memorably phrased it, *Graecia capta ferum victorem cepit*, "Conquered Greece conquered its fierce victor" (*Epistles* 2.1.156).

2

Space and Time

LANDSCAPE AND CLIMATE

Greek history, not to mention the Greek character, owes much to the imperatives of the landscape. It is a landscape that is unfriendly to man. The mountains are forbidding, the vegetation sparse, the trees few, the soil poor and stony, and the climate harsh. Only a few of the valleys—one fifth of the total land surface—are capable of supporting agriculture and cattle rearing on a significant scale. Because of the thinness of the soil, cows and sheep are relatively rare, and the most common livestock are goats. None of the rivers is navigable and only a few have estuaries wide enough to serve as ports. Though these rivers may be raging torrents in the winter, irrigating the lowlands, most dry up in the summer.

Despite the fact that Greece was probably more thickly wooded in Classical antiquity than it is today, it has always been a poor country agriculturally and incapable of supporting a large population. Most of the land is mountainous and few of the fertile plains are large. From early times many states found it necessary to import wheat from abroad, including Athens, whose soil is too thin to support wheat. Her only important agricultural product was the olive. To compensate for this deficiency, however, her territory was rich in marble and silver. To this day Attica continues to have extensive marble quarries, though her silver mines are no longer active. Sparta's agricultural land was so small that already by the seventh century B.C. she had conquered the plain of Messenia, which lies to the west.

It was the prominence of the mountain ranges, combined with the difficulty of land travel, that helped to generate the fierce individualism that is a hallmark of the Greek character. Though the Greeks shared a common language, common social structures, and a common religion, in other respects they observed little sense of unity. Only when faced with an external threat, as at the time of the Persian invasion, did they temporarily succeed in forming an alliance and implementing a joint strategy. Even so, the cohesiveness of that alliance was constantly being undermined by the competing interests of its different members.

Another factor that played a vital part in shaping the Greek character was the sea. The perilousness and unpredictability of this element is a central motif in Homer's *Odyssey*; it is due to the wrath of the sea god Poseidon that Odysseus loses all his companions and is prevented from returning home to Ithaca for nine years. It was precisely because they were compelled to trade owing to their lack of natural resources that the Greeks came to develop a flexible response to the challenges of the outside world, whereas landlocked states that had no contact with the sea were, by contrast, inherently conservative and backward. This principle is demonstrated by the difference in character between Athens and Sparta, the two dominant powers in the Greek world in the Classical Period. Whereas Sparta, an inland state, remained conservative and unenterprising, Athens, whose power and wealth were based on the sea, became the cultural leader of the Greek world.

The climate of Greece has been likened to that of southern California. The summers are hot and dry, whereas in the fall westerly winds occur with frequent outbursts of rain. Twice as much rain falls in the west of Greece as in the east. The coastal region is mild but snows lie in the mountains throughout the winter. The poet Hesiod, a born complainer, found little to recommend it. In *Works and Days* (line 639f.), he tells us that his father, who came from Asia Minor, "settled near Mount Helikon [in Boeotia] in a wretched village called Askra, bad in winter, oppressive in summer, good at no time." Objectionable though the climate was to Hesiod personally, it is nonetheless sufficiently mild to enable the population to live much of its life outdoors.

Only the region as far north as Thessaly was regarded as properly Greek by the Greeks themselves. Macedonia, which lies above Thessaly, was considered semibarbaric, notwithstanding the fact that its inhabitants spoke Greek. The Greek world was not, however, limited to the mainland. As a result of colonization it also came to include the so-called Ionian cities along the west coast of Asia Minor (modern Turkey); the islands of the Aegean, of which there are more than two thousand in all; the islands off the west coast of Greece; the cities along the east coast of Sicily; and coastal cities in southern Italy, Libya, and Egypt. In the Hellenistic Period, the limits of the Greek world become almost impossible to define, since Alexander

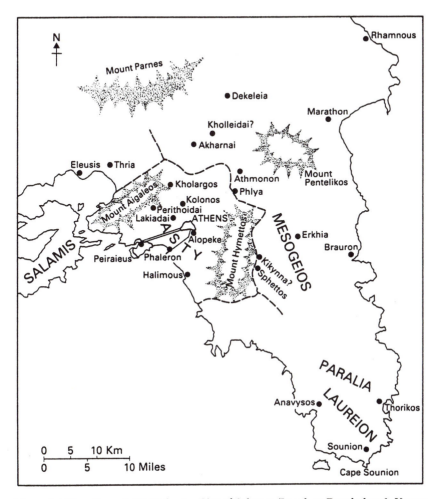

Map of Attica. From J. W. Roberts, *City of Sokrates* (London: Routledge & Kegan Paul, 1984).

the Great established Greek colonies in a predominantly non-Greek world that stretched as far east as the Hindu Kush.

THE CITY OF ATHENS

Like any other Greek polis, the Athenian state was a combination of urban center, or *asty*, and countryside, or *chôra*. Ancient Athens is today best known for the magnificent buildings erected on the Acropolis. This is a small, artificially leveled hilltop no more than 300 meters by 200 meters that was the home of Athens' patron goddess Athena and other major state gods. Here stands the monumental gateway known as the Propylaia, the Parthenon or temple of Athena Parthenos, and the Erechtheion or temple of Poseidon-Erechtheus, all justly renowned as the crowning achievements of Classical architecture. These monuments should not, however, so overwhelm us that we lose sight of the image of Athens as a city—a city, moreover, that possessed many of the same problems as any modern urban development, as well as others that were peculiar to the ancient world.

Civic Amenities Despite the grandeur of its civic buildings, in many respects Athens resembled a country town rather than a city. Most of the amenities that we take for granted today were virtually nonexistent. Only a few major roads were paved. The majority of private dwellings were modest in scale and appearance. There was only a very rudimentary and highly inefficient method of waste disposal. There were no public toilets. There was no street lighting. There was no fire brigade. There were no hospitals. The police force, such as it was, consisted of publicly owned slaves, whose job primarily was to keep the peace, not to detect or to prevent crime. Water was brought to the city from distant springs by means of terra-cotta pipelines that fed public fountains. With one or two notable exceptions, the majority of fountain houses were simple reservoirs cut into the living rock.

It was the duty of municipal law enforcement officers known as *astynomoi* to determine that certain minimum standards of hygiene and safety were upheld. Their tasks included ensuring that dung collectors did not deposit dung within a radius of ten stades (approximately half a mile) of the circuit wall, that buildings did not encroach upon the streets, and that the bodies of those who expired upon the public highways were collected for burial. The checking of such abuses, particularly the proper disposal of dung, must have been an uphill battle; disease was an ever-present hazard, especially during the summer months.

City Limits From 479 B.C. onward, and possibly earlier, the limits of Athens' growth were defined by a circuit wall built on top of a stone socle with mud brick in its upper courses. This wall, hurriedly constructed after the defeat of the Persians, was pierced by at least seventeen gates. Through these gates passed roads connecting the city with the outlying districts of Attica—Acharnai to the north, Eleusis to the west, Piraeus to the south. The most famous of these gates was the Dipylon, or Double Gate, so named because it consisted of an entrance at each end of a long corridor that was designed to entrap the invader. Outside the Dipylon lay the Kerameikos or Potters' Quarter, where the most impressive grave monuments have been discovered. Reconstructed according to its Classical plan, the Kerameikos is today a tranquil oasis of peace amid the bustle of modern Athens. In the Erida-

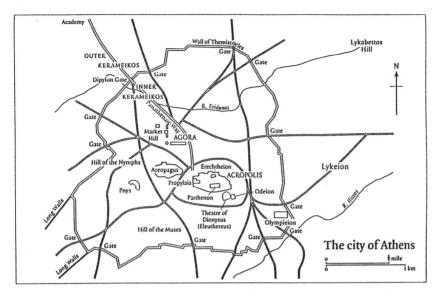

The City of Athens. From P. E. Easterling, *The Cambridge Companion to Greek Tragedy* (Cambridge, U.K.: Cambridge University Press, 1997), p. xvii. Courtesy of Cambridge University Press.

nos brook that ambles through it, frogs frolic playfully as they did in antiquity.

The road from the Dipylon Gate joined the Panathenaic Way, one of the few paved roads in Athens. This was the route taken by the Panathenaia or All-Athenian Festival, held annually in honor of Athena. As it wound its way up to the Acropolis, the Panathenaic procession passed through the Agora, a flat, open space roughly rectangular in shape and lined on all four sides with administrative buildings.

The Agora

The Agora, which has no real equivalent in the modern world, occupied a central position in the life of the community until the destruction of Athens by a barbarian people known as the Herulians in A.D. 267. It was the civic, commercial, administrative, social, and political heart of the city. The Altar of the Twelve Gods in the northwest corner of the Agora marked the spot where all roads converged and from which measurements to other parts of Attica were taken. Temporary stalls selling agricultural produce and manufactured goods were also set up here. In addition, the Agora provided the setting for most trials. Its unique flavor is conveyed in a fragment from a lost play by the comic dramatist Euboulos, who lists the following items for sale (quoted in Athenaios, *Professors at Dinner* 14.640b): figs, issuers of summonses to attend the law courts, grapes, turnips, pears, apples, witnesses, roses, medlars, haggis,

The Athenian Agora, c. 500 B.C. Courtesy of the American School of Classical Studies at Athens: Agora Excavations.

honeycombs, chickpeas, lawsuits, beestings, curds, myrtle berries, ballot boxes, bluebells, lamb, water clocks, laws, indictments.

Amply provided with colonnaded walkways or stoas, of which the re-constructed Stoa of Attalos on the east side is the finest example, the Agora was also a place for Athenians to engage in their favorite pastime—lively and animated discussion. Here at the end of the fifth century B.C. the phi-losopher Sokrates was invariably to be found. Here, too, a century later gathered the Stoics, philosophers who took their name from the Painted Stoa, remains of which have recently been identified in the northwest cor-ner of the Agora. The Agora was also a place to pass the time of day, as suggested by the verb *agorazein*, which comes to mean to "loaf about." Groups of Athenians, as well as foreigners, had their favorite meeting places. As the speaker in a law-court oration by Lysias states (24.20), "Each of you is in the habit of frequenting some place, a perfumer's shop, a bar-

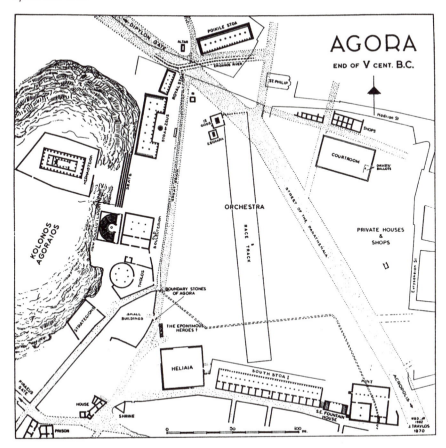

The Athenian Agora, c. 400 B.C. Courtesy of the American School of Classical Studies at Athens: Agora Excavations.

ber's shop, a cobbler's and so forth." The Dekeleians, for instance, gathered at the barber's shop beside the Herms, whereas the Plataians could be found at the cheese market on the last day of the month.

One of the most popular spots was the monument to the Eponymous Heroes, which stood in the southwest corner of the Agora close to the law courts. This monument honored the heroes who gave their names to the ten Athenian tribes that were created by Kleisthenes. Its base served as a public notice board which provided news about military conscription, forthcoming trials, agendas for public meetings, proposed legislation, and other public matters. Other important secular buildings located in the Agora include the public mint, the *Bouleutêrion* or Council House, the *Metrôön* or Public Record Office, and the *Tholos*. This last was a circular building which served as the living quarters for the fifty members of the council who were permanently on duty day and night to deal

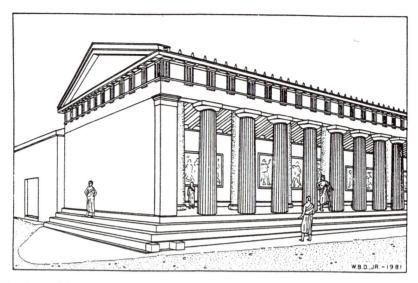

The Painted Stoa. Courtesy of the American School of Classical Studies at Athens.

with emergencies. Yet despite its importance, the Agora possessed only very rudimentary civic amenities. Storm water and sewage were disposed of by means of a stone channel which modern archaeologists have rather grandiosely named the Great Drain.

The Acropolis The Acropolis, which means "high part of the city," dominates the countryside of Attica for miles around. In early times it functioned as a palace, a sanctuary, and a fortress.

Its massive surrounding wall dates to the late thirteenth century B.C. The Acropolis continued to be used for defensive purposes until the 460s B.C., when a new wall was built to encompass a larger area. All its temples were destroyed by the Persians in 479 B.C., and little trace of them survives today apart from a few fragments of architectural sculpture. For forty years the Acropolis remained in its ruined condition as testimony to Persian barbarity until 447 B.C. when an ambitious building program was instigated on the initiative of Perikles, financed by the surplus tribute paid by Athens' allies.

As one enters the Acropolis through the Propylaia or Monumental Gateway today, one finds oneself facing the diminutive Erechtheion on the left and the massive Parthenon on the right. The Parthenon stands starkly isolated at the highest point of the rock, surrounded by a wasteland of broken marble. Yet the Acropolis played host to many other temples, of which virtually no trace has survived. In order to appreciate the effect that it would have presented in antiquity, one must imagine a forest of dedicatory statues, jockeying for position like insistent petitioners.

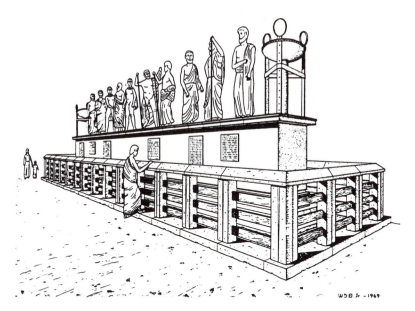

Monument to the Eponymous Heroes. Courtesy of the American School of Classical Studies at Athens.

Before the beginning of the sixth century B.C. Athens possessed few public buildings. Nor, so far as we know, was any **Urban** part of the city specifically laid aside for civic activity. Around **Growth** the beginning of the sixth century B.C., however, the city began to expand dramatically, albeit in a haphazard fashion and without reference to any functional master plan or guiding architectural principle. By the next century its population had grown to such an extent that it could no longer gather in the Agora for public meetings. The *ekklêsia* or assembly was therefore moved to a hill overlooking the Agora, called the Pnyx. The Theater of Dionysos, located on the south slope of the Acropolis, was also enlarged at this date. To the west, the Odeion of Perikles was built—a vast, roofed building capable of accommodating an audience of 5,000. Much later, in A.D. 169, the Theater of Herodes Atticus was constructed, and the entire southern slope of the Acropolis became a vast cultural center, rather like the Kennedy Center in Washington, D.C., or the South Bank Arts Complex in London.

Although fifth-century B.C. Athens was an urban entity, her growth and development did not bring about an exodus from the countryside. Even at the outbreak of the Peloponnesian War most of the population still resided outside Athens, as Thukydides tells us (2.16.1). It is difficult to gauge the extent to which those living in the countryside were incorporated into the life of the city. Though most Athenian citizens would have needed to travel to Athens at least once or twice a year for official

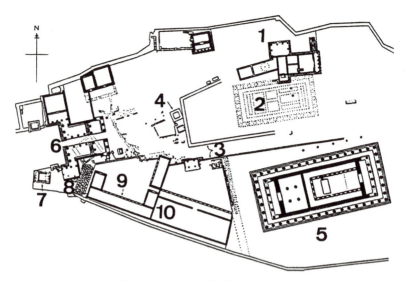

Plan of the Acropolis: (1) Erechtheum, (2) Old Temple of Athena, (3) sanctuary wall, (4) site of statue of Athena Promachos ("Fighting in the front rank"), (5) Parthenon, (6) Propylaea or gateway, (7) Temple of Athena Nike (Victory), (8) Mycenaean wall, (9) sanctuary of Artemis Brauronia, (10) Chalkotheke or treasury. From Evi Melas, *Temples and Sanctuaries of Ancient Greece*. Translated by F.M. Brownjohn (London: Thames and Hudson, 1973), p. 10.

business, it is highly improbable that many of them would have done so on a regular basis, even though the distance to Athens from the furthest demes was only thirty miles.

A City of Contrasts   Athens would have struck the modern eye as a curious amalgam of public magnificence and private squalor. It was a city to be admired for the breathtaking beauty of its public buildings, for which there was hardly any equal in the entire Greek world. In regard to its housing and public amenities, however, it was inferior to many of its contemporaries. It may strike one as remarkable that the Athenians, who adorned their city with some of the most splendid buildings ever constructed, were prepared to tolerate such discomfort in private. It says everything about the difference in mentality between them and us that no one ever suggested that their priorities should be reversed.

TIME AND THE SEASONS

Dividing Up the Day   The Greek day was divided into twelve hours of daylight and twelve hours of darkness; the daylight hours were longer in the summer than in the winter. Hours were not subdivided into halves and quarters. In fact, the only way to tell the time accurately was by means of the sundial, which was introduced into Greece in the sixth century B.C. The natural divisions of the day—dawn, midday, and dusk—served for most purposes.

Only in the Athenian law courts was accurate timekeeping necessary; from the fifth century B.C. onward, speeches had to be timed down to the last second. This was done with the aid of a water clock known as a *klepsydra*, a clay vessel which could be filled up to the level of an overflow hole just below the rim. When the speaker began his delivery, a plug was removed from a small hole at the base of one of the jugs. As soon as the water ceased to flow, the speaker would be required to sit down. This simple device guaranteed that both parties spoke for exactly the same amount of time.

Hesiod's *Works and Days*, which was composed in the seventh century B.C., is a kind of farmer's almanac. It uses **Marking the** signs from the natural world, such as heliacal risings and **Passage of the Seasons** settings, to mark the passage of the seasons, which in turn serve as a guide to the farming year. The time for plowing and harvesting, for instance, is indicated by the rise of a constellation known as the Pleiades:

> When the daughters of Atlas [the giant who supports the earth on his shoulders] are rising [i.e., early in May], begin the harvest, and when they are setting begin your plowing. These stars are hidden for forty nights and forty days, but they appear again as the year revolves again, which is when iron [i.e., for the blade of the plow] must first be sharpened. (lines 383–87)

Similarly, the moment to harvest grapes coincided with the appearance of particular stars:

> When Orion and Sirius are in the middle of the sky, and rosy-fingered dawn sees Arcturus [i.e., in September], then cut off all the grapes . . . and bring them home. (lines 609–11)

Hesiod also uses animal behavior as an indicator of the changing seasons:

> When the house-carrier [i.e., snail] leaves the ground and climbs up plants [i.e., in the middle of May], fleeing the Pleiades, then is not the time to dig vineyards, but to sharpen your sickles and rouse your slaves. (lines 571–73)

The blossoming of plants served as a further guide:

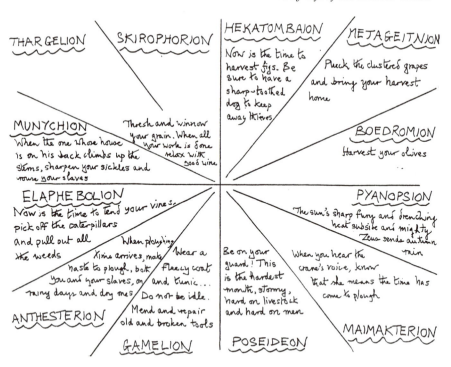

The farmer's year according to Hesiod (after Claudia Carrington, *Omnibus* 17 [March, 1989]). Reprinted with permission.

When the artichoke comes into flower [i.e., in June], and the chattering cicada sits in a tree and pours down his sweet song in full measure from under his wings and wearisome heat is at its height, then goats are fattest and wine is sweetest. Women are in heat, but men are at their weakest, because Sirius saps the head and the knees, and the flesh is dry because of the heat. (lines 582–88)

Reckoning the Years   There was no universal method of reckoning the passage of years in the Greek world. Rather, each community adhered to its own system. So when the historian Thukydides was trying to indicate the year in which the Peloponnesian War broke out, he tells his readers that hostilities began "fourteen years after the capture of Euboea, forty-seven years after Chryses became priestess of Hera at Argos, in the year when Ainesias was ephor at Sparta, and in the year when Pythodoros was archon in Athens" (2.2.1).

The earliest preserved date in Greek history is 776 B.C., the year when the Olympic Games were first celebrated. However, Olympiads, which marked the four-year intervals between successive celebrations of the games, were not adopted as a basis for chronology until the third century B.C. Nor did city-states seek to establish the year of their foundation. All that they were interested in proving was that their city had been founded earlier than its rivals, since this could lend legitimacy to territorial claims.

Athens' written records begin in 683 B.C., which was when she instituted a system by which a magistrate known as the eponymous archon gave his name to the year. There was, however, nothing inherently significant about this date. It merely marked the adoption of a procedural convenience. Moreover, although the Athenians annually celebrated the birthday of their principal state deity, Athena Polias, on the twenty-eighth of the month of *Hekatombaion* (i.e., shortly after the summer solstice), they did not know the year in which the goddess had been born. They also held a festival called the *Synoikia* earlier in the month in commemoration of the *synoikismos* or unification of Attica, which they ascribed to their legendary king Theseus. However, since Theseus' reign could not be dated, this event did not provide a fixed date either. It was not until the Hellenistic Period that a determined attempt was made to establish a foundation date for Athens. The author of an inscribed marble column, known as the *Marmor Parium*, who claimed to have "written up the dates [of Athenian history] from the beginning," maintained that Kekrops, the first king of Athens, came to the throne 1,218 years prior to the setting up of the inscription in 264/3 B.C. In the same century the geographer Eratosthenes devised a dating system that took as its departure the fall of Troy, which he assigned to 1183 B.C.

The Athenians did not celebrate the New Year, mainly because their calendar, which was based on the phases of the moon, was in a state of almost constant turmoil. A lunar calendar is extremely convenient in a subliterate society for arranging the dates of monthly festivals, payment of debts, and so forth. As a basis for marking the passage of the seasons, however, it is virtually useless, because the lunar year is eleven days shorter than the solar year. Since, however, the success of the harvest was thought to depend on ritual activity performed at precise moments of the year, the Athenians, like other Greeks, had to intercalate (or add) an extra month from time to time in order to keep their calendar in line with the annual circuit of the sun. In fact, over a nineteen-year cycle, they had to intercalate seven extra months.

Though the Greeks were spared the anxiety that is associated with an approaching millennium, they did in a general way have an appreciation that the world's biological clock was running down. One indication that the earth **The End of the World** was in biological decline was the alleged diminution of human stature and capability. In the *Iliad*, for instance, Homer claims that the heroes who fought at Troy were giants compared with the men of his day. A

Greek warrior called Diomedes, for instance, effortlessly picked up a stone "which two men could not lift, of the kind that mortals are today" (5.302–4). Belief in the earth's biological decline was not confined to the hyperbolic medium of Greek epic. Herodotos tells us that in Egypt a sandal had been preserved two cubits in length which had once belonged to the hero Perseus. Likewise, the image of a giant footstep made by Herakles was allegedly engraved on a rock in Scythia (2.91.1; 4.82).

A particularly bleak prophecy appears in Hesiod's *Works and Days*, which may well reflect deteriorating economic and social circumstances in the Greek world at this time. The poet informs his audience that they are presently living in the Age of Iron and that it is their lot "never to cease from labour and sorrowing by day, and dying by night" (lines 176–78). Yet if conditions seem bad now, they are destined to become much worse, for the time is fast approaching when infants will be born with the marks of old age upon them. Human life span, in other words, will have so contracted that infancy and old age will be virtually indistinguishable from one another.

> The father will have nothing in common with his sons, nor sons with their father, nor a guest with his host, nor friend with friend, nor will a brother be beloved as before. Men will dishonour their parents as they age rapidly. They will blame them, speaking harsh words. Stiff-necked, they will think nothing of the gods. Nor will they repay to their aged parents the gift of their own nurturing. (lines 182–88)

When that apocalyptic moment is reached, which reflects a decline in moral standards in line with the earth's biological decline, Zeus will annihilate the human race. Even so, the forlorn wish which prefaces the poet's description of the Age of Iron—"O that I was not among men of the fifth race, but had either died before it or been born after it" (line 174f.)—seems to hint at a cyclical repetition involving a return to the Golden Age. Hesiod does not appear to have regarded the invention of iron as marking an improvement in technology, nor does he seem to have been of the opinion that technological advance in itself represents a threat to the future of this planet, though the seeds of this prevalent modern theory certainly lie embedded in the myth.

3

Language, Alphabet, and Literacy

THE ORIGINS OF THE GREEK LANGUAGE
AND LINEAR B

By the thirteenth century B.C. at the latest, the inhabitants of the Greek mainland and the island of Crete were speaking Greek. Though its origins are unclear, Greek belongs to the Indo-European family of languages, which extends from Iceland to Bangladesh. Until the Hellenistic Period it existed in a number of different dialects, the most important of which were Aeolic, Doric, Ionic, and Attic. These dialects do not, however, invariably correspond to ethnic divisions within the Greek "race." For instance, the inhabitants of Halikarnassos, modern Bodrùm on the Turkish coast, who were Dorians, spoke in an Ionic dialect. Following the conquests of Alexander the Great, a dialect called *koinê*, or "common," became the educated tongue of the entire Hellenistic world. *Koinê* is the dialect in which the New Testament is written.

The evidence for the existence of the Greek language in the Bronze Age derives from a prealphabetical Greek script called Linear B, so named in order to distinguish it from an earlier, still undeciphered script called Linear A, which may or may not have been Greek. Linear B was based on the principle that each sign represented one syllable. Clay tablets engraved in Linear B by means of a sharp instrument have been found at Mycenai, Tiryns, Thebes, Pylos, and Knossos (Crete). With the collapse of the Mycenaean world in c. 1200 B.C., the script died out and the art of literacy was lost.

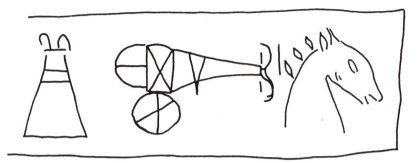

Clay tablet showing Linear B ideograms for cuirass, chariot, and horse. From J. T. Hooker, *Linear B: An Introduction* (Bristol, U.K.: Bristol Classical Press, 1980). Reprinted by permission of Schocken Books and Bristol Classical Press.

Greece subsequently remained illiterate for over four hundred years. Then, in the early eighth century B.C., the Greeks came into contact with a seafaring people called the Phoenicians, who inhabited the coast of

One of the earliest known inscriptions written in Greek. The lettering has been scratched on the cup from right to left in the Phoenician manner.

Syria. They adapted the Phoenician alphabet to their own language by adding seven vowel sounds (i.e., *a*, short and long *e*, *i*, short and long *o*, and *u*) to the original sixteen consonants, making it a much more flexible script. Many of the Phoenician names for the letters entered the Greek alphabet virtually unchanged, including *aleph* (alpha) meaning "ox-head" and *beth* (beta) meaning "house." The same letters also functioned as a numerical system and were used for musical notation.

The earliest surviving examples of the Greek alphabet are dated c. 740 B.C. Though some states had their own local variants, the alphabet had become standardized by the early fourth century B.C. The Greek alphabet was destined to become the basis for many European scripts, including Latin, modern Greek, and Cyrillic.

The Greek Alphabet

A	α	alpha	a
B	β	beta	b
Γ	γ	gamma	g (always hard as in "get," not as in "gent")
Δ	δ	delta	d
E	ε	epsilon	short e (as in "get")
Z	ζ	zeta	z
H	η	eta	long e (as in "ate")
Θ	θ	theta	th
I	ι	iota	i
K	κ	kappa	k
Λ	λ	lambda	l
M	μ	mu	m
N	ν	nu	n
Ξ	ξ	xi	x
O	ο	omicron	short o (as in "top")
Π	π	pi	p
P	ρ	rho	r
Σ	σ, ς	sigma	s
T	τ	tau	t
Y	υ	upsilon	u
Φ	φ	phi	ph
X	χ	chi	ch
Ψ	ψ	psi	ps
Ω	ω	omega	long o (as in "porter")

There is no aspirate or letter "h" in Greek; instead, "h" is indicated at the beginning of a word by the sign ʽ, as in the word Ἅδης (Hades). We call this a "rough breathing." The absence of an "h" sound is indicated by the sign ʼ, as in the word Ἀχιλλεύς (Achilleus). This is called a "smooth breathing."

Because Greek is an inflected language, the significance of each word is determined not by its order in the sentence but by its ending. Each noun, pronoun, and adjective consists of a stem, which never changes, and an ending which does. Endings take the form of cases. For example, the genitive case is the case of possession, as in the phrase "the bone *of the dog*" or "the *dog's* bone." Because Greek is an inflected language, it tends to be more economical than English in the number of words it employs. In addition, the definite and indefinite article (i.e., the, a, or an) are frequently omitted, particularly in verse.

Here is a transcription, transliteration, and translation of Book I, line 1 of Homer's *Iliad*.

Greek	Μῆν-ιν	ἄ-ει-δε,	θε-ά,	Πηλ-η-ϊ-άδ-εω	Ἀχ-ιλ-ῆ-ος
Transliteration	**Mên-in**	**a-ei-de,**	**the-a,**	**Pêl-ê-i-ad-eô**	**Ach-il-ê-os**
Part of speech	noun	verb	noun	adjective	noun
Case of noun	accusative	—	vocative	genitive	genitive
Word meaning	anger	sing of	goddess	of Peleus' son	of Achilles
Translation	"Sing, goddess, of the anger of Achilles, son of Peleus."				

Verb: The verb **a-ei-de** is in the imperative voice, which means that the person who is speaking (in this case, the poet himself) is giving a command. The command is addressed to **the-a**, "goddess." The person who is given the command goes into the vocative case, the case of address. This is indicated by the **-a** on the end of **the-a**.

Object: The object of the verb **a-ei-de** is the noun **mên-in**, "anger," which is in the accusative case. This is expressed by the ending **-in**. But anger has to belong to someone, and in this case that someone is Achilles, or **Ach-il-ê-os**, whose name is in the genitive case, the case of possession. This is expressed by the ending **-os**.

Polysyllabic words: Many Greek words consist of numerous syllables ; **Pêl-ê-i-ad-eô** is a prime example. The reason for its length is that **Pêl-ê-i-ad-eô** conveys three ideas. The beginning of the word, **Pêl-ê-**, is the stem of the proper name, **Peleus**. The middle part of the word, **-i-ad-**, carries the meaning "son of," in this case "son of Peleus." The last part of the word, **-eô**, is the case ending. It tells us that the entire word is in the genitive case. So the whole word means "of the son of Peleus."

Word order: Because word order does not determine sense, the Greek language is free to use word order for emphasis. **Mên-in**, "anger," is the leading idea in the line and indeed the leading idea in the entire poem. It therefore stands at the beginning because the beginning and end of every line are places of special emphasis. For the same reason, the last word in the line is **Ach-il-ê-os**, "of Achilles," since Achilles is the principal character in the poem. So **Mên-in** and **Ach-il-ê-os**, which belong together grammatically, enclose the whole line like the cornerstones of a building. In addition, the adjective **Pêl-ê-i-ad-eô** and the noun that it qualifies or describes, **Ach-il-ê-os**, stand next to each other, as in English usage.

Pronunciation: There is much discussion about how Greek was pronounced. A basic fact to note, however, is that all vowels can be either long or short. Those marked with an accent in the transliteration are long (**Mên-**, **Pêlê-**, and the **ê-** in **Ach-il-ê-os**). Diphthongs, vowels that are pronounced together as one sound such as **ei-**, are also long.

LITERACY

It is not known what percentage of the Greek population could read and write. What is abundantly clear, however, is that mass literacy never existed on the scale that it exists today. William Harris, in *Ancient Literacy* (1989), has estimated that no more than 30 percent of the Greek population was literate at any one time. Levels of literacy inevitably varied from place to place, and from one social group to another. One of the highest levels was achieved by Classical Athens, whose democratic constitution was based on the principle that a majority of the (male) citizenry could read the often lengthy and extremely detailed documents that were recorded on stone. In Sparta, by contrast, where few written records were kept, most of the population was probably completely illiterate. Literacy is likely to have been practically nonexistent among women, those who belonged to the lower social classes, and slaves, apart from those whose job it was to keep accounts of financial transactions or to read aloud to their masters and mistresses.

PAPYRI

The commonest Greek writing material was *cyperus papyrus*, a plant that grows in the swamps of Lower Egypt, which was used for writing in Egypt from 3000 B.C. onward. The Greeks called this plant *biblos*, from which the word "Bible" derives. Stalks of papyrus were laid out in horizontal and vertical strips and were then entwined and pressed flat to form a scroll. The earliest surviving Greek papyrus, a commentary on the Orphic poems, dates from the fourth century B.C. It was found at Derveni, near Thessaloniki, in Macedonia. The overwhelming majority of papyri have come to light in Egypt, whose dry soil provides ideal conditions for their preservation. The largest cache has been retrieved from the rubbish dumps of a town called Oxyrhynchos (the name means "the city of the sharp-nosed fish"), situated about 100 miles south of modern Cairo. Oxyrhynchos has so far yielded over 50,000 papyri. They include tax returns, death certificates, and private letters. Many are written on scraps that contain fragments of Greek literature on the reverse.

It is thanks to papyrology (i.e., the study of papyri) that many lost works of Greek literature have come to light. Among the most important finds are Sophokles' satyr play *Detectives*, Menander's comedy *The Ill-Tempered Man*, and Aristotle's *Constitution of Athens*.

Papyrology provides us with a slice of Greek life that would otherwise be completely unknown to us. It is the life of the Greek population which settled in Egypt following its conquest by Alexander the Great. It sometimes comes across to us in heart-rending detail. We hear, for instance, of a slave called Epaphroditos, eight years old, who fell to his death out of a bedroom window when he was leaning out to watch the castanet players down below in the street. On a more light-hearted note we also hear of a schoolmaster called Lollianos who complained that he never received his salary "except sometimes in sour wine and worm-ridden corn."

OSTRAKA

Since papyri were relatively expensive to purchase, broken pieces of pottery, known as *ostraka*, frequently served for writing as well. From *ostrakon* comes *ostrakismos*, which give us our word "ostracism." An *ostrakismos* was a vote cast by the Athenian assembly to banish one of two leading politicians whose rivalry was judged to be harmful to the state. If more than 6,000 votes were cast, the leading candidate would be exiled from Athens for ten years. The ballot papers took the form of *ostraka* on which the citizens wrote the name of the candidate of their choice—or rather nonchoice. Thousands of *ostraka* have been preserved in the soil of Greece because, unlike papyri, they are practically indestructible.

THE LIBRARY OF ALEXANDRIA

Book rolls written on papyri were in general circulation around the end of the fifth century B.C. They were on sale in the Athenian Agora and were exported all over the Greek world. Since they were copied by slaves, they were relatively inexpensive to purchase. Sokrates says that a copy of the complete works of the philosopher Anaxagoras could be purchased for one drachma "at most" (Plato, *Apology* 26d). Even so, the book-buying public is likely to have been extremely small in size. Aristotle is said to have owned the largest private collection of books.

Public libraries were an invention of the Hellenistic Period. The largest was the Mouseion, or House of the Muses, in Alexandria, from which our word "museum" derives. Founded in 259 B.C. by King Ptolemy I, it is said to have possessed over half a million scrolls, perhaps the equivalent of 100,000 books. (To give an indication of the sheer quantity of learning that existed in antiquity, we may note that when the first Bible rolled off Johannes Gutenberg's press in 1456, it is estimated that there were fewer than 30,000 books in all of Europe.) For several hundred years the Mouseion remained the foremost repository of learning in the world. Among its famous librarians were Aristophanes of Byzantium, who annotated the earliest editions of Greek literature, and Aristarchos of Samos, who established the definitive text of both the *Iliad* and the *Odyssey*. Though the library was accidentally burnt during Julius Caesar's siege of Alexandria in 48 B.C., it continued to function until A.D. 641 when it was closed down on the orders of an Arab general. Throughout its existence, it played a vital part in preserving the culture of antiquity. If it had never existed, our knowledge of the ancient world would be immeasurably poorer. As the Hellenistic Period progressed, libraries became a feature of many towns. As today, their use was regulated by strict rules. The library in Athens, which was the gift of a Roman called T. Flavius Pantainos, contains an inscription which states: "No book shall be taken out, since we have sworn. It shall be opened from the first hour to the sixth."

Somewhat paradoxically, however, what has survived of Classical literature owes nothing to the great libraries of antiquity and everything to the fact that manuscripts were copied and recopied, initially during the Roman empire and later during the Middle Ages, first onto papyrus and subsequently onto parchment. Even so, merely a fraction of the total output of antiquity has survived. To give an example, we have only 7 of a total of 123 plays written by Sophokles—the ones that were selected as set books for school examinations in the late Roman empire.

4

The People

SOCIAL ORGANIZATION

The basic social unit throughout the Greek world was the family, although there was no word exactly equivalent to "family." The nearest equivalent is *oikos* (or *oikia*), which more accurately translates as "household." An *oikos* denoted **The Household** all those living under the same roof: the master and mistress, their children and other dependents, and all their household slaves. It also included the estate and all its livestock. The head of the *oikos* was the oldest male, who was also in charge of the religious practices that were conducted in the home.

The next largest unit was the *genos* (pl. *genê*), a word best translated as "noble kin group." Members of the same *genos* **The Genos** traced their descent from a common ancestor, who in many cases was either mythical or divine. We know of the existence of about sixty Athenian *genê*; the most prominent of these was the Alkmaionidai, to which both Kleisthenes and Perikles belonged. All of Athens' most venerable cults were administered by *genê*, and the election to their priesthoods remained hereditary throughout history. The priesthoods of both Athena Polias (Of the city) and Poseidon Erechtheus, the two principal state cults, were restricted to a small *genos* known as the Eteoboutadai. Precisely what *gennêtai* (i.e., members of the same *genos*) did in common apart from worship is not known. Until the reforms of Kleisthenes at the end of the sixth century B.C., *genê* effectively controlled the political process. Even after the democratic reforms carried out in c. 462 B.C., they still continued to wield considerable influence.

The Phratry   Whereas only aristocrats belonged to a *genos*, all Athenians were members of a phratry. "Phratry," from which our word "fraternal" is derived, means "brotherhood." Until Kleisthenes' reforms, membership in a phratry was the basis of Athenian citizenship. The blood ties between *phrateres* (i.e., members of the same phratry) are likely to have been much looser than those that bound together members of the same *genos*. *Phrateres* gathered together to perform religious ceremonies. They were also under an obligation to afford protection to one another. In particular, if one of their members was murdered, they were required to seek legal redress on the victim's behalf. The Athenian population was divided into at least thirty phratries. Phratries are first mentioned in Homer and may be of Mycenaean origin. They also existed in Sparta, Argos, Delphi, Syracuse, and on the island of Chios.

A baby boy was admitted into his phratry in the first year of his life at a festival known as the Apatouria. Admission was contingent upon a vote of all the members of the phratry, who were required to substantiate the father's claim that his child was the legitimate offspring of Athenian parents. The boy was later reintroduced to his phratry at the age of fourteen. The ceremony of induction, which included a sacrifice, was accompanied by a ritual cutting of the candidate's hair, an action that symbolically marked the end of his growing years. It is not known whether girls were also admitted to phratries, nor is it known what procedure was used to determine whether a girl was the legitimate offspring of Athenian parents.

The Deme   The territory of Attica, including the city of Athens, was divided into 139 local districts known as demes, many of which dated back to very early times. Some may even have predated the foundation of Athens. It was Kleisthenes who converted the demes into political units, each with its own local assembly, its own cults, its own *demarch* or local mayor, and its own treasury. Demes varied considerably in size and importance. Some were little more than hamlets, whereas others, such as Acharnai, situated on the northern borders of Attica, were very substantial settlements in their own right. A few even had their own theatre. Each functioned as a kind of miniature polis or city-state. Every deme was required to keep a register, in which were recorded the names of all its demesmen who had reached the age of eighteen. This register served as an official record of the citizen body. For all public purposes, an Athenian citizen was required to identify himself by his "demotic," or the adjective that designated the deme in which he was registered. He retained his demotic even if he went to live elsewhere in Attica. This meant that each Athenian family was identified in perpetuity by the demotic that it possessed at the time of Kleisthenes' reforms.

All Greeks believed themselves to be descended from one of two racial groups. Dorian communities, so named because **The Tribe** they traced their descent to the Dorian invasion, divided themselves into three tribes, and Ionian communities, who took their name from their mythical founder Ion, son of Apollo, into four. The Athenians claimed to be Ionians, whereas the Spartans claimed to be Dorians. To what extent these tribal divisions corresponded to a genuine racial division is unknown.

Kleisthenes introduced a system based on ten tribes, which were named after ten eponymous Attic heroes. These tribes, into which the whole Athenian body was divided, now became the basis of all civic administration. Though the Athenians continued to acknowledge the existence of the four Ionian tribes, these now ceased to play any significant part in the administrative process. The ten Kleisthenic tribes formed the basis for election to the council, or *boulê*, which consisted of five hundred citizens, fifty of whom were elected annually by lot from each of the ten tribes. No Athenian was permitted to serve in the council more than twice during his lifetime. Its function was to prepare the agenda for the assembly and advise the magistrates. For one tenth of the year, that is to say, for thirty-five or thirty-six days, each of the fifty members of each of the ten tribes served on an executive committee known as a *prytany*. Each *prytany* was responsible for the welfare of the state throughout its period of office. Its members, who were on call twenty-four hours a day, slept and ate in a circular building known as the Tholos, situated on the west side of the Agora. Each day a new member was elected by lot to serve as the chairman of the *prytany*. This meant that every Athenian had an equal chance of assuming the highest executive office in the land for the duration of a single day.

In most Greek communities citizenship was limited to free-born adult males over the age of either eighteen or twenty-one. **The** It is estimated, however, that no more than between 6 and 10 **Citizen** percent of any population were actually citizens. The most de- **Body** tailed information about the size of a citizen body relates to Athens. Thukydides (2.13.6–8) tells us that at the outbreak of the Peloponnesian War there were 13,000 hoplites on full-time duty, 16,000 of "the oldest and the youngest" who manned the garrisons, 1,200 cavalry, and 1,600 archers. This gives us a citizen body of approximately 32,000. If we multiply that figure by four to include women and children, we arrive at a total of about 120,000 Athenians. There is no evidence to indicate that men outnumbered women or vice versa except at the time of the Peloponnesian War when there was a drastic shortage of males. The evidence for the shortage of males lies in the fact that the offspring of common-law wives were now recognized as legitimate, which was not the case at other times. The population had been seriously reduced by the plague that ravaged Athens from 430 to 426 B.C., but it recovered and probably remained at around 120,000 until the end of the fourth century, when it began progressively to decline.

Evidence for the size of the population of other Greek states is even more meager. Argos is thought to have had a citizen body roughly the same size as Athens, whereas Corinth's was only half that of Athens. Sparta, by contrast, had a very small citizen body. Herodotos (7.234.2) tells us that, even in 480 B.C., her fighting force numbered only 8,000. By 371 B.C. her citizen body had dwindled to a mere 1,500. The reason for this sharp decline is not fully understood and may be complex. It is conceivable that it had as much to do with disenfranchisement as it did with depopulation. In particular, many Spartans may have become impoverished and found themselves unable to contribute to the dining clubs that were a condition of citizenship. The most populous Greek states in the Classical period were in southern Italy and Sicily. Judging by the extent of the archaeological remains, the largest was Syracuse. In the period of the Roman empire, three Greek cities, notably Alexandria, Antioch, and Ephesos, had populations of at least 250,000.

Athenian citizens were divided into classes according to the economic productivity of their land. The highest property class was known as the *pentakosiomedimnoi*, so named because their land yielded 500 bushels of corn annually. The next was the *hippeis* or cavalry, whose yearly yield was 300 bushels. These were followed by the *zeugitai* or "yokemen," whose yield was 200 bushels, so named because they served in close rank (i.e., yoked together) in the army. The lowest group of all was the *thêtes*, literally "hired laborers." The right of citizenship went hand in hand with the requirement to serve in the army, although military service was regarded as a privilege rather than a duty. From the time of Solon onward all Athenian citizens had the right to attend the assembly. The belief nonetheless persisted that the attainment of full citizen rights was dependent upon wealth. The political importance of the *thêtes*, the most impoverished section of Athenian society, rose dramatically when Athens became a naval power, since it was they who constituted the bulk of the sailors. Even so, members of this group were not permitted to stand for political office, either as magistrates or as members of the council, until the second half of the fourth century B.C.

The Sense of Nationhood   Though the Greeks differentiated themselves from those who did not speak Greek by the term *barbaroi*, the idea of "Greekness" played little part in politics. They never had an agreed capital, a single ruling family, or even a clearly defined boundary. As we noted earlier, although they did occasionally form alliances against a common enemy, these were invariably fragile and short lived. On the cultural front, the idea of Greekness was promoted by common blood, a common language, a common set of gods, and a common set of institutions. On an everyday basis, however, being a Greek was far less significant than being an Athenian or a Corinthian or a Macedonian.

WOMEN

At the opening of the *Odyssey*, Odysseus' son Telemachos delivers this stern rebuke to his mother Penelope who, understandably pained by allusions to her missing husband, has just asked the bard Phemios to choose a theme other than that of the Greeks' homecoming from Troy:

> Go inside the house, and do your own work, the loom and the distaff, and bid your handmaidens be about their work also. But discussion is the concern of men, of all men, but of me most of all. (lines 356–59)

Telemachos' reprimand summarizes perfectly the bipolarity of Greek society, which was both patrilineal and patriarchal. Women, though necessary for propagation, served few other useful functions. They were to be subdued and secluded, controlled and confined. Greek society was sexist and chauvinistic, and there is more than enough evidence to support this view. And yet the picture is not quite so simple and straightforward as all that, for there are indications that Greek men did not have it entirely their own way.

Despite Telemachos' claim about the dominant role of men in Homeric society, his father Odysseus constantly finds himself in a position of weakness and inferiority vis-à-vis women. As in the real world, so in the world of the poem, **Odysseus' Women** female power takes many guises: beauty, intelligence, cunning, resourcefulness, wisdom, and charm. The women whom Odysseus encounters exercise their power in ways that are usually indirect, sometimes magical, and often dangerous. They possess access to privileged information. They control hidden forces that can assist or impede him on his way. They counterfeit and deceive. And they can kill.

The power that wives wield is aptly symbolized by the different fates of Odysseus and his commander in chief. Whereas Odysseus was blessed in the possession of a wife, Penelope, who remains faithful to him for twenty years and has the skill to ward off no fewer than 108 suitors, Agamemnon was murdered on his return from the Trojan War by his wife Klytaimnestra, who had taken a lover in his absence. The question, however, remains: to what extent does this picture of women's power in early Greece mirror reality and to what extent does it constitute a fantasy on the part of the poet?

The Bride   Though we do not have any documentary evidence regarding age at marriage, literary sources suggest that girls in their early to mid-teens typically married men who were old enough to be their fathers. Hesiod, in *Works and Days*, recommended that a man should be "not much less than in his thirtieth year" and a girl "in her fifth year past puberty" (lines 695–99). Hesiod's view, though that of a peasant farmer, is by no means unique. Solon was of the opinion that the right time for a man to marry was between the ages of twenty-seven and thirty-four. Similarly, Plato claimed that a man was at his peak for marriage in his thirtieth year. Some brides would have been even younger than the age recommended by Hesiod, particularly those who came from wealthy families, as we know from a law code from Gortyn on Crete, which decreed that heiresses should be married "in their twelfth year or older."

Arranged marriages were the norm in Greek society, though a mature suitor would negotiate on his own behalf with his future bride's parents. In the following passage, a fictional character calls Ischomachos, who is intended to be typical of many upper-crust Athenians, informs his wife how he came to choose her as his bride:

> Have you ever wondered why it was that I married you and why your parents gave you to me? It wasn't just because I wanted someone beside me in bed at night. You realize that, don't you? What happened was as follows. Your parents were looking for a suitable son-in-law and I was looking for a suitable wife. I chose you and they, from among a number of possibilities, chose me. (Xenophon, *Household Management* 7.11)

Evidently, his wife's wishes did not figure in the negotiations. Regrettably, we are not informed about how she reacted on being told of her husband's passionless courtship of her parents. Although Ischomachos was able to exercise independence in the choice of his bride, younger men were required to follow their fathers' wishes.

Such evidence as we possess suggests that wealth and status, rather than emotional attachment, were the principal criteria for choosing a wife. Mercenary and cynical though this system may seem to us, we need to bear in mind that there were very few opportunities for the creation of wealth in ancient Greece. A marriage alliance was thus primarily an opportunity both to produce offspring and to increase the family's finances. A girl would almost invariably have been provided with a dowry, since without one she risked ending her life "unwed and barren"

Woman seated in a high-backed chair or *klismos*. From Thomas Hope, *Costumes of the Greeks and Romans* (New York: Dover, 1962). Reprinted by permission of Dover Publications.

(Sophokles, *Oedipus the King*, line 1502). Dowries varied considerably in size. The aristocratic politician Alkibiades received the huge sum of ten talents when he married the sister of Kallias, one of the wealthiest men of his day. Since the function of the dowry was to provide maintenance for the wife, legal restraints were imposed upon its use. In the event of divorce, for instance, the husband was required to return it intact to his wife's father or legal guardian. If for any reason he was unable to produce the entire sum, he was required to pay interest on it. The wife's personal possessions were also returned to her family. The orator Isaios informs us that when Menekles divorced his wife he not only returned the dowry, but also her jewelry and clothing. The clear purpose of this law was to ensure that a divorcee did not become financially destitute.

Athenian law also imposed strict regulations upon the marriage of a daughter whose father died leaving no male heir behind. (Athenians were required by law to leave the bulk of their estates to their sons.) Such a woman was known as an *epiklêros*, which literally means "attached to the *klêros* or estate." The estate in question did not actually belong to her but merely accompanied her when she married. Since it was the duty of the nearest male relative to claim an *epiklêros* as his wife, an *epiklêros* might, and presumably occasionally did, marry her own uncle. So strictly was the law upheld that in some cases existing marriages were dissolved in order to comply with it. Its purpose was to keep property within the family and thus prevent the amalgamation of several *oikoi*. For much the same reason, marriages were often contracted between relatives, especially among the wealthy.

The Wedding Ceremony   Marriage created a much more violent disruption in the life of a woman than it did in the life of a man. The bride not only was removed from her family at an age when she was scarcely past playing with her dolls, but also had to take on a number of onerous duties, chief of which was to produce an heir for her husband as soon as possible. One of the most moving Greek myths, that of the abduction of Demeter's daughter Persephone by Hades, the grim god of the underworld, explores the underlying tensions generated by this violent disruption. Persephone is innocently plucking flowers in a meadow when she is snatched away to become the bride of an aged and forbidding stranger whom she has never seen before. Though the myth in the version that has come down to us, an anonymous epic poem known as the *Homeric Hymn to Demeter*, focuses upon the grief of Persephone's mother Demeter rather than upon the trauma experienced by her daughter, it nonetheless reveals a profound insight into the institution of marriage from the female point of view.

The most popular time for getting married was in the winter month of Gamelion, which actually means "the time of wedding." The ceremony began with a sacrifice to the gods of marriage, Zeus and Hera, to whom the bride dedicated a lock of her hair. She then dedicated her childhood possessions to the virgin goddess Artemis.

On the day of the wedding, an Athenian bride took a ritual bath in water. This was poured from a special vase known as a *loutrophoros*, which means literally "a carrier of *loutra* (sacred water)." This bath prepared her for her new life. It was followed by a feast held at the house of the bride's father. Here the bride, who was veiled, sat apart from all the men, including the bridegroom. Beside her sat an older woman called a *nympheutria*, who guided her through the ceremony. Instead of a tiered wedding cake with fruit filling covered in icing sugar, little cakes covered in sesame seeds were served to the guests. These were believed to make women fertile. Toward evening the bridegroom led his bride, still veiled, from her father's house in a wagon drawn by mules or oxen. The bride sat in the middle with the groom on one side and the best man, or *paranymphos*, on the other. A torchlight procession preceded the wedding party along the route, and wedding hymns were sung to the accompaniment of the flute and lyre. On arrival at the bridegroom's house, the pair were showered with nuts and dried figs by other members of the household. They now entered the bridal chamber and the bride removed

Scene from a red-figure *pyxis* (ointment jar) depicting a wedding procession leaving the bride's house. The *pyxis* is shown beneath. From I. Jenkins and S. Bird, *An Athenian Childhood* (London: British Museum Publications, 1982). Courtesy of British Museum.

her veil. The door to the bridal chamber was closed and a hymn called an *epithalamion* was sung outside. Its macabre purpose, according to a late source, was to cover the cries of the bride as she underwent the violence of penetration. A Greek wedding was a private ceremony, which did not require the services of a state official or priest.

The first and overriding duty of a Greek wife was to provide her husband with offspring, preferably male offspring, **A Wife's** in order to ensure that his household did not die out. In the **First Duty** absence of any reliable method of birth control, there would be little opportunity for respite between pregnancies. In addition to the pressure that came from the husband and the husband's family, there would also have been pressure from society at large, since every Greek community expected its citizens to beget legitimate children in order to keep the population at parity. Because of the high level of infant mortality, it is estimated that each married couple would have had to produce four or five children in order to achieve even this modest target. The obligation to become pregnant was further reinforced by medical theory, which taught that abstinence from sex was injurious to health. A text ascribed to Hippokrates, the legendary founder of Greek medicine, states:

> Women who have intercourse are healthier than those who abstain. For the womb is moistened by intercourse and ceases to be dry, whereas when it is drier than it should be it contracts violently and this contraction causes pain to the body. (*Seed* 4)

Giving birth was an extremely risky undertaking partly because the standards of hygiene were deplorably low, and partly because women often became pregnant while still pubescent. Miscarriages were extremely common, as were the deaths of women in labor. Echoing no doubt the judgement of many Greek women, Medea in Euripides' play of that name sums up the perils of childbirth as follows: "I would rather stand in battle-line three times than give birth once" (line 250f.).

The failure to become pregnant was typically regarded with grave suspicion or interpreted as a biological problem from which the woman was suffering. Conversely, once a woman had provided her husband with a male heir, her standing and respect within the household increased considerably. An Athenian husband who discovered his wife in bed with her lover and slew the latter on the spot justified his action to the jury by stating that after the arrival of his firstborn he had bestowed upon his wife complete control of his estate in the belief that "the two of us had now achieved a condition of complete intimacy" (Lysias 1.6). Given the importance of producing offspring, it is hardly surprising that concern about fertility and pregnancy features prominently among the miraculous cures that are inscribed on stones in the healing sanctuary of Asklepios at Epidauros in the northeast Peloponnese. One inscription, for instance, states: "Agamede from Chios. She slept in the sanctuary in order to have children and saw a dream. A snake seemed to lie on her belly and as a result five children were born."

Another tells of the curious case of a certain Ithmonike of Pellene, who dreamt that she petitioned Asklepios to make her pregnant with a girl. The god agreed to grant her request and asked Ithmonike if that was all that she wanted. Ithmonike said it was and in due course became pregnant. After remaining pregnant for three years, she returned to Epidauros to ask the god why she had not yet given birth. Asklepios mischievously replied that he had made her pregnant as requested, whereas what she had really wanted was to give birth. The story has a happy ending, however. Immediately after leaving the sanctuary, Ithmonike gave birth to a girl.

In later times, obstetrics aroused considerable interest in medical circles. The most famous work on the subject is the *Gynaecology*, which was written by a physician called Soranos in the early second century A.D. It provides us with a highly detailed account of the practices surrounding labor, childbirth, and nursing.

Household Chores   In the Funeral Speech delivered over the Athenian dead in the first year of the Peloponnesian War, Perikles states, "Women's greatest glory is not to be talked about by men, either for good or ill" (Thukydides 2.45.2). Likewise, in Euripides' *Trojan Women*, Andromache, the wife of Hektor, declares, "There is one prime source of scandal for a woman—when she won't stay at home" (line 648f.). Patronizing though such statements may appear to be from our perspective, they also reveal an overriding concern on the part of Greek husbands concerning their wives' fidelity. Ischomachos, whom we met earlier, tells us that he gave his wife the following advice soon after they were married:

You must stay indoors and send out the slaves whose work is outside. Those who remain and do chores inside the house are under your charge. You are to inspect everything that enters it and distribute what is needed, taking care not to be extravagant. . . . When the slaves bring in wool, you must see that it is used for those who need cloaks. You must take care of the grain-store and make sure that the grain is edible. One of your less pleasant tasks is to find out whenever one of the slaves becomes sick and see that they are properly looked after. (Xenophon, *Household Management* 7.35–37)

As this passage indicates, it was the mistress of the house who was in charge of the domestic arrangements and who was held accountable if anything went amiss.

In addition to running the home, a wife was expected to contribute to its economy by plying the distaff and working the loom. Spinning and weaving were regarded as essential accomplishments in a woman, not least because most garments were made in the home.

Garments were made as follows. First the wool was cleaned and scoured. Then the matted fibers were separated from one another with a comb. This was done with the aid of a semicircular instrument known as an *epinitron*, which fitted over the thigh and knee, providing a slightly roughened surface upon which to tease out the wool. The wool was then dyed in a vat. Next it was spun by hand using a distaff, spindle, and terra-cotta spindle whorls in what is known as the drop-and-spin method. Finally, the wool was woven into fabric on the loom. The warp was suspended from a crossbar, and its strands, known as the weft, were threaded together by means of a shuttle. The weft was held taut at its ends by loom weights made of terra-cotta or lead.

Men spent most of the day outside the home, shopping, conversing, deliberating, attending the assembly or the law courts, and visiting in other public places. On the few occasions when respectable women went out of doors, by contrast, they were invariably accompanied by their slaves or female acquaintances.

Escaping from the Daily Grind

There were, however, a number of socially approved outlets for women, all connected with religion. Though most festivals were attended by both men and women, there were a few, such as the Thesmophoria, from which men were rigorously excluded. Funerals provided another important occasion for women to associate with one another. Women played the major part in preparing the body for burial, as they do in most Mediterranean countries to this day. It may seem odd to suppose that some women actually looked forward to the next death in the family as an opportunity to meet with their relatives and friends, but such was undoubtedly the case. The defendant in Lysias' *On the Murder of Eratosthenes* (1.8) claims that his adulterous wife first met her lover at a funeral.

A frustrated Greek wife and her would-be lover had to seize whatever chance they could find. Women were also permitted to leave the home to make visits to the cemetery to attend to the needs of the dead.

The following extract from *Idyll 15* by the Syracusan poet Theokritos provides a fascinating insight into the lives of two women who are planning to use the excuse of a festival in honor of Adonis, the beloved of Aphrodite, to spend the day together. The poem, which was written in the first half of the second century B.C., is set in Alexandria, Egypt, but the dialogue could be imagined as taking place almost anywhere in the metropolitan Greek world.

Gorgo: Is Praxinoa in?

Praxinoa: Gorgo, my love, what a long time it's been since I saw you—yes, I'm in. I'm surprised you made it, though. (*To her slave*) Eunoa, go and get a chair and cushion for the lady.

Gorgo: Oh, don't bother. I'm quite all right.

Praxinoa: Sit down.

Gorgo: What a silly thing I am! I was nearly crushed alive getting here. There are chariots, boots, and men in uniforms everywhere. And the road is endless. You are always moving farther and farther away.

Praxinoa: It's that stupid husband of mine. He buys this house out in the wilds—it's not even a house—it's just a hovel—purely to stop us from seeing each other. He's spiteful, just like all men.

Gorgo: You shouldn't talk about your husband like that when the baby's here. You see how he's looking at you. (*To the baby*) Don't worry, Sopyrion, sweetie, she isn't talking about Daddy.

Praxinoa: Heavens above! The child does understand.

Gorgo: Nice Daddy.

Praxinoa: The other day I told that Daddy of hers to pop out and get some soap and red dye and the idiot came back with a cube of salt! (lines 1–17)

The Legal and Political Status of Wives
Athenian women had no political rights. Legally, too, their position was one of inferiority. A law quoted by the fourth-century B.C. orator Isaios decreed that "No child or woman shall have the power to make any contract above the value of a *medimnos* of barley" (10.10). (A *medimnos* was sufficient to sustain a family in food for about a week.) They were not permitted to buy or sell land, and although they were entitled to acquire property through dowry, inheritance, or gift, it

was managed for them by their legal guardian (i.e., their father, male next of kin, or husband). Women thus remained perpetually under the control of one man or another, whatever their age or status. A wife seeking a divorce would most commonly be represented in the courts by her next of kin. If she sought to represent herself, the law afforded her no protection from further abuse, as we learn from an anecdote told by Plutarch about Hipparete, Alkibiades' wife, who became so distressed by her husband's philandering that she went to live with her brother. When she lodged a complaint against him in the courts, however, Alkibiades "seized hold of her and dragged her back home through the Agora, with no-one daring to stop him or rescue her" (*Life of Alkibiades* 8.2–4). If a divorce was granted, no formalities were required other than the return of the dowry to the wife's *oikos*. The husband, too, was free to claim back whatever he had contributed, as the following deed of divorce from Hellenistic Egypt indicates. Though the document is dated to the beginning of the fourth century A.D., contracts of this kind may well have been drawn up in earlier times as well.

> Soulis, gravedigger, to Senpais, daughter of Psais and Tees, gravedigger, greetings. Because it has come about as the result of some evil spirit that we are estranged from one another in respect to our common life, I, the said Soulis, hereby admit before sending her away that I have received all the objects given to her by me . . . and that she is free to depart and marry whomever she wishes. I, the said Senpais, acknowledge that I have received from the said Soulis all that was given to him by way of dowry. (*Select Papyri* 1 no. 8 in Loeb Classical Series)

Because of the large age difference between men and women at marriage, many wives became widows by the time they **Widows** reached their late twenties or early thirties. Young widows were expected to remarry, whereas older widows probably enjoyed considerable freedom. In view of the fact that the dowry which a wife brought with her had to be returned to her natal household (i.e., to the head of the family into which she was born) in the event of her husband's death, widows, like divorcees, were guaranteed some degree of economic security.

Athenians could also enter into a less formal and less binding arrangement with a partner of the opposite sex **Common-Law** known as a *pallakê*, close to the modern equivalent of a **Wives** common-law wife. Such unions were made primarily with foreigners, prostitutes, and women who had no dowries. The prostitute Aspasia, virtually the only woman in fifth-century B.C. Athens who is known to us other than by name, was the *pallakê* of Perikles. A *pallakê* was placed under the authority of the man with whom she lived in much the same way as a legitimate wife. There were, however, two important differences: such a union did not involve the transfer of a dowry, and the offspring were not regarded as citizens and so had no claim on the man's *oikos*. In the last decade of the Peloponnesian War, however, this regulation was suspended due to the shortage of Athenian manpower. Citizens were therefore permitted to have a legitimate wife, as well as a *pallakê*.

The Working Woman

So far we have considered only the lives of well-to-do women. The wives and daughters of the poor, as well as many spinsters and widows, were not able to lead lives of seclusion and would therefore have been frequently seen in the streets. The orator Demosthenes tells us that one of the effects of the poverty that afflicted Athens after her defeat in the Peloponnesian War was that many women had to go out to work, typically as wet nurses, weavers, and grape pickers (57.45). In Aristophanes' *Thesmophoriazousai*, a widow with five children describes how she earns a precarious living by weaving chaplets (lines 446–49).

Virtually the only profession available to freeborn women in the Greek world was that of prostitute. It is important to bear in mind, however, that the English word conjures up a very limited picture of the range of services that women performed under this general title. As the Greek word *hetaira*, which means "female companion," suggests, they charged for their companionship rather than their sexual favors. The ideal *hetaira* was gifted, charming, and intellectually accomplished. *Hetairai* were the only women permitted to attend private gatherings known as *symposia*. The *hetaira* of Aspasia was so respected that Sokrates and his friends would call on her to elicit her opinions on political and philosophical matters. Such was her influence over Perikles that the latter's decision to lead an expedition against the island of Samos is said to have been taken on her advice (Plutarch, *Life of Perikles* 24.1–3). In addition, many brothels existed in Athens, largely staffed by slaves. In fact, the state acted as pimp by farming out the right to collect taxes from prostitution to enterprising individuals, in the same way, say, that it farmed out the right to collect harbor dues.

Conclusions

To offer any final assessment regarding the condition and status of women in the Greek world is impossible. Since we possess no testimony by the women themselves, all we have to go on are statements made by men about women. Furthermore, our ability to make an objective judgement is complicated by contemporary assumptions about the role and status of women in our own society—assumptions, moreover, which continue to be in a state of flux. Certain unpalatable facts are not in dispute, however. For instance, a girl's chances of survival were poorer than those of a boy from birth on, her life expectancy was shorter than that of a male, her opportunities for acquiring an education were virtually nonexistent, the law regarded her as a minor whatever her years, and, should she choose to abandon her traditional role as mother and housekeeper, virtually only one profession—the oldest of all—was available to her.

At the same time, there is evidence to suggest that men did not invariably have the upper hand. Just to give a humorous example, Sokrates' wife Xanthippe is said to have doused the philosopher in water on one occasion and to have stripped him of his cloak in public on another (Diogenes Laertios 2.36–37). Relationships between the sexes were no doubt complex, as they have been throughout history. As Andromache observed, "I offered my husband a silent tongue and gentle looks. I knew when to have my way and when to let him have his" (Euripides, *Trojan Women* 655f.). Even so, we should probably not attach too much credence to a remark ascribed by Plutarch to the Athenian politician Themistokles, who claimed that his son was the most powerful person in Greece on the grounds that the Athenians commanded the Greeks; he, Themistokles, commanded the Athenians; his wife commanded him; and his son commanded his wife (*Life of Themistokles* 18.5).

PARENTS AND CHILDREN

In the absence of hospitals most births took place in the home or out of doors. Male physicians were present only when there **Birth** were fears for the mother's life. Medical texts indicate that the presence of male physicians would have caused embarrassment and shame to women in labor. The most important assistant was the *maia*, or midwife, who combined medical expertise with proficiency in ritual.

Birth and religion were in fact inseparably bound together. Women in labor were placed under the protection of Eileithyia, or "She who comes." The goddess was so named because her arrival was believed to enable birth to take place. Artemis, herself a virgin who rigorously shunned sexual intercourse, was also prominent in the birthing ritual. It was necessary to appease the goddess' anger by invoking her in prayer before delivery and by dedicating clothing in her shrine afterward. Perhaps as an indication that the house was polluted by birth, an olive branch was hung on the front door when a boy was born, and a tuft of wool in the case of a girl. The walls were smeared with pitch in order to prevent the pollution from seeping into the community.

On the fifth day after birth, the newborn baby was officially introduced into the home and placed under the protection of the household deities. The ceremony, which was called the *Amphidromia* or "running around," was so named because the child's father would run around the domestic hearth holding his infant in his arms in order to consecrate it to Hestia, goddess of the hearth. Relatives would bring gifts for the newborn, including charms for protection against bad luck or the evil eye. Probably on the tenth day after birth, the child would officially be given his or her name. The majority of first-born boys were named after their grandfather, as is still the custom in Greece to this day.

The Newborn Baby Officially Enters the Home

In all periods it was customary for the well-to-do to secure the services of a wet nurse to breast-feed their infants. The following contract from Hellenistic Egypt dated to 13 B.C. lays down terms of hire:

Nursing

> Didyma agrees to nurse and suckle outside at her own home in the city with her own milk that is to be pure and unsullied for a period of sixteen months . . . the foundling slave girl . . . that Isidora has given to her. She is to receive from the said Isidora as pay for the milk and the nursing ten silver drachmas and half a litre of oil every month. (*Select Papyri* 1, no. 16 in Loeb Classical Library)

Nurses feature prominently in Greek tragedy, which suggests that they were important members of the household. The most sympathetically drawn is Orestes' nurse Kilissa, who makes a brief but memorable appearance in Aeschylus' *Libation Bearers*. In the following passage she is fondly reminiscing about the chores that she had to perform on behalf of her royal charge many years ago:

> How I devoted myself to that child from the moment that his mother gave him to me to nurse as a newborn babe! He kept me up every night, crying and screaming. He was a perfect nuisance and all for nothing. They're brainless things, you see, children. You have to nurse them as if they're animals and follow their moods. A babe in swaddling clothes can't tell you what the matter is— whether it's hungry or thirsty or wants to go to the potty—though of course babies can't control themselves. It just comes out and you can't do anything about it. You learn to tell the future in my profession, but, heavens above, I was wrong often enough and then I had to wash its clothing. I was a nurse and a washer-woman rolled into one. (lines 751–60)

Baby's feeding bottle. The inscription reads, "Drink, don't drop!"

Though most nurses were slaves, a few were impoverished freeborn women. Soranos in *Gynaecology* (2.19.1) recommended that the ideal nurse should be "self-controlled, sympathetic, well-tempered, Greek, and tidy." Servile or free, many won the confidence and gratitude of their masters and mistresses, as is indicated by the fact that they often retained a position of trust in the household even in old age. The following humorous sepulchral inscription testifies eloquently to the enduring bond that existed between a nurse and her former charge:

> Mikkos looked after Phrygian Aischre [the name means something like "Commoner"] all her life, even in old age. When she died he set up this monument for future generations to see. Thus the old woman departed from this life, having received due recompense for her breasts.

Despite the keen desire for children, inevitably some pregnancies were unwanted. One solution was to undergo an **Unwanted** abortion. Those who resorted to this measure were primarily **Babies** unmarried girls, prostitutes, and slaves. Though the Hippokratic Oath contained a prohibition against giving a pessary to cause an abortion, it is unclear whether the ban was due to ethical or medical considerations. Abortion would have been extremely dangerous, not least because of the risk of infection. Soranos recommended the procedure only if a woman's life was in danger. There were also legal objections. An Athenian law quoted by Lysias made it a criminal offense for a pregnant woman whose husband had died to undergo an abortion, on the grounds that the unborn child could have survived to claim its father's estate. Most objections were based on the fear of the polluting effect of an aborted fetus. A sacred law from the sanctuary of Artemis in Cyrene, for instance, decreed that "if a woman has a miscarriage or abortion when the foetus is fully formed the household is polluted as if by death [i.e., heavily], whereas if it is not fully formed, the household is polluted as if by childbirth [i.e., lightly]." Aristotle, who advocated performing an abortion only "before the foetus received life and feeling," seems to have been mainly concerned with the risk of increased pollution that a later abortion would cause (*Politics* 1335b 24–26). Not until the third century A.D., however, was a law introduced which established an outright ban on abortion as a crime against the rights of the parents.

Though the Greeks had certain reservations about terminating an un-wanted pregnancy, they showed little concern for the rights, as we would phrase it, of the newborn child. They did not, however, go so far as to kill unwanted babies, for the simple reason that to do so would cause pollution and involve the murderer in blood guilt. Instead, the unwanted infant was carried outside the city and abandoned to its fate. The legend of Oedipus tells of an infant who was abandoned because of a prophecy that he would kill his father and marry his mother. In order to reduce his chances of survival still further, his father took the added precaution of nailing his ankles together, from which in later time he received the name Oedipus or "Swollen Foot." In Sparta the abandon-ment of handicapped and sickly infants was required by law. Plutarch informs us that the father of a newborn child had to present his offspring for inspection before the council of Spartan elders. If it was strong and lusty, the council ordered him to raise it, but if it was not, the father was ordered to expose it at the foot of Mount Taygetos "in the belief that the life which nature had not provided with health and strength was of no use either to itself or to the state" (*Life of Lykourgos* 16.1–2).

Girls were abandoned more frequently than boys, partly because their usefulness in the home was more limited than that of boys, and partly because they had to be provided with a substantial dowry in order to attract a suitable husband. For this reason, families with more than two daughters were probably somewhat rare. In a lost work, Poseidippos, a comic writer of the third century B.C., puts the following revealing re-mark into the mouth of one of his characters: "If you have a son you bring him up, even if you're poor, but if you have a daughter, you aban-don her, even if you're rich." The same preference for a son is poignantly revealed in a letter written on a papyrus from Hellenistic Egypt. The writer, a soldier who was billeted in Alexandria, informs his pregnant wife that if she gives birth to a boy she should raise him, but if to a girl she should expose her. Evidently the mother's feelings were regarded as irrelevant. The lower value placed on girls is also strikingly illustrated by Herodotos' comment about the Spartan king Kleomenes who, he says, "died childless, leaving only one daughter, Gorgo, behind" (5.48). Other groups that were at risk of being exposed included the deformed and those who were the product of rape or incest.

Some estimates actually put the level of female exposure in Athens at as high as 10 percent. However, almost everything that we know about the practice derives from literary sources. It is certain, too, that some exposed infants would have survived, as is indicated in the contract with the wet nurse Didyma, quoted above. Infertility was a serious problem in the Greek world, and many childless couples would have been only too happy to act as the foster parents of an unwanted child. This was the experience of the infant Oedipus who, having aroused the pity of the servant entrusted with the task of exposing him, grew up believing that he was the offspring of the king and queen of Corinth, his adoptive parents.

In the fourth year of its life, an Athenian child was brought to the Anthesteria, or Flower Festival, which took place in early spring. Here it was presented with a wreath to wear on its head, a small jug known as a *chous*, and a small cart. **A Child's First Years** This was also when it experienced its first taste of wine. Since wine was the gift of Dionysos and the drinking of wine was, as we shall see later, invariably accompanied by religious ritual, the Anthesteria performed the function of a kind of rite of passage, marking an important transitional moment in a child's life.

Athenians felt particular tenderness toward children who died before attending their first Anthesteria. A *chous* was placed beside them in the grave, evidently to compensate them for the fact that they had not received one in life. In the graves of even younger children, feeding bottles have been found. In some cases the black glaze around the spout has worn away, indicating that the bottle had been used before the baby died. Infant mortality—deaths during the first year of life—was extremely high in Greece, perhaps accounting for more than a quarter of all live births. Diarrheal diseases resulting from a lack of clean drinking water and the absence of a satisfactory waste disposal system—the two main killers in the developing world today—were major causes.

Many funerary monuments commemorate the deaths of small children. One bears an inscription which informs us that the deceased, whose name was Philostratos, bore the nickname Little Chatterbox, and that he was "a source of joy" to his parents "before the spirit of death bore him away." Another shows a pudgy child of about three stretching out his hands in the direction of a bird which his sister is holding. The inscription on the gravestone states that the monument was erected in honor of Mnesagora and her little brother Nikochares "whom the doom of death snatched away," perhaps as the result of a joint accident or an illness to which they both succumbed.

Toys and Games   Most toys were made in the home. There is archaeological evidence for miniature horses on wheels, boats, spinning tops, and rattles. Dolls with movable limbs were also very popular. In the following passage from Aristophanes' *Clouds*, Strepsiades, a doting father, tells how his precocious son used to construct his own toys:

> Oh he's clever all right. When he was only knee-high to a grass-hopper, he made houses out of clay and wooden boats and chariots from bits of leather, and he carved pomegranates into the shape of little frogs. You just can't imagine how bright he was! (lines 877–81)

A favorite game, especially among girls, was knucklebones, in which knucklebones are tossed and an attempt is made to catch them on the back of the hand, without dropping any. If any are dropped, the player must attempt to pick them up without dropping those already in her hands. Another popular game, which resembled checkers, was played on a board with black and white squares. The best throw was three sixes, which was proverbial for good luck. Ball games were extremely popular, despite the fact that it was impossible to manufacture a truly spherical ball. Children used to blow up a pig's bladder and try to make it rounder by heating it in the ashes of a fire. Some ancient ball games are still in vogue today. In one a player was selected to throw the ball and the others had to drop out one by one as they were hit. Boys at puberty and girls at marriage customarily dedicated their toys to the gods.

Growing Up   Both boys and girls spent a great deal of time in the company of their mothers and slaves. Fathers, who were absent much of the time, played only a minor role in the rearing of their children, until they reached puberty. In Sparta, where men spent most of their time communally with their peers, the matricentral tendency of the home was especially pronounced. Spartan mothers had a reputation for putting extreme moral pressure upon their sons. One is said to have remarked to her son as she handed him his shield before he departed for war that he should return, "Either with this or on this" (Plutarch, *Moral Sayings* 241f). What she meant was that he should not disgrace himself by throwing away his shield in flight.

The following speech, attributed to Sokrates by Xenophon, provides an especially moving tribute to motherhood:

> It is she who is impregnated, she who bears the load during preg-nancy, she who risks her life for her child, and she who supplies it with the food with which she herself is nourished; and then, having

brought it into the world with much labor, she nourishes it and cares for it, although she has received no good and the child does not recognize its benefactress and has no means of signaling its desires. But a mother guesses what it needs and likes and tries to satisfy it, and rears it for a long time, toiling day after day, night after night, not knowing what gratitude she will receive in return. (*Memorabilia* 2.2.5)

Though the mother was the primary figure in a child's growing years, the one with authority was the father or legal guardian. This authority was formidable and entitled him, for instance, to enslave his daughter if he caught her in an act of illicit sexual intercourse.

Despite the fact that the Greek family was a much stronger unit than ours is today, it was by no means spared all the ills that afflict contemporary society. **Juvenile Delinquency** Though we do not hear about the children of broken homes, many must have grown up in acute poverty. Paradoxically, however, juvenile delinquency seems to have been more common among the well-to-do than among the poor. A detailed description is preserved in a speech by Demosthenes, which was written on behalf of a young man called Ariston around the middle of the fourth century B.C. Ariston claims to have been the victim of an unprovoked attack while walking home late one night through the Agora. He subsequently indicted the father of his chief assailant, a man called Konon, who played a leading part in the assault. In the speech that he delivered while prosecuting Kimon, he describes the attack as follows:

First they tore my cloak off me, and then, tripping me up and pushing me into the mud, they struck me so violently that they split my lip and caused my eye to close up. They left me in this sorry condition, so that I could neither get up nor utter a word. While I was lying there, I heard them making a number of abusive comments, many of which were so offensive that I would shrink from repeating them in your presence. One indication of Konon's insolence and proof of the fact that he was the instigator of the whole affair, I will tell you. He began to make a sound in imitation of the song made by fighting cocks when they have scored a victory, while his associates encouraged him to move his elbows around against his sides as if they were wings. After this I was picked up naked by some passers-by, for my assailants had carried off my cloak. (54.8–9)

Ariston warns the jury that the kind of defense that they are likely to hear from Konon is that there are many young men in Athens from good backgrounds who become infatuated with prostitutes and then come to blows over them with other young men. He will argue, in other words, that such behavior should be treated with indulgence by the jury. Ariston, however, maintains that rivalry over prostitutes had nothing to do with the attack and that his assailants held a personal grievance against him. He claims that there was a history of bad blood between Konon's son Ktesias and himself. When they were serving as *ephebes* (or cadets) on the borders of Attica, Ktesias and his brother amused themselves by emptying the contents of their chamber pots over the heads of the personal slaves of their fellow soldiers. Unfortunately we do not have the speech for the defense, so it is impossible to determine what part Ariston himself might have played in stirring things up. What is evident, however, is that rivalry among privileged youths featured prominently in a society which encouraged a high degree of competitiveness among all social groups.

There is no evidence to suggest that Greek society produced a disaffected youth culture that set its face against the values of society as a whole. We hear of only one isolated instance of violence against property. This was perpetrated in Athens in 415 B.C. by the so-called *Hermokopidai*, or "Herm-mutilators." Herms were stone pillars surmounted by a carved head. The rest of the pillar was in block form except for a carved phallus. They stood at street corners and served as boundary markers. The *Hermokopidai* disfigured the faces of these pillars and removed their phalluses. The crime, however, was not a mindless prank. On the contrary it had a political objective, for it was intended to prevent the sailing of the Athenian expedition to Sicily. Since Hermes was the god of travelers, the destruction of his image was naturally interpreted as an extremely bad omen, as was no doubt the vandals' intention. The identity of the perpetrators remains unknown, however, and we do not actually know for certain whether they were youths.

THE ELDERLY

Life Expectancy Though estimates about life expectancy in the Greek world vary considerably, it is possible that it was little more than half the level common in Western society today. The major source of evidence for age at death is skeletal, which is at best only approximate. Greek funerary monuments, unlike Roman ones, rarely record age at death except in the case of those who survived to extreme old age and for whom the recording of their years was thus a matter of personal pride. Yet despite the brevity of human life, three score years and ten none the less constituted the proper quota of years, as is indicated in a fragmentary poem by the Athenian lawgiver Solon: "If a man finally reaches the full measure of his years [i.e., seventy], let him receive the apportionment of death, without dying prematurely." Maximum life expectancy also seems to have been the same as it is today. The oldest Athenian known to us was a certain Euphranor, whose gravestone records that he lived to the ripe old age of 105. Women's life expectancy was about ten years lower than that of men. There were many reasons for the disparity. First, other than in Sparta, girls were not as well fed as boys. This had the effect of rendering them more susceptible to disease and in certain cases of permanently impairing their health. Second, the early age at which many girls became pregnant—shortly after puberty—imposed severe strains upon their bodies, as did the frequency with which they became pregnant. In addition, many women were required to do manual work, often of a highly demanding nature. Men, by contrast, tended to lead less strenuous lives than women, except when they went to war, which was mainly a seasonal activity.

One of the most memorable literary portraits of old age is that of Nestor, king of Pylos, who is a major character in the *Iliad*. Nestor claims to have "seen two generations pass away . . . and now be ruling over the third" (1.250–52). Though given to delivering lengthy homilies about the su- **Literary Portraits of the Elderly** periority of the men of his generation to those of the present, Nestor nonetheless commands respect from the Greek chiefs. Indeed, Agamemnon goes so far as to declare that if he had ten men of his quality advising him on strategy, Troy would soon be captured. In Attic Comedy the elderly are often caricatured as irascible and vituperative. A notable example is Philokleon, who appears in Aristophanes' *Wasps*. Philokleon is depicted as a superannuated delinquent who looks back wistfully on his youth with all the venom of a frustrated old age.

We have no means of knowing what percentage of the Greek population was able to retire. Nor is there any way of estimating to what extent the Greeks regarded retire- **Retirement or Death in Harness?** ment as an attractive or even possible option. Though we occasionally hear of the head of the household handing over the management of his property to his son, we do not know of a single Greek who actually looked forward to retirement. Nor is there any hint as to the fate of elderly or infirm slaves. While domestics such as nurses and pedagogues would probably have been treated humanely in their declining years, the prospects for those who did not have a personal relationship with their masters must have been grim indeed.

The Greeks regarded the care of the elderly, which they called *gêroboskia*, as a sacred duty, the responsibility for which rested exclusively with the offspring. Greek law laid **Caring for the Elderly** down severe penalties for those who omitted to discharge their obligations. In Delphi, for instance, anyone who failed to look after his parents was liable to be put in irons and thrown into prison. In Athens those who neglected either their parents or their grandparents were fined and partially deprived of their citizen rights. There were no public facilities for the aged—the very idea of an old people's home would have been utterly alien to the Greeks.

In Athens it was customary for a childless man to adopt a male heir of adult years to whom he would leave the entirety of his estate. In return the adopted son would look after him in old age, give him a proper burial, and pay regular visits to his tomb. The adopted son would lose all legal connection with the family into which he had been born, including the right to inherit. In this way, if he had an heir himself, he would prevent his adoptive father's household from dying out. To a limited degree this arrangement may have served to redistribute wealth, since the majority of adopted sons would presumably not have relinquished their entitlement to inherit from their natal homes without the expectation of an improvement in their financial prospects. Adoption was as much a practical as a sentimental arrangement, into which both parties entered with a firm calculation of their own advantage.

The majority of elderly Greeks probably remained physically and mentally alert until their final illness. Few households can have had the time, energy, or resources to look after those who were bedridden and incapacitated. Even the aged would have been expected to play some part, however small, in their economic well-being. Odysseus' father Laertes, who makes himself useful by working in the vineyard on his own farm, is likely to have been typical (*Odyssey* 24.205ff.).

Respect for the Elderly Even in the aristocratic world evoked by the Homeric poems, the elderly seem to have been concerned about the degree of respect that they received from the younger generation. Harking back to a supposedly Golden Age when youths were inherently deferential to their elders, Nestor remarks at the beginning of one of his long speeches, "In former times I associated with better warriors than you and they never made light of me" (*Iliad* 1.260f.).

Though Athenians were required by law to look after their parents, contempt for the elderly seems to have become something of a national characteristic by the late fifth century B.C. This was in marked contrast to Sparta, where old people were held in high esteem. This difference in attitude is in part a reflection of the conservative temperament of the Spartan people. In Xenophon's *Memorabilia*, Perikles despairingly demands, "When will the Athenians respect their elders in the same way that the Spartans respect theirs, instead of despising everyone older than themselves, beginning with their own fathers?" (3.5.15). According to Herodotos (2.80), it was a characteristic of Spartan youths to stand aside for their elders when they passed them in the street and to rise when they entered the room.

Greek physicians do not seem to have been much concerned with the welfare of the elderly. There is little discussion of the ailments of the elderly in medical treatises, still less about how to treat them. Given the **Medical Neglect of the Elderly** absence of effective painkillers, many old people presumably ended their days in extreme discomfort. A Hippokratic treatise entitled *Aphorisms* lists the following ills to which old age is subject:

> Difficulty in breathing, catarrh accompanied by coughing, problems of the urinary tract, arthritis, nephritis, dizzy spells, apoplexy, cachexia, itching of the whole body, insomnia, watery discharge from the bowels, the eyes and the nostrils, dullness of vision, glaucoma, and deafness. (3.31)

It is unlikely, however, that many elderly persons would have sought to take their own lives in order to end their misery, since suicides were thought to constitute an unhappy category of the dead. Only among the Stoic philosophers was it regarded as a point of honor for the very aged to terminate their existence before entering upon their dotage.

THE DISABLED

Probably most Greeks became affected by at least partial disablement by the time they had reached middle, let alone old, age due to the demands and **The Prevalence of Disability** stresses of life in the ancient world. The price of survival to what we would identify as middle age for the average man or woman was an unpalatable assortment of rotting and rotten teeth, failing eyesight, increasing deafness, constant back pains, vicious stomach ulcers, and unpredictable bowel movements. Disorders of the foot were the commonest form of injury, as we know from the fact that these inspired the largest number of votive offerings in healing sanctuaries. As there were only very limited means of alleviating any disability whether slight or severe, a relatively mild disability like, say, astigmatism or a badly set fracture, would often be as constricting as a major one. Among the poor, the onset of disability would have meant a serious reduction in economic circumstances, which would have contributed further to the pace of their decline. It goes without saying that those who were most at risk of becoming disabled as a result of both sickness and injury were slaves. Since no professional medical care was available for those who were bedridden, it would also have been the slaves who tended to the needs of the seriously disabled. Those who could afford round-the-clock medical attention probably received as good as anything offered today in the intensive care ward of a modern hospital. To use an example from the Roman world, we hear from Pliny the Younger of a certain Domitius Tullus, who "could not even turn in bed without assistance." Domitius, evidently a cussed old sod, was often heard to say that "every day he licked the fingers of his slaves," evidently because he required them to spoon-feed him (*Letters* 8.18).

In addition to those who became disabled in later life, many infants would have suffered permanent debility from contaminated drinking water, which encourages the spread of cholera and typhus. Viral diseases such as meningitis, measles, mumps, scarlet fever, and smallpox, which produce damaging side effects such as deafness and blindness, are also likely to have been common. Malnutrition, which impedes the growth and composition of bones, is likely to have been especially prevalent among girls. Fewer congenitally deformed infants would have survived to adulthood than is the case today, however, in part because the Greeks had little compunction about withholding the necessities of life from those deemed incapable of leading a full and independent existence. In Sparta, as we have seen, the abandonment of deformed infants was required by law. Likewise Aristotle recommended that there should be a law "to prevent the rearing of deformed children" (*Politics* 7.1335b, 19–21).

Attitudes Toward the Disabled   Reports of persons exhibiting gross deformities were probably widely circulated in the Greek world, as the name of the one-eyed giant Polyphemos ("Much talked about") suggests, even though Homer never specifically describes the giant's synophthalmia. Already in Hesiod we encounter the belief that the birth of a congenitally deformed infant was an expression of divine ill-will (*Works and Days* 235). Moreover, oaths frequently contained the proviso that, if they were broken, the oath breaker would give birth to children who were "monsters." Such a belief would surely have acted as an inducement to abandon a deformed child rather than let it live as a permanent reminder of its parents' shame.

The absence of physical blemish was a requirement for holding a priesthood. However, there is no evidence to indicate that the Greeks took official notice of abnormal births, nor that they constituted a distinctive category of divination. This was in marked contrast to Rome, where the birth of a deformed child was regarded as portentous in the extreme. Given the religious importance attached to physical wholeness, it is likely that the deformed were stigmatized as second-class citizens, such as the hunchbacked Thersites, whose humiliation at the hands of Odysseus is greeted with approval by the entire Greek army (*Iliad* 2.211–77). No provision was made to facilitate the participation of the physically disadvantaged in ceremonies and rituals of a civic or religious nature. Few individuals of whom we have record are known to have been congenitally deformed. A rare exception is the Spartan king Agesilaos, who was both diminutive and congenitally lame. Hunchbacks, cripples, dwarfs, and obese women were popular entertainers at drinking parties.

The majority of the disabled and chronically deformed probably begged or claimed the indulgence of a well-to-do relative. The only state that is known to have made any provision for its disabled was Athens, which provided a very small pension for those who were financially insolvent. The primary candidates, no doubt, were those who had been injured or maimed while fighting for their country. Even so, there was a deep suspicion of malingerers, and those claiming disability pensions were required to undergo a physical examination by the council or *boulê*. There also existed an Athenian law that enabled meddlesome citizens to bring charges against persons whom they suspected of claiming welfare under false pretenses.

"No one is responsible for the fact that I am deformed except my own parents," moans the crippled fire god Hephaistos in Book 8 of the *Odyssey*, "and I wish they had never given birth to me" (line 311f.). Nowhere else in Greek literature do we hear a similarly heart-rending utterance from a disabled person. Though the disabled were numerous, they have left little trace in the historical record. Evidently they saw no advantage in trailing their misery before the public eye. The defendant in Lysias' *Oration* 24, whose right to public support was challenged by a fellow citizen, provided the jury with no description of his affliction, even though appeals to pity were a conventional feature of Athenian law court speeches. Physical pain and discomfort were not the only burdens that the disabled had to endure. They were also routinely exposed to shame, ostracism, stigma, guilt, disgrace, and ridicule. Judged overall, it seems likely that the disabled were expected to suffer in silence, make as few demands upon society as possible, and remain hidden behind closed doors, since their presence constituted a source of shame both to their families and to themselves. Their plight is easily overlooked when we conjure up the image of godlike physical perfection bequeathed to us by the Greek world.

Conclusions

SLAVES

The vast majority of Greeks from Homer to Aristotle regarded slavery as an indisputable fact of life. Its existence at the heart of the Classical world is thus a source of considerable disquiet to those who admire Greek culture for its supposedly enlightened humanism. It is important to appreciate, however, that slavery was not an absolute condition but one that admitted many different statuses. It included at one end of the scale chattel slaves, those who in Aristotle's telling phrase had the same status as "an animate or ensouled piece of property" (*Politics* 1253b 33), and at the other end those who lived independently and remitted a part of their income to their masters.

The Origins of Slavery   The origins of slavery are not precisely understood, but the institution was certainly in existence by the end of the eighth century B.C. In the world evoked by the Homeric poems most slaves were obtained by piracy, kidnapping, or warfare. Odysseus' swineherd Eumaios, for instance, was captured and sold into slavery as a child. Enslavement is the fate that awaits the female members of the royal household when Troy is taken. It would also have been the fate of women and children in historical times when a besieged city fell. In seventh century B.C. Greece, slavery appears to have been widespread even among the poorest section of society. Hesiod, in *Works and Days* (line 405f.), is of the opinion that an ox and a bought woman are an essential part of a small farmer's holding.

The Size of Athens' Slave Population   Slaves were particularly numerous in Athens and may well have outnumbered those in any other Greek community. Thukydides (7.27.5) claims that "more than 20,000," most of them manual workers, absconded to Dekeleia in northern Attica when it was occupied by the Spartans in 413 B.C. All other evidence is anecdotal. In Classical times the possession of at least one slave was regarded as a necessity. In a lawsuit written by Lysias the speaker states, "I have a trade but I don't earn much. I find it difficult making ends meet and I can't save enough money to buy a slave to do the work for me" (24.6). It is a mark of his meanness that Theophrastos' *Tight-Fisted Man* refuses to buy his wife a slave girl and instead hires one from the women's market (*Characters* 22.10). The majority of well-to-do Athenians probably owned two or three slaves, whereas the wealthy possessed between ten and twenty. A few, however, owned a great many more. Nikias, one of the richest men in Athens in the late fifth century B.C., owned 1,000 slaves, whom he leased out to fellow citizens at the rate of one obol per slave per day (Xenophon, *Revenues* 4.14). The only surviving slave census relates to Athens in the late fourth century B.C. The total, which is put at 400,000, exceeds all bounds of credibility.

The Racial Diversity of Athens' Slaves   Athenian slaves were imported from a wide variety of regions including Thrace, Scythia, Illyria, Colchis, Syria, Caria, and Lydia. Such diversity was probably fairly typical. The purchase price of a slave varied according to his or her skills and looks. Obviously an educated slave who could read and write fetched considerably more than one who was only good for menial duties. Likewise a pretty young girl cost much more than an ugly old hag. Slaves with management skills were extremely expensive. Nikias, whom we mentioned above, paid a talent

(6,000 drachmas) for a slave to manage his silver mines. A slave in good health probably cost the equivalent of half a year's salary. The inscription relating to the sale of confiscated property that belonged to the Mutilators of Herms in 414 B.C. prices a Syrian male at 240 drachmas, a Thracian female at 220 drachmas, and "a little Carian boy" at 72 drachmas. Though most Athenian slaves were purchased from abroad, some were bred in captivity, as indicated by the following remark made by Ischomachos in Xenophon's *Household Management*: "As a general rule, if good slaves are permitted to breed, their loyalty increases, whereas when bad slaves live together as husband and wife they are more liable to cause trouble" (9.5).

Domestic slaves served in practically every capacity, including that of washerwoman, cook, porter, cleaner, tutor, **Domestic** escort, messenger, nurse, and companion. No doubt in the **Slaves** larger households there was some division of labor, as for instance among the female slaves in the palace of the Homeric king Alkinoös, "some of whom grind the yellow grain on the millstone, while others weave the web and turn the spindle" (*Odyssey* 7.104f.). Whether slaves were also employed in large numbers as agricultural laborers is unclear.

On becoming a member of an Athenian household, a slave underwent an initiation ceremony similar to that which a bride underwent on first entering her new home. This was intended to place the slave under the protection of Hestia, the goddess of the hearth. The poems of Homer suggest that close ties arose between master and slave. When, for instance, Odysseus reveals himself to his faithful slaves Eumaios and Philoitios on his return to Ithaca after twenty years, they throw their arms around him and kiss him (*Odyssey* 21.222–25). Scenes of mistress and maid figure prominently on Athenian grave monuments, testimony to the fact that the two spent much time together in the *gynaikeion*, or women's quarters. In Classical Athens slaves were occasionally buried in family plots beside their masters and mistresses.

Overall the treatment of slaves varied greatly from one household to the next. Though Athenian slaves were protected by the law against violent abuse, in practice it was virtually impossible for them to lodge a complaint against their masters, since they could not represent themselves in court. Starvation and flogging were regular punishments for bad behavior. A runaway slave was branded with a hot iron upon capture. If a slave was required to be a witness in a lawsuit, his or her testimony could be accepted only under torture.

Though we lack any account written by a slave telling us what he or she felt about his or her condition, Aristophanes in *Frogs* provides us with an insight into the kind of gossip that slave owners imagined their slaves engaging in when out of earshot:

Slave A: I'm absolutely thrilled when I can curse my master behind his back.

Slave B: What about grumbling as you're going outside after being beaten?

Slave A: That's great!

Slave B: What about not minding your own business?

Slave A: That's terrific!

Slave B: You're a man after my own heart. What about eavesdropping when he's having a private conversation?

Slave A: That's enough to drive me wild with delight!

Slave B: What about gossiping to your friends about what you discover? Do you like that?

Slave A: Do I like it? By Zeus, that's enough to make me wet my knickers! (lines 746–53)

Publicly Owned Slaves
The most privileged Athenian slaves were owned by the state. They included the notaries, jury clerks, coin testers, and executioner. In addition, a large number of publicly owned slaves toiled as road menders. As building accounts make clear, slaves sometimes worked on building projects alongside Athenian citizens. Athens' force of Skythian archers, who kept the peace, was also the property of the state.

Living Separately
Because Athenian citizens refused to satisfy the demand for wage labor in the second half of the fifth century B.C., the conditions and opportunities for a limited number of slaves improved dramatically. Such slaves, who paid a commission to their owners, were described as "living separately" (*chôris oikountes*). They included the managers of shops and factories, bankers, captains of trading vessels, bailiffs, and artisans. One was a certain Pasion, who rose to be one of the wealthiest men in Athens. Pasion, who worked as a banker, was eventually granted Athenian citizenship because he gave generously to the state at a time of crisis. Overall, however, the Athenians were niggardly in freeing their slaves, even when they had served them dutifully all their life.

Industrial Slaves
The most dangerous and exhausting work performed by Athenian slaves was in the silver mines of Lavrion in southeast Attica. Inscriptions reveal that the vast majority of industrial slaves were barbarians. Xenophon (*Memorabilia* 2.5.2) informs us that the price of slaves who served in this capacity could be as low as 50 drachmas. Work in the mines continued uninterruptedly for twenty-four hours a day. From the discovery of miners' lamps containing oil, it has been estimated that shifts were ten hours in length.

Though it had its critics, the institution of slavery was never seriously challenged in the ancient world. Even phi- **Conclusions** losophers such as the Cynics and Stoics, who professed to believe in the brotherhood of mankind, were muted in their opposition. In the *Politics*, Aristotle goes so far as to justify slavery as part of the order of existence, though he makes a distinction between what he calls slaves by nature, those born in captivity, and slaves by law, those captured in war. Aristotle proposed this distinction in response to those who regarded the very existence of slavery as "contrary to nature" (1253b–1255b).

Our understanding of slavery in the Greek world is bedevilled by both modern Christianity and Marxism. Each imposes value judgements upon the institution, and these value judgements tend to distort our investigation of its place in ancient society. Christianity deplores slavery as barbaric and inhumane. Marxist historians identify slaves with the subjected European proletariat of the nineteenth century. Friedrich Engels even went so far as to allege that the moral and political collapse of the ancient world was chiefly caused by slavery. Neither the Christian nor the Marxist viewpoint does full justice to the realities of life in the ancient world, however. Abhorrent though the institution of slavery was in many respects, it nonetheless provided some measure of economic security. Thus when Achilles wishes to convey the worst social condition imaginable, he instances that of a man who works as a day laborer, rather than that of a slave (*Odyssey* 11.489f.). With the exception of Spartan agriculture and Athenian silver mining, there is little evidence to suggest that the Greeks depended on slavery for what Marxists call their means of production. Overall, therefore, it remains questionable whether the achievements of Greek civilization were made possible by slavery.

FOREIGNERS AND BARBARIANS

The status of being a foreigner, as the Greeks understood the term, does not permit any easy definition. Primarily it signified such peoples as the Persians and Egyptians, whose languages were unintelligible to the Greeks, but it could also be used of Greeks who spoke in a different dialect and with a different accent. Notable among this latter category were the Macedonians, whom many Greeks regarded as semibarbaric, as the following judgement upon Philip II of Macedon by the Athenian politician Demosthenes indicates:

He's so far from being a Greek or having the remotest connection with us Greeks that he doesn't even come from a country with a name that's respected. He's a rotten Macedonian and it wasn't long ago that you couldn't even buy a decent slave from Macedon. (*Third Philippic* 31)

Prejudice toward Greeks on the part of Greeks was not limited to those who lived on the fringes of the Greek world. The Boeotians, inhabitants of central Greece, whose credentials were impeccable, were routinely mocked for their stupidity and gluttony. Ethnicity is a fluid concept even at the best of times. When it suited their purposes, the Greeks also divided themselves into Ionians and Dorians. The distinction was emphasized at the time of the Peloponnesian War, when the Ionian Athenians fought against the Dorian Spartans. The Spartan general Brasidas even taxed the Athenians with cowardice on account of their Ionian lineage. In other periods of history the Ionian-Dorian divide carried much less weight.

Metics   "Metic," which comes from the Greek word *metoikos* meaning "one who dwells among," denoted a foreigner with the right to live permanently in the host country of his or her choice. Classical Athens, because of her empire, wealth, and commercial importance, attracted a vast number of metics. In this she was rather unusual, as Perikles pointed out (Thukydides 2.39.1). Approximately three-fifths of the metic population lived in demes located in or around Athens, nearly one-fifth in the port of Piraeus, and the remaining fifth in demes situated in the countryside and along the coast. At least sixty different Greek and non-Greek states are represented among their ranks, as we know from sepulchral inscriptions. In the fifth century B.C., metics perhaps accounted for as much as 10 percent of Athens' entire population, or about from 20,000 to 30,000. It should be emphasized, however, that their numbers fluctuated in line with Athens' changing fortunes and prosperity. Very likely many left before the outbreak of the Peloponnesian War in 431 B.C. Athens was not the only Greek state that encouraged the immigration of foreigners, but it was undoubtedly the one that attracted them in greatest numbers. The Spartans were notoriously xenophobic and actively discouraged foreigners from residing in their territory even on a short-term basis.

It was due to the large influx of metics around the middle of the fifth century B.C. that Athens introduced a law debarring the offspring of a union between an Athenian citizen and a metic woman from claiming citizenship. The state also revised her citizen register at this time and struck off a number of suspected metics who were believed to be claiming citizenship under false pretenses. Though Athenians could marry metic women, metic men were subject to a fine of 1,000 drachmas—the equivalent of about three years' salary—for cohabiting with an Athenian woman. Each metic had to have an Athenian sponsor, called a *prostatês*, and be registered in a deme. He or she was required to pay an annual poll tax called a *metoikion*. Men were liable to service in the military but in the navy only in times of emergency. They were also required to undertake liturgies. Metics were not permitted to own land unless they had obtained a special grant called an *enktêsis*. This entitled them either to purchase a home or establish a sanctuary for the worship of a foreign deity.

It was through their private cultic associations that metics were able to consort together and retain their distinctive identity. Many such associations also functioned as dining clubs. One of these was devoted to the worship of the Phrygian god Sabazios, an exotic deity whose nocturnal rites included ecstatic dances accompanied by the flute and kettledrum. The cult of Sabazios aroused such animosity when it was first introduced into Athens that it was the butt of humor in no fewer than four comedies by Aristophanes. In one play, Sabazios, together with other foreign deities, is booted out of Athens. In the middle of the fourth century B.C., however, the Athenians received an oracle ordering them to desist from persecuting the followers of Sabazios. This had the desired effect, and in time the Athenians themselves became worshipers of Sabazios. An inscription dated to the very end of the second century B.C. records the names of fifty-one members of the cult, no fewer than thirty-six of whom were Athenian.

Religion apart, to what extent were the Athenians tolerant of foreign influences, let alone in the business of absorbing them? We know that some Athenians affected the Spartan style of dress by wearing short cloaks and growing their hair long. In addition, the Athenians' fascination with the sophists, who were teachers of rhetoric, is often quoted as an instance of their appetite for foreign ideas. As the sophists and Spartans were Greek, however, they hardly count as foreign.

It is sometimes suggested that the Greeks more or less invented racism single-handedly by holding up their culture **Barbarians** as a shining example of everything that was noble and praiseworthy, while at the same time rubbishing everybody else, particularly the Persians. The truth, however, is rather more complex. Even if the Greeks considered their culture to be superior to others, that does not mean that they were out-and-out racists. Moreover, some Greeks saw much to admire in Persian culture. The historian Herodotos was so enamored of the Persians that he was dubbed *philobarbaros*, or "barbarian lover." Overall, the Greek attitude toward the Persians was probably a complex mixture of fascination, envy, and contempt.

The notion of the barbarian was not inherent in Greek culture. There is no trace of racial prejudice against the Trojans in Homer's *Iliad*. In fact, the regard for civilized values on the part of the Trojans is equal, if not superior, to that of the Greeks. The word *barbarophônoi*, meaning "of barbarous diction," appears only once in the *Iliad*, in reference to a contingent of Karians, a semi-barbarous people who fought on the side of the Greeks. Not until Aeschylus' *Persians*, which was produced in 472 B.C., are barbarians depicted as a stereotypical group with a homogeneous culture. This change came about as a result of the Persian invasion of Greece—an event that bred terror and loathing in the Greek population, similar in intensity to that felt toward the hated Hun by the Allies in World War I. The stereotype was also disseminated through art, notably in portrayals of the battle between the Lapiths and Centaurs, which we find on the metopes of the Parthenon. The lascivious and aggressive Centaurs stand for the Persians and the innocent and abused Lapiths for the Greeks. Depictions of this mythological encounter, in which right clearly triumphed over wrong, served to bolster Greek self-esteem and self-righteousness in the aftermath of the Persian invasion.

Precisely what the category barbarian amounted to in practical terms is difficult to determine. The most plausible origin of the word is "the people who mutter ba-ba-ba." Barbarians, in other words, were people who could not speak Greek. Non-Greek speakers were excluded from participation in the Olympic Games and from certain other religious ceremonies, such as the Eleusinian Mysteries. In time, however, barbarian also came to acquire the pejorative meaning of "ignorant, brutal, and savage."

"Typical" barbarian behavior included drinking neat wine, beer, and milk; wearing effeminate clothing; and practicing circumcision. Thukydides (1.6.1–3) was of the belief that contemporary barbarians behaved similarly to the earliest inhabitants of Greece, in that they carried weapons around with them and wore loincloths when exercising. The most despised feature of barbarian society, however, was the subjugation of its population to one man, as the following brief exchange from Aeschylus' *Persians* indicates. It takes place at the royal capital of Susa shortly after the Persian queen received news of her son's defeat at the battle of Salamis.

> *Queen*: Who is their leader? Who commands their army?
>
> *Chorus*: They declare themselves to be the slaves of no-one and to serve no-one.
>
> *Queen*: How then can they withstand an enemy invasion?
>
> *Chorus*: Well enough to destroy King Dareios' large and powerful army. (lines 241–44)

Despite the highly negative view of barbarian culture that many Greeks held, there is no evidence to suggest that barbarians were unwelcome or subjected to mistreatment if they traveled to Greece. On the contrary, they figure prominently among Athens' metic population in the fourth century. The Sidonians, who were Phoenicians, actually enjoyed a privileged status that was not extended to other metics: they were exempted from the metic tax and other financial burdens.

The outermost reaches of geographical knowledge were thought to be inhabited by monstrous races, descriptions **Ultimate** of whom were brought back by travelers. They include the **Monstrosity** Astomoi or Mouthless Ones, who have holes in their faces instead of mouths; the Skiapods or Shadowfeet, a one-legged people who lie on their backs shading their heads from the sun with a single huge foot; and the Kynokephaloi or Dogheads, who communicate by barking.

The blinding of the Cyclops Polyphemos by Odysseus and his men. From *Homer* by Martin Thorpe (Bristol, U.K.: Bristol Classical Press, 1973). Reprinted by permission of Duckworth Publishers.

No figure quite so succinctly epitomizes the horror of the foreign, however, as the Cyclops Polyphemos, whom Odysseus encounters in Book 9 of the *Odyssey*. Solitary, monstrous in size, possessing a single eye in the center of his forehead, stupid, contemptuous toward the gods, hostile toward strangers, ignorant of seafaring and agriculture, Polyphemos is everything that the Greeks despised. Who could fail to be repulsed by the description of the regurgitated pieces of human flesh that surface at the corners of his giant maw, as he sleeps off a dinner that consisted of Odysseus' companions? And who could fail to applaud when Odysseus blinds his single eye with a stake, before escaping from the cave by grabbing onto the belly of Polyphemos' favorite ram?

This interpretation nonetheless ignores one or two important details that are less than complimentary to the hero. In the first place, the encounter with the Cyclops could have been avoided altogether if Odysseus had listened to his companions, instead of being guided by his own insatiable curiosity. It was his curiosity that prompted him to wait for the Cyclops in his cave, and this in turn led to the deaths of several of his companions. Again, after he escaped, it was his irrepressible ego that caused him to reveal his name to the Cyclops, enabling the Cyclops to curse him in the name of his father Poseidon and delay Odysseus' homecoming by many years. In short, the encounter leaves us with the distinct impression that a canny Greek is by no means intellectually light-years ahead of an ignorant and uneducated Cyclops. Already in Homer's day, the category "barbarian" was problematic.

THE SPARTAN ALTERNATIVE

Spartan society was unique in that the needs of the family were wholly subordinated to the requirements of the state. It was a militaristic society, whose primary objective from the seventh century B.C. onward was to foster a high degree of conformity and discipline. It therefore differed radically from Athenian society, to which it is unflatteringly contrasted in Perikles' Funeral Speech (Thukydides 2.37–39). Perikles' view notwithstanding, there were a good many Greeks who admired the Spartan system. Xenophon (*Constitution of the Spartans* 10.4), for instance, an Athenian who was born a generation later than Perikles, has this to say about it: "The state of Sparta with good reason outshines all other states in virtue, since she alone has made the attainment of a high standard of nobility a public duty" (line 10.4).

It would be extremely difficult to write a detailed account of Spartan daily life, since its people have left behind so few traces of themselves. Most of what we know about their society comes from philosophers and historians, and they were hardly concerned with the practicalities of daily life. What is beyond dispute, however, is that Sparta was extremely conservative, as we know from the fact that its constitution remained unchanged for hundreds of years. Virtually from birth onward, the obligation to the state overrode any duty to self or family. Appropriately, therefore, the only two types of Spartans who were accorded the distinction of being honored with tombstones that recorded their names were soldiers who died in battle and women who died in labor.

Upbringing The Spartan home was hardly a home in our sense of the word, since children spent most of their time with their peers. Even the first years of a boy's life were not completely free of discipline, as Plutarch informs us: "Spartan nurses taught Spartan babies to avoid any fussiness in their diet, not to be afraid of the dark, not to cry or scream, and not to throw any other kind of tantrum" (*Life of Lykourgos* 16.3).

From the age of six onward boys were removed from the care of their parents and subjected to a tough system of state education known as the *agôgê*, or training. The aim of the *agôgê*, which had something of the character of a Victorian boarding school, was to instill obedience, discipline, and resourcefulness. It probably had the further consequence of turning the child first into a brat, then into a bully. Boys were divided into packs and placed under the general control of an educational director known as a *paidonomos*. The boys were whipped for minor offenses and never given enough food in order to encourage them to thieve. Plutarch describes the process as follows:

> Learning how to read and write was not considered important. Mainly their education consisted in learning how to carry out orders, how to test themselves to the limits of their endurance, and how to succeed at wrestling. So their training got tougher and tougher as they got older. Their heads were close-shaved, and they learnt how to march barefoot and go naked when training. (*Life of Lykourgos* 16.6)

The courage that this kind of training was designed to produce is indicated by the well-known story of a boy who was apprehended with a stolen fox under his cloak. Rather than admit his crime to his captors and undergo the humiliation of punishment, the boy vehemently denied the charge. His courage cost him his life because the fox gnawed through his entrails while he was being interrogated. Although physically weak babies were exposed at birth there must have been a number of perfectly fit and healthy children who were bullied mercilessly and who found this brutal system quite intolerable.

When a youth reached the age of sixteen (or possibly eighteen), he became a member of the *krypteia*. This, as its name from the Greek verb *kryptô*, meaning "conceal," indicates, was a kind of secret police force. Its purpose was to intimidate the subjected helot population. During this period he lived out in the wilds and had to fend for himself.

At the age of twenty a youth's education came to an end and he graduated to the *eirênes*, a word of uncertain etymology. He was now liable for military service, though he did not yet possess full rights of citizenship. Even now, however, he was still required to lead a communal life, eating with his peers and sleeping in army barracks. Only occasionally would he be allowed to sleep with his wife. Even on his wedding night a Spartan bridegroom was permitted to spend only a short time with his bride; he was required to return to his army barracks before dawn.

Citizenship

On reaching thirty a Spartan finally became a full citizen, or *homoios*, which means "peer." He now enjoyed something resembling a home life, though he was still required to take a number of his meals away from home. Qualification for Spartan citizenship, in fact, depended on membership in a *syssition*, or dining club. Each *syssitos*, or member of a *syssition*, made a monthly contribution to his dining club. He would not only regularly dine and relax in the company of his fellow *syssitoi*, but also fight alongside them in time of war. The size of a *syssition* is not known. Plutarch (*Life of Lykourgos* 12) suggests that the number was as low as fifteen, but modern estimates put it much higher, perhaps as high as three hundred. Only when he attained sixty was a Spartan finally released from military obligations, though, like many other retired servicemen, he probably continued to feel as much at home in the army as he did at home.

Women Although Spartan home life was extremely restricted, women actually enjoyed more freedom than their counterparts in many other parts of the Greek world. Girls were allowed to mix freely with boys. They also underwent an intensive physical training program, which included discus and javelin throwing, and wrestling. The purpose of this training program was to ensure that they became fit breeders of Spartan babies. The extreme value that was put on child rearing in Spartan society is indicated by the fact that wives could be "loaned" to an interested third party with the agreement of the husband, presumably in order to exploit their fecundity in cases where the husband was elderly or infertile. Another unique feature of Spartan society is that women were permitted to own their own property.

Spartan Helots When the Spartans conquered Lakonia and Messenia, they reduced the entire population to servile status. Known as *heilôtai*, or helots, a word that is probably connected with a verb meaning "to capture," Spartan slaves were required to till the land and pay half their produce to their masters, who were thus freed to discharge their military duties. We have no means of estimating the size of the helot population, but it almost certainly outnumbered that of the citizen body. Such was the animosity felt toward the helots that the Spartan ephors annually declared war on them. Helots had no political or legal rights and could be executed without trial. They could be freed only by a decision of the Spartan assembly. Their condition was so wretched that the poet Tyrtaios describes them as "asses worn down with great burdens." They were the property of the state and assigned by it to individual citizens, who did not have the right to dispose of them. Since, perhaps uniquely among slave populations, they were allowed to propagate without restriction, helots were racially homogeneous. For this reason the Spartans were constantly fearful of helot revolts and took extreme measures to safeguard against them, as this chilling incident reported by Thukydides indicates.

On one occasion [in 424 B.C.] the Spartans issued a proclamation to their helots offering freedom to those who judged themselves to have shown the most bravery in war. Their purpose was to make test of them, since they believed that those who came forward first to claim their freedom would also be the ones who were most likely to give them trouble. Two thousand were selected. They were crowned and did the rounds of the temples, thinking that they had been liberated. Not long afterwards, however, the Spartans eliminated them. To this day nobody knows exactly how any of them perished. (4.80.3–5)

The majority of Spartans seem to have been content to lead lives of the utmost frugality and simplicity. They had virtually no means of acquiring wealth, since the Spartan economy was wholly agrarian. Though we do not know whether every citizen possessed a *klêros* or holding assigned to him by the state at birth, most of the population were no doubt at the same point in the economic scale. When abroad and off the leash, however, Spartan generals were as greedy as the rest. A common, though no doubt occasionally trumped-up, charge leveled against them was that of accepting bribes from the enemy.

The Economy

Sparta was not the only polis that put a premium on military discipline, but it was the one that did so to an extreme degree. Since the lives of all its members were dominated by warfare, there can have been little time for relaxation and pleasure. How the Spartans occupied themselves when they were not either exercising or fighting remains a mystery. Perhaps they were simply too exhausted to bother. From the sixth century B.C. onward, they had little interest in cultivating the arts. Clearly the pursuit of happiness was not a recognized Spartan ideal. The austerity of their lifestyle gives us our word "Spartan." Hardly surprisingly, the Spartans also had a reputation for extreme economy in the use of language, and the term "laconic" derives from the Spartan aversion to long speeches. In the hands of the Spartans, however, brevity could be put to good effect. When Philip II of Macedon sent the Spartans a letter threatening to raze Sparta if he captured the city, the ephors are said to have sent him back just one word in reply: "If".

Conclusions

5

Private Life

HOUSING

The residential area of Athens consisted of narrow, winding streets and small, poorly constructed houses. Most of it lay to the northeast of the Acropolis. Somewhat paradoxically, it was not until the fourth century B.C., when Athens' economy was declining, that houses began to be constructed in a more luxurious style. One ancient commentator called Herakleides was so contemptuous of Athens that in a fragmentary work he wrote, "Most of the houses are mean, the pleasant ones few. A stranger would doubt, on first acquaintance, that this was really the renowned city of the Athenians."

The cost of purchasing a house varied enormously. In Xenophon's treatise *Household Management*, Sokrates says to his wealthy friend Kritoboulos, "I expect that if I found a good buyer, everything including the house itself would fetch 5 minai [i.e., 500 drachmas], whereas your house would sell for more than a hundred times that amount" (2.2–4).

The best-preserved Athenian house was found in the Attic countryside near the modern town of Vari, a few miles to the southeast of Athens. Though it is a farmhouse, its plan is probably similar to that of many prosperous houses in Athens: a central courtyard with rooms leading off on all four sides. There was only one entrance to the house from the road. A south-facing verandah provided a place to work and relax, shaded from the summer heat or winter rain. Judging from the thinness of its walls, it is unlikely that the Vari House had a second storey. In the

An Athenian house. Courtesy of the American School of Classical Studies at Athens.

southwest corner, however, the foundations are considerably thicker, suggesting that a tower of two or more storeys once existed here. This probably served as either a workroom or storeroom.

Building materials were extremely crude. Even the more sturdily constructed houses had lower courses of irregularly shaped stones simply piled on top of one another. Exterior walls were made of baked or unbaked mud brick, sometimes coated with lime. For the most part, walls were so thin and poorly constructed that instead of breaking in by the front door, thieves merely knocked a hole through them. The word most commonly used for a burglar means literally a "wall digger." As the orator and politician Demosthenes once remarked, "Are you surprised, men of Athens, that burglary is so common when thieves are bold and walls are merely made of mud?"

Interior walls were generally covered with a coat of plaster, whitewashed on top. Some wealthy Athenians decorated their rooms with frescoes. There was evidently a shortage of good interior decorators in fifth-century Athens, however, for the politician Alkibiades took the drastic step of locking his house painter inside his house for three months until he had finished the job. Floors consisted of beaten earth or clay, occasionally covered in animal skins or reed matting. From the fourth century B.C. onward, they were commonly decorated with mosaics made out of small pebbles. Roofs were made of wood with terra-cotta tiling. Windows were very small and set close to the ceiling to afford maximum protection against the weather. In the winter they were covered with boards or sacking to keep out the wind and rain, supplemented by shutters if the householder could afford them, since wood was both scarce and expensive. When the Athenians residing in the countryside evacuated to the city at the outbreak of the Peloponnesian War, they took their wooden doors and shutters with them.

The houses of the poor consisted of only one room, divided up into different living spaces by makeshift partitions. However, since Greek husbands regarded it as a matter of honor that their wives not be exposed to the public gaze even when at home, those who could afford it provided them with a separate living area known as the *gynaikeion* or women's quarters. A *gynaikeion* can usually only be identified in the archaeological record from the discovery of associated finds such as loom weights. It would generally have been situated at the back of the house or, if the house possessed two storeys, in the upper storey. There were, however, some exceptions. The speaker in an oration by Lysias describes his domestic arrangements as follows:

My small house has two storeys. The layout was the same upstairs as downstairs, with the women's quarters upstairs and the men's quarters downstairs. Then our child was born, whom my wife decided to nurse herself. However, every time she wanted to bathe it, she had to come downstairs at the risk of falling down the staircase. So I decided to move upstairs and put the women downstairs. I soon adjusted to the new arrangement and my wife was frequently able to sleep with the baby, so that she could breast-feed it and stop it from crying. (1.9–10)

In time, well-appointed houses also came to acquire an *andrôn* or men's quarters. The most favored location for the *andrôn* was on the north side of the courtyard, which was warmed by the winter sun. The *andrôn* was the setting for the symposium or drinking party.

Lamps provided the main source of artificial lighting. Curiously there are very few references to lamps in the Homeric poems, even though many of the scenes are set at night (*Odyssey* 19.34). From the sixth century B.C. onward, small terra-cotta lamps become extremely common in the archaeological record. They were provided with a wick that floated in olive oil. Several were required to illuminate a single room and often they were set on tall stands.

As wood does not survive in the Greek soil, we know most about furniture from illustrations on vases and sculpted gravestones. One of the most popular items was a chair with a curved back and curved legs known as a *klismos*. Three-legged tables also appear regularly, as do a variety of small stools. A basic necessity was the *klinê*, which did double duty as a couch by day and a bed by night. Cupboards were unknown but wooden chests, used for the storage of clothing and bed linen, were popular. Musical instruments and other objects are sometimes shown hanging from walls. Small terra-cotta statuettes served as popular adornments.

All water had to be fetched from outside. Many houses possessed a well in the courtyard which was cut into the bedrock sometimes to a depth of over thirty feet. In later times wells were lined with cylindrical drums made of terra-cotta to prevent their sides from crumbling into the water. From the middle of the fourth century B.C., however, following a sizeable drop in the water table in Athens, bell-shaped cisterns became popular. These were designed to catch the rainwater that drained off the roof. The quality of the water obtained in this way must have varied greatly at different times in the year.

Many Athenians, and Greeks in general, relied on the nearest public fountain for their drinking water. Collecting the daily supply of water was an arduous and time-consuming task. For the most part it was performed by slaves, though in the case of the poor, this chore fell to the mistress of the house. The public fountain was a popular place to gather and gossip, as scenes on vases indicate.

The earliest bathtub to come to light, which is of Mycenaean date, was found in the so-called Palace of Nestor at Pylos. Nearby it stood two large jars about four feet high, which probably contained water for the bath. In later times small terra-cotta bathtubs became common. Given the scarcity of water, however, only wealthy Greeks were able to immerse themselves in a full bath. Personal standards of hygiene thus varied considerably from one social class to another. Few houses possessed drains for the disposal of waste water.

Men seem to have had few qualms about relieving themselves in public. In the opening scene of Aristophanes' *Women in Assembly*, Blepyros relieves himself in the street as soon as he rises. More sophisticated Greeks used a chamber pot called an *amis*. This was shaped rather like a salt container with an opening in the front. Women used a boat-shaped vessel called a *skaphion*. Though babies could be dangled out of the window in an emergency (see Aristophanes' *Clouds*, line 1384), well-regulated houses possessed potties. One potty, which was found in the Agora, is provided with two holes for the baby's legs and a hole in the seat. Its detachable stand enabled its contents to be removed without disturbing the baby. Urination was not without its dangers. Hesiod gives the following tips about how to avoid giving offense to the gods:

> Do not urinate standing upright facing the sun but remember to do it either when the sun has set or when it is rising. Do not make water either on the road or beside the road as you go along and do not bare yourself. The nights belong to the blessed gods. A good man who has a wise heart sits or goes to the wall of an enclosed court. (*Works and Days* 727–32)

Facilities for the disposal of refuse were almost nonexistent. As a result rubbish piled up in the streets in vast quantities, creating a terrible stench and constituting a serious health hazard, particularly in the summer months. Where houses were built close together, as in Athens and the Piraeus, the streets were ankle-deep in filth. Mosquitoes, rats, and flies were plentiful, carrying all manner of diseases and causing epidemics. One of the worst epidemics occurred in 430 B.C. when the entire population of Athens was cooped up inside the city walls. The Athenians claimed that the outbreak was caused by the Spartans poisoning their reservoirs. Though there appears to have been no substance to the charge, they were correct in their belief that the contamination of their water supply was the chief cause of the spread of the disease.

We also hear of cramped and poorly constructed apartment blocks called *synoikiai*. These were surely death traps owing to the prevalence of earthquakes and the frequency of fires. *Synoikiai* were especially common in the port of Piraeus, where many poor people and foreigners resided. Domestic slaves were housed mainly in shacks some distance from the main house.

DRESS

Judged by our standards, Greek clothes were uniform and utilitarian in the extreme. It was virtually impossible to make a fashion statement by adopting an exotic or provocative style of dress, though the wealthy aristocrat Alkibiades was distinguished by special shoes that were named for him and a purple robe (Athenaios, *Professors at Dinner* 12.534c). Most clothing was made on the loom in the home under the supervision of the mistress of the house. Almost every garment was rectangular in shape and required little stitching. Since very few items of Greek clothing have survived, our knowledge derives mostly from vase paintings and sculpture.

In earlier times Athenian women wore the peplos, a long, heavy woollen garment which revealed little of the figure be- **Women** neath. The peplos hung from the body folded over at the top by about a quarter of its length. The turned-down material was attached to the shoulders by means of two long dress pins, and the garment was supported at the waist by a belt. Parts might be dyed purple or enlivened with woven geometric motifs. Embroidered decoration was, however, rare.

In the middle of the sixth century B.C., the peplos was replaced by a lighter and finer garment made of linen called the *chitôn*. Since the chitôn hugged the figure more tightly than the peplos, it was more revealing of the figure, which may reflect a modest change in attitude toward women's sexuality. The chitôn, being worn without any overfold, was held in place by a series of pins along the length of the arms. Whereas

Woman wearing a *peplos* (left) and woman wearing a *chitôn* (right). From I. Jenkins and S. Bird, *Greek Dress*. Greek and Roman Daily Life Series no. 3 (London: British Museum Education Service, n.d.). Courtesy of British Museum.

the peplos was sleeveless, the chitôn had loose, elbow-length sleeves. It, too, was fastened around the waist by a belt.

The Athenians were of the opinion that the peplos was a Doric invention, whereas the chitôn was Ionic. More likely the change was a reflection of the increased wealth of the Athenians in the middle of the sixth century B.C., since linen, being more costly to produce than wool, had to be imported. As Herodotos reports, however, the Athenians gave a more sensational explanation for it. They claimed that after a disastrous defeat at the hands of the Aiginetans, only one Athenian managed to escape. When he returned with news of the disaster, the wives of the men who had died in the battle were so outraged by the fact that he alone had escaped that they stabbed him to death with the pins of their dresses, demanding as they did so what had befallen their husbands. Herodotos concludes:

> So this man died but the Athenians thought that what the women had done was more terrible than the disaster itself. As they could find no way of punishing them, however, they made them change their dress to the Ionic style . . . which did not require any brooches. (5.87)

Bronze dress pins eighteen inches in length have come to light in excavations. They would have been more than adequate to the task of stabbing. The peplos remained popular in other parts of Greece, however, especially in the wintertime for which it was ideally suited.

The simplest male attire was a short tunic rather less than knee-length. This *exômis*, which means "off the shoulder," was held in **Men** place by means of a brooch or knot tied at the shoulder. The *exômis* was worn by manual workers, including slaves. On formal occasions, however, men wore a chitôn. Another popular garment was the *himation*, which was worn either over the chitôn or without any undergarment. This was a rectangular piece of cloth that was generally wound over the left shoulder and under the right, with the surplus material hanging over the left forearm. There was, however, practically no limit to the different ways of attaching it to the body. *Himatia* were often dyed and embroidered with a patterned border around the edge. In vase paintings and sculpture, those wearing a *himation* are often depicted leaning on a stick, which suggests that it was favored by older men. Women also wore *himatia*, usually draping them over the right shoulder and under the left arm in the same way as men. Over the course of time, the dress worn by Athenian men became simpler and less ornate. According to Thukydides, "The Spartans were the first to adopt a moderate costume . . . and in other respects, too, the propertied class [of Athens] changed their way of life to correspond as closely as possible to that of ordinary men" (1.6).

Earrings, hairpins, necklaces (worn tight around the neck), bracelets, diadems, and rings were frequently worn **Accessories** by well-to-do women. These were made out of a variety of materials, but the commonest were gilt terra-cotta, copper, and lead. More expensive items were made of silver and gold, though it is noteworthy that few pieces of gold jewelry have survived from the Archaic period. In the Classical period, however, goldsmiths produced highly intricate work, utilizing techniques such as filigree, granulation, and chasing. Infants were commonly provided with amulets to ward off evil. The only item of jewelry commonly worn by men was the signet ring, used to put a seal on private documents and merchandise. Expensive pieces were frequently buried with their owners.

As an undergarment men wore a loincloth known as a *perizôma*. A simple cloth band called a *strophion* served as a brassière for women. Other accessories used by women include the fan or *rhipis*, a flat object with a wooden handle. Another was an umbrella, or *skiadon*, used as a shield against the sun rather than as a protection against the rain. Both men and women pulled up the fold of their *himation* to serve as a kind of hood. On their travels men wore a flat, broad-brimmed hat made out of felt or straw, called a *petasos*, which they tied under the chin. When not in use, this often hung loose at the back of the neck. Workmen and slaves wore a conical cap called a *pilidion*. Women were less inclined to cover their heads than men, though in the Hellenistic Period they are often depicted wearing a sunhat with a broad brim and a pointed crown. The simplest form of footwear was the sandal. On long journeys men wore short lace-up boots, turned over at the top. Fashionable women sometimes wore platform heels. In the home both men and women usually went barefoot. All shoes and sandals were manufactured out of leather.

Perfume was popular among both men and women. It was generally manufactured by boiling the petals of flowers. Athletes applied perfume to their bodies after exercise, as is indicated by grave reliefs which show them carrying a small bottle attached to their wrists by means of a thong. Guests at a symposium also liberally sprinkled themselves with perfume. A highly prized perfume container was the *alabastron*, so named because it was carved out of alabaster.

Makeup   Contrary to today's taste, it was a sign of beauty in a woman to have a pale complexion, which is why women on vases are frequently depicted with whitened faces. Their paleness was a natural consequence of spending most of their time indoors. However, some women sought to enhance their natural appearance by applying makeup. They also applied round spots to their cheeks, and darkened their eyebrows with the soot produced by lamps. Eyes, eyelashes, and lips were also painted a variety of colors. Not everyone approved, however. In Xenophon's treatise *Household Management*, Ischomachos makes the following observation:

> One day I noticed that my wife had put makeup on. She had rubbed white lead onto her face to make her complexion look paler than it really was and rouge onto her cheeks to make them look rosier than they really were, and she was wearing platform shoes to make her look taller than she really was. (9.19.2)

This drew the following stern lecture from Ischomachos:

> You are to assume, my dear, that I do not prefer white paint and red dye to your real color, but just as the gods have made horses so as to give pleasure to horses, cows to cows, and sheep to sheep, so humans find the natural body most delightful. (9.19.7)

Ischomachos concludes his puritanical homily,

> Mix flour, knead dough, and shake and fold the cloaks and the bedclothes. This will increase your appetite, improve your health, and add redness to your cheeks. (9.19.11)

Hair   Women arranged their hair in a variety of styles. Some plaited it in long tresses, others piled it up in the form of a bun either at the nape of the neck or on the top of the head. Athenian women only "let their hair down"—literally—on special occasions, notably at festivals and funerals. This gave them license to indulge in much freer behavior than was at other times permitted to them. Often women bleached their hair or dyed it. Female slaves wore their hair short and covered it in a hairnet called a *kekryphalos*.

Freeborn men of all periods favored beards and moustaches, whereas slaves were often completely shaven. The Homeric heroes braided their hair and wore it long. This, too, is how men's hair is depicted in Archaic sculpture. In the Classical period the Athenians cut their hair much shorter, whereas the Spartans remained conservative in their preference for long hair. Plutarch writes,

> In wartime the Spartans relaxed the harshest aspects of their train-
> ing and did not prevent young men from beautifying their hair and
> their armor and their clothing, happy to see them like horses pranc-
> ing and neighing before competitions. For this reason men grew
> their hair long from adolescence onwards. Especially in times of
> danger they took care that it appeared glossy and well-combed,
> remembering a certain saying of Lykourgos concerning hair, that it
> made the handsome better-looking and the ugly more frightening.
> (*Life of Lykourgos* 22.1)

FOOD AND DRINK

The Greeks did not just eat to live; on the contrary, from earliest times, dining had enormous social importance. Homer tells us in the *Iliad* that as long as Achilles grieves for his dead comrade Patroklos he refuses all offers of food and drink. The hero's eventual acceptance of nourishment signals the abatement of that grief. Each day ends with a description of the warriors dining. Dining fills a bodily need and provides a necessary interruption to war. In historical times the conditions of soldiers were less agreeable. On short campaigns Athenian hoplites were required to bring their own provisions with them, whereas rowers were fed on a sparse diet of barley meal, onions, and cheese. At home the whole family probably dined together. The most lavish dining parties were the symposia, which are discussed later in this chapter.

The basic Greek diet was both frugal and monotonous. Athenians ate two meals a day—a light lunch, known as *ariston*, and dinner, known as *deipnon*, their main meal. Well-to-do Greeks ate reclining on couches, leaning on an elbow and using their free hand to take food from a small table in front of them. This had important consequences for the preparation of food, which had to be served in small pieces. Though knives and possibly spoons were commonplace, forks were unknown. Many Greeks probably made do with their fingers. A piece of flat bread would also have conveniently served as a kind of spoon.

In summer, meals were prepared in the open over a wood fire or charcoal grill, as is the case today in many rural parts of Greece. In winter cooking was done inside the house on a portable brazier, which also provided the only source of heating. Since chimneys were unknown, the only way that the smoke could escape was through a hole in the roof. For this reason charcoal was preferred, since it creates far less smoke than wood. Almost all cooking utensils were made of unglazed or partly glazed clay. The most common were kettles, saucepans on stands, shallow frying pans, casseroles, and grills. Though such mundane objects are rarely put on display in museums, they often have more to tell us about daily life in ancient Greece than the most beautiful painted pottery. Boiling and roasting were the most common ways of cooking, but much food was served raw.

From the end of the fifth century B.C., the Greeks began to develop an interest in culinary art. The lead in this was taken by Sicily, a region famed for its luxury, where a number of cookbooks were produced. *Professors at Dinner*, written by Athenaios, a Greek from Egypt, in c. A.D. 200, culls numerous extracts from these books and provides a vast storehouse of information on the subject of dining. As in the modern world, the most celebrated chefs tended to be men.

Cereals Homer characterizes the human race as "bread-eating," and bread remained the basis of the Greek diet throughout antiquity. It has been estimated that cereals provided 70 percent of the needed daily caloric intake. As a result of a serious shortage in cereal production over extensive areas of the eastern Mediterranean in 328 B.C., it became necessary to make free distributions of grain. This, however, was an exceptional occurrence, for which there was perhaps no parallel until the Common Era.

The grain was separated from the chaff in a shallow mortar by pushing a flat stone back and forth across the millstone. The mortar was either made of baked clay or improvised from a hollowed-out tree trunk. There were two kinds of bread: *maza*, made from barley flour, and *artos*, a white bread made from wheat. Because barley was more plentiful than wheat, *artos* was something of a luxury, largely confined to the wealthy or served to the populace at festivals. The Greeks ate bread with honey, cheese, and olive oil. They also cooked it up in a porridge or broth. The word *opson* described any type of food that was eaten with bread or other cereal.

Meat Meat was a rarity, particularly for those living in the city. Though most Greeks ate a simple casserole of game or poultry on a fairly regular basis, the only occasion when they would have tasted roasted meat was on feast days. The climax to every religious festival was the ritual slaughter of a large number of animals, including bulls, cows, sheep, goats, and oxen. This may be another reason why meat was rarely served in the home, since it was so closely associated with ritual.

Though the ostensible purpose of a sacrifice was to honor the gods, the Greeks gave the least edible parts, namely the thigh pieces, to the gods. The rest they devoured themselves. All those who attended a sacrifice received a portion of meat, the choicest parts of which were reserved for the priests.

Fish, both fresh and dried and salted, seems to have been re-garded as more of a delicacy than meat, judging by the fact that **Fish** it is more frequently mentioned in cookery than meat. Some of the best fish, including mackerel, sturgeon, tuna, sea bream, and mullet, was imported from the Black Sea region. In Athens a particularly com-mon seafood was the anchovy or sardine, which was harvested close to the Attic coast. Archestratos of Gela, a mid-fourth century B.C. poet who had a reputation for being a master cook, speaks of it as follows:

> Value all small fry as shit apart from the Athenian variety. I'm referring to sprats, which the Ionians call foam. Get hold of it fresh from the sacred arms of Phaleron's beautiful bay. What you find in wave-girt Rhodes is also good, if it happens to be local. If you'd care to taste it, you should also buy leafy sea anemones. Mix this in and bake it all in a pan, grinding the fragrant flowers of the greens in olive oil. (quoted in Athenaios, *Professors at Dinner* 285b)

A favorite delicacy was eels from Lake Kopaïs in Boeotia. Aristophanes facetiously suggests that one of the greatest hardships that the Athenians had to face during the Peloponnesian War was the lack of Kopaïc eels, since the Boeotians had sided with the enemy. Kopaïc eels were accorded a quasi-religious status by the Boeotians, as we learn from a Hellenistic historian called Agatharkides:

> The Boeotians sacrifice to the gods Kopaïc eels of extraordinary size, putting garlands on them, and praying over them, and casting barley seeds upon them, just as they do with other sacrificial vic-tims. When a foreigner expressed amazement at the custom, a Boeotian replied that he had only one explanation for it, that one should observe ancestral customs. It wasn't his business to justify such things to other people. (quoted in Athenaios 297d)

Popular vegetables included cabbages, asparagus, carrots, radishes, cucumbers, pumpkins, chicory, celery, and arti- **Vegetables,** chokes. Onions, garlic, and olives were also eaten in large **Fruit, and** quantities and provided the staple diet for those serving in **Other** the army and navy. Legumes, though high in protein, do not **Foodstuffs** appear to have been regarded as an important foodstuff. Fruits included grapes, figs, apples, pears, and dates. Nuts were generally harvested wild. Almonds, walnuts, hazelnuts, and chestnuts were among the most widely distributed.

Olive oil, used in the preparation of many meals, was the principal source of fat. It also served in religious rituals and was applied to the body after exercise. The importance of olives to Attica is indicated by the fact that the goddess Athena caused an olive tree to spring up miraculously on the Acropolis when she was competing with Poseidon for the guardianship of the land. The use of butter was regarded as a mark of the barbarian. Cheese, which was mainly produced from the milk of sheep and goats, did not figure prominently in the Greek diet. Salt was used both as a preservative and as a condiment. Silphium, sage, and rosemary also served as additives. In place of sugar, which was unknown, the Greeks used honey and dried figs. The honey that came from Mount Hymettos in Attica was particularly highly prized in antiquity, just as it is today. Beehive pots have actually come to light at the Vari House (see p. 83). Notable absentees from the Greek diet included potatoes, rice, tomatoes, citrus fruits, and bananas.

Wine   The favorite Greek drink was wine, which was almost invariably served diluted and often artificially sweetened. The Greeks preferred to drink in quantity only after they had finished eating. The islands of Chios, Lesbos, Rhodes, and Samos had the reputation for producing the best wine. Wine was transported in clay storage jars called amphorae. The handles of these amphorae were stamped with seals bearing the name of the merchant and that of the city in which the wine was produced, rather like the label on a modern bottle of wine. Beer was associated exclusively with barbarians. Milk, though used in cooking, was not a common beverage. It is thus a sign of savagery in the *Odyssey* that the Cyclops Polyphemos drinks goat's milk and has never tasted wine.

Let us end this section with a celebration of the good life as seen through the eyes of Archestratos:

> As you sip your wine let these delicacies be brought to you, pig's belly and sow's matrix, seasoned with cumin and vinegar and silphium, together with the tender species of roasted birds, as each is in season. Pay no attention to those Syracusans who drink like frogs and don't eat anything. Don't follow their example but eat what I recommend. All other delicacies are a sign of abject poverty—I mean boiled chickpeas, beans, apples, and dried figs. The flat cake made in Athens deserves praise, though. If you can't get hold of that, demand some Attic honey, as that will set your cake off really well. This is the life of a freeman! Otherwise one might as well go below the earth, even below the pit [into which condemned crim-

inals are cast] and Tartaros [the lowest region of Hades] and be buried measureless fathoms underground! (quoted in Athenaios 101c–e)

DRINKING PARTIES

When the Greeks wanted to relax at the end of the day, the choices available to them were extremely limited. Institutions such as the cinema, the theatre, the concert hall, the jazz club, and the dance hall had no ancient equivalent. So far as we know, no enterprising individual ever had the bright idea of charging admission to a place of public entertainment. There does not seem to have been anything comparable to the local pub or coffee bar. Confronted with such a barren landscape— as we at least would see it—the Greeks had no alternative but to entertain themselves. This they did foremost through the symposium, a word which means literally a "drinking together." A symposium was not, however, the ancient equivalent to a few guys getting together to shoot the breeze and down a few drinks. On the contrary, it was a highly ritualized institution with its own precise and time-hallowed rules.

Strictly speaking, "symposium" refers to the communal drinking of wine that took place at the conclusion of a dinner. Only after the tables containing food had been cleared away, garlands of flowers distributed, libations performed, and a hymn sung, was it permitted to begin drinking. Symposiasts did not sit on chairs but reclined on couches, a custom which the Greeks probably learned from the Near East around the turn of the seventh century B.C. Though a symposium served a variety of purposes, for definition we can hardly do better than quote Plutarch, a Greek writer living in the Roman era, who described it as "a passing of time over wine, which, guided by gracious behaviour, ends in friendship" (*Moral Precepts* 621c).

The most famous drinking party of all time was held at the house of a young tragic poet called Agathon in 416 B.C. **Agathon's** The pretext for the party was Agathon's first victory in the **Symposium** dramatic festival held earlier in the day. Because some of the company were suffering from hangovers, they elected to consume only a modest amount of wine. They also decided to dispense with the services of a flute-girl whom Agathon had hired for the evening. Instead they entertained themselves by each delivering an encomium in praise of Eros, the offspring of Aphrodite, goddess of love. The last to speak was Sokrates. Just when he reached the end of his delivery, a young aristocrat called Alkibiades burst into the room. Alkibiades, already somewhat the worse for drink, tried to make the other guests tipsy by forcing them to consume large quantities of wine. Eventually he settled down and agreed to follow the procedure adopted by the company by delivering a speech in praise of Sokrates. The party continued till dawn, by which time everyone had fallen asleep with the exception of Sokrates and Aristophanes, who were still conversing on the subject of poetry. Sokrates alone was completely unaffected by the alcohol that he had consumed, and around dawn, he rose, departed, took a bath, and went about his daily business.

Agathon's symposium is described by Plato in a work entitled *Symposium*, perhaps his most charming dialogue. The image it conveys, however, one of learned gentlemen delivering well thought-out speeches over a bowl of wine, can hardly be taken as typical of Athenian practice. Presented with the choice of either producing an impromptu encomium or listening to a flute-girl, the majority of Athenians would have undoubtedly opted for the latter. Nor can there have been many drinkers who had the ability to conduct an elevated discourse when flushed with wine.

As we know from references in literature, any excuse could be used to party in ancient Greece: birth, marriage, or death, the departure or arrival of a loved one from abroad, a feast day, a birthday, or merely a change in the seasons. Probably in most cases, however, no pretext was required. Given the lack of alternative entertainment, we might suppose that drinking parties were an everyday occurrence. We do not know, however, whether they were exclusive to aristocratic society or whether poorer Athenians also held symposia.

Guests It was customary for the host to inscribe the names of his guests on a wax tablet, together with the day and hour appointed for the symposium, and then hand the tablet to a slave who would make the rounds of the guests' houses. The usual hour for convening was the ninth. Generally, the ideal number of guests was nine, including the host. In Athens in the fourth century B.C., however, symposia grew so large that it became necessary to appoint a commission to ensure that the number of guests did not exceed the legal limit. Since wives and daughters were not permitted to attend symposia, the only females present were hired companions known as *hetairai*.

Rooms Reserved for Drinking The growing importance of the symposium was such that, from the fourth century B.C. onward, well-appointed houses possessed a special room for reclining and drinking known as an *andrôn* or men's quarters. An *andrôn* can be identified in the archaeological record by its off-center doorway, so located in order to enable the room to accommodate the couches, which were arranged alongside one another and set against the walls. The basic *andrôn* held four couches, though some were considerably larger. The couches were made of either wood or stone. In front of

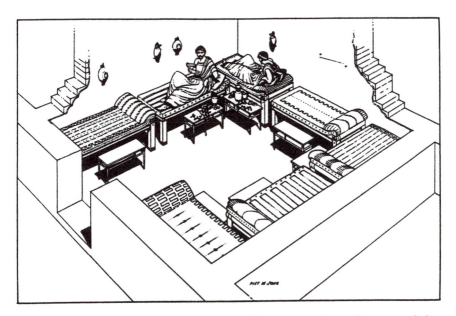

An *andrôn* or men's dining room set up for a symposium. Courtesy of the American School of Classical Studies at Athens.

each was a three-legged table on which food was laid out and the drinkers placed their cups. As private houses became more elegant, *andrônes* acquired mosaic floors and their walls were hung with tapestries.

The taking of wine was a religious act, akin to the taking of communion by Christians. This religious aspect is prominent in descriptions of the origin of wine. A Greek poet of the Roman era called Nonnos tells us that a vine sprang from the body of a youth named Ampelos, the favorite of Dionysos, when the god was lamenting the death of his beloved. As Dionysos drank the fruit of the vine, which was infused with the beauty and grace of the dead youth, he gradually forgot his sorrow. The myth thus explains why wine causes human beings to forget their cares. **Remembering the Gods**

Every stage of the symposium was marked by a traditional religious observance. Before being mixed with water, a few drops of wine were drunk in honor of the *Agathos Daimôn* or Good Spirit. In a fragment from a lost work, Theophrastos states that the purpose of this toast was "to serve as a reminder, through a mere taste, of the strength of the god's generous gift." He continues, "Having bowed three times, they take it from the table, as though supplicating the god that they may do nothing indecent or have too strong a desire for the wine." This toast was followed by three libations, to Zeus Olympios and the other Olympian gods, to the heroes, and to Zeus Soter (Savior). While these libations were being performed, a hymn was sung to the gods. Before the party broke up, a triple paean was sung to Apollo. This was followed by a hymn to Hygieia, the personification of health, which began thus: "Hygieia, most revered of the blessed gods, with thee may I dwell for the rest of my life and may thou be a gracious inmate of my house." A purificatory rite was performed both before the commencement of the symposium and at its close. So ingrained was the sense of religious occasion that Hesiod, as he sits alone under his shady rock in the heat of summer, his belly filled with good food, does not omit to perform a libation before drinking a cup of wine (*Works and Days* 592ff.).

The Master of Drinking There were strict rules to which all symposiasts were required to adhere in order to ensure that the drinking did not get out of hand. Several Greek writers even compiled books of symposiastic laws, though none has survived. The philosopher Theophrastos, however, provides us with a number of instances of bad form. It was, he tells us, the mark of an uneducated lout to drop his cup while the rest of the company was at prayer and burst out laughing, to tap or whistle in accompaniment to the flute-girl, or to spit across the table at the wine pourer.

The enforcement of these rules was in the hands of the symposiarch, or master of drinking. The ideal symposiarch, according to Plutarch, had to be "the quintessence of conviviality," neither inclined to drunkenness nor averse to drinking. He had to be aware how each of his fellow symposiasts was affected by wine in order to determine what was conducive to the promotion of good cheer. He should be cordial and friendly, and objectionable to no one. Election to this office was made on the throw of dice, which meant that it generally fell to one of the guests. The symposiarch had the authority to inflict a penalty on any drinker who infringed on the rules. In exceptional circumstances he could even order a guest to depart. As the Greeks did not drink undiluted wine, his inaugural duty was to determine the proportion of parts of wine to water—an important decision that would affect the tone of the whole evening. In addition, he decreed how many cups should be drunk, since only on rare occasions, as at Agathon's symposium, were symposiasts permitted to drink as much or as little as they wished. The purpose behind this rule was to ensure that everyone attained approximately the same degree of inebriation. Finally, the symposiarch proposed the entertainment and fixed penalties for those who failed to distinguish themselves in the games and competitions.

Despite these precautions, however, much no doubt happened that was not in accordance with the rules. A popular Greek saying, "I hate a drinker with a good memory," suggests that whatever was said or done

Scene at a symposium. From *Religion and the Greeks* by Robert Garland (Bristol, U.K.: Bristol Classical Press, 1994). Reprinted by permission of Duckworth Publishers.

by a symposiast when under the influence of alcohol was not to be held against him when he sobered up.

For everyday use, the Greeks drank out of glazed un-decorated mugs. The well-to-do, however, possessed a **Serving the** special set of drinking cups and wine containers, which **Wine** they reserved for use at a symposium. Basic drinking equipment included a dozen or so *kylikes* or drinking mugs, a *kratêr* or mixing bowl, a *psychtêr* or wine cooler, an *oinochoê* or jug for pouring wine, and a *hydria* or jug for pouring water. The pottery was frequently decorated with figured scenes, often of very refined draughtsmanship. These scenes provide a major source of information about conduct at these gatherings.

Though the proportion of wine to water varied from symposium to symposium, there was usually a preponderance of water. Homer praises a much-diluted blend and Hesiod went so far as to recommend three parts of water to one part wine.

One of the most popular symposiastic entertainments was the capping game. The rules were as follows: either the first player **Games** recited a well-known line from poetry and the second had to cap it by quoting the verse that followed, or alternatively the first player recited a whole passage of poetry and the next had to deliver a similar passage from a different poet on the same theme.

The Greek equivalent to darts was called *kottabos*. A piece of wood was fixed into a depression in the floor or attached to some other means of support and a cross-beam was placed on top of it with a vessel balanced at each end. Under each vessel stood a pan of water with an object fixed upright in the center. Players were required to flick a drop of wine from their cups into one of the vessels. The object was to cause the vessel to topple off and strike the object in the center of the pan. The winner was the one who spilled the least wine and made the most noise.

Dancing was also popular. One of the most famous symposiastic dances was the *kordax*, of which Theophrastos writes, "Only a madman would dance when sober" (*Characters* 6.3). Unfortunately we have no description of the *kordax*, though we do of other energetic dances that it probably resembled. At the end of Aristophanes' *Wasps*, the Chorus encourages the elderly Philokleon thus, "Whirl around, punch yourself in the belly, hurl your leg sky-high, become a spinning top!" (lines 1526–30).

Hired Entertainers

In Plato's *Protagoras*, Sokrates makes the following haughty pronouncement:

> Where the drinkers are men of worth and culture, you will find no girls piping or dancing or harping. They are quite capable of enjoying their own company without such frivolous nonsense, using their own voices in sober discussion and each taking his turn to speak or listen, even if the drinking is heavy. (347c)

It is questionable, however, whether Sokrates was quite such a killjoy as Plato suggests. Xenophon, who, like Plato, was a personal friend of Sokrates and also wrote a dialogue entitled *Symposium*, paints a strikingly different picture of the great philosopher when he was in his cups. In it we encounter a Sokrates who delighted in the acrobatics of the hired entertainers and who even deigned to make a spectacle of himself by attempting to emulate their agile movements. Whatever the truth about Sokrates' liking for live entertainment, hired entertainers were in great demand among the drinking fraternity as a whole. They included flute-girls, dancing girls, tumblers, and buffoons.

One of the earliest laws regulating hours of labor in the Greek world refers to the hire of flute-girls according to three separate shifts: from dawn until noon, from noon until nightfall, and from nightfall until dawn. This law, passed in Kolophon (Asia Minor), was intended to protect professional entertainers against the excessively lengthy symposia to which the inhabitants of that city were addicted. Flute-girls were also subject to price control. The Aristotelian *Constitution of Athens* informs us that, in fourth-century B.C. Athens, they were forbidden by law to charge more than two drachmas for their services (50.2).

The Political Dimension

The fact that a number of drinking songs were politically inspired suggests that many symposia were convened by those of the same political leanings. The most famous of these songs celebrated the murder of Hipparchos, the brother of the Athenian tyrant Hippias, in 514 B.C. The perpetrators of this deed were two young men called Harmodios and Aristogeiton, and a song in their honor by an anonymous author became a kind of Athenian national anthem.

> I shall carry my sword hidden in a branch of myrtle like Harmodios and Aristogeiton when they slew the tyrants and established Athenian democracy. Dearest Harmodios, you are not dead, but they say you live in the Isles of the Blest, where swift-footed Achilles lives and godlike Diomedes, the son of Tydeus.
>
> I shall carry my sword hidden in a branch of myrtle like Harmodios and Aristogeiton, when they slew the tyrant Hipparchos at the festival of Athena. Your fame shall live on the earth for ever, dearest Harmodios and Aristogeiton, since you slew the tyrant and established Athenian democracy.

At the conclusion of a symposium, or when moving from one symposium to another, it was customary for drinkers to *kômazein*, or to roam about the streets in a gang. It was just such a gang of *kômastai*, headed by Alkibiades, that crashed Agathon's party. "No sooner had they sat down than the whole place was in an uproar," Plato writes in *Symposium*. "Order went out of the window and they compelled everyone to drink huge quantities of wine." Assaults by drunken *kômastai* were not uncommon. The myth of the attempted abduction of Lapith women by the Centaurs, wild creatures half-human and half-horse whose bestial natures got the better of them under the influence of alcohol, is the archetypal drinking party gone wrong. It became a stock joke that the worst behaved guests at a symposium were the philosophers. In *Symposium*, written by the second century A.D. satirist Lukian, a philosopher of the Cynic school called Alkidamas was the chief instigator of a bloody rumpus that led to a broken head, smashed jaw, gouged-out eye, and several broken teeth. Comic writers tended to see the more humorous side of drunkenness. Euboulos, in a fragment from a lost play, describes its effects as follows:

Drunken and Rowdy Behavior

> The first cup is to health, the second to love and pleasure, the third to sleep, the fourth to violence, the fifth to uproar, the sixth to drunken revel, the seventh to black eyes, the eighth to the summoner, the ninth to bile, and the tenth to madness and throwing chairs around.

The symptoms of drunkenness were of scientific interest to Aristotle, who wrote a lost treatise on the subject containing the following observation:

> Under the influence of all other alcoholic beverages, people who become drunk fall in all directions, namely to the left, to the right, on their faces, and on their backs. But those who drink barley wine only fall on their backs and lie supine.

Conclusions   In Plato's *Laws*, an Athenian who claims to have made the symposium the subject of sociological inquiry observes:

> I have never yet seen or heard of one that was properly conducted from beginning to end. Here and there a few minor details may not have been amiss, but by and large I have found universal bad management. (639e)

The *Laws* was Plato's last work, written a few years before his death, and this statement is no doubt a reflection of the bitterness of his old age. It has to be viewed in connection with his own disenchantment with the society around him. Apart from their social importance, symposia played a key role in the educational, cultural, and political life of the Greeks.

EDUCATION

Boys   Prior to the fifth century B.C., education was in the hands of private tutors; therefore, only the very wealthy could afford it. Most schools were extremely small, accommodating perhaps no more than about ten or fifteen pupils. We do hear, however, of a few exceptions. Herodotos (6.27) tells us of a school on the island of Chios which had 120 pupils. In 494 B.C. the roof caved in while the boys were learning their letters; tragically, only one survived.

Most Athenian boys began their schooling around the age of seven. They continued as long as their parents could afford to pay their fees—or as long as the parents did not require their sons to be economically productive. There is no record of the fees that were charged. Because democratic Athens required its citizens to be functionally literate, very few boys were completely unlettered. Aristophanes makes it clear in *Knights* (188f.) that even an ignorant lout such as a sausage seller knew how to read and write. As Protagoras points out in Plato's dialogue of that name, it was a general rule that "the sons of the most wealthy went to school earliest and left latest" (326c). Not until the Hellenistic Period was a system of universal public education established in some cities for all boys, thanks to foundations that funded teachers' salaries.

Basic Athenian education consisted of reading and writing, physical training, and music. Reading and writing were taught by the *grammatistês*. Pupils practiced their letters on waxed tablets using a pen called a *stylos*. Broken sherds of pottery, called *ostraka*, served as scrap paper. The *grammatistês* also provided them with a grounding in literature, by requiring pupils to learn passages from epic, lyric, and dramatic poetry. Memorization was a key element in the educational process. Nikeratos, who figures in Xenophon's *Symposium*, claims that his father made him learn by heart the whole of the *Iliad* and *Odyssey*—some 27,000 lines in all (3.5). Learning by rote sometimes paid off in later life. The Athenians who were taken prisoner by the Syracusans after the disaster of the Sicilian expedition were removed from the stone quarries and given domestic work if they were able to recite passages of Euripides. The most popular musical instrument was the lyre or *kithara*, which was taught by a musician known as a *kitharistês*. It was regarded as such an important part of education that in Aristophanes' *Wasps*, the hero Bdelykleon seeks to excuse a dog's thievery on the grounds that "he never learnt the lyre" (line 959). Physical education, which took place under the instruction of a teacher known as a *paidotribês*, is discussed later. Only a few children learned how to draw. Little attention was given to mathematics.

Although the Athenian state did not require children to be educated or involve itself in the school curriculum, it legislated to ensure that proper standards of conduct were upheld. The orator Aischines cites an Athenian law which forbade parents to send their children out of the home before daybreak and insisted that they be collected before sunset. With the exception of slaves called *paidagôgoi* who accompanied their young masters to school and sat behind them in the classroom, no adult was allowed to enter the school. If any did, it was a capital offense (1.9–12). Class size was prescribed by law. Publicly sponsored competitions sought to encourage high standards of accomplishment. At the festival known as the Apatouria, for instance, prizes were given to boys for recitation.

The education of Athenian girls was almost completely neglected. The majority received merely a basic training in how to **Girls** run the household, generally from their mothers. Girls may even have been actively discouraged from becoming literate in order to keep them "unspoiled." A fragment from a lost play by Menander states axiomatically, "He who teaches his wife how to read and write does no good. He's giving additional poison to a horrible snake." Though some women were able to play a musical instrument, as we see from depictions in Greek art, few would have been sufficiently well-informed to express an opinion about the political issues of the day. Xenophon's fictional Ischomachos therefore probably speaks for a number of middle-class Athenians when he declares,

> When I married my wife, she was not yet fifteen and had been so carefully supervised that she had no experience of life whatsoever. A man should be content, don't you think, if his wife comes to him knowing only how to take wool and make clothes and supervise the distribution of spinning among slaves. (*Household Management* 7.5–6)

Apprenticeship   Herodotos (6.60) informs us that in Sparta some trades and professions were exclusive to certain designated families, including those of herald, flute player, and cook. In Athens, too, many skills and professions were handed down from father to son, due partly to the fact that the lawgiver Solon prescribed that an Athenian father should teach his son a skill if he expected to be supported by him in old age. For instance, the Athenian sculptor Praxiteles was the son of a sculptor and both his sons and grandson were sculptors as well.

HEALTH AND SICKNESS

Like other aspects of Greek life, medicine never wholly divorced itself from its religious roots. It is not therefore accidental that the growth of the cult of the healing god Asklepios at the beginning of the fifth century B.C. exactly parallels the birth of the tradition of scientific medical inquiry. Sickness and its cure were now for the first time identified as areas of both professional and divine concern.

The rise of scientific medicine was due largely to the influence of Hippokrates of Kos, a somewhat shadowy figure about whom little is known for certain yet to whom many early medical writings have been ascribed. Among these is a book entitled *Aphorisms*, which begins with the statement, "Life is short. Art is long. Opportunity is brief. Experiment is dangerous. Judgement is difficult." It serves as a fitting comment upon the onerousness of the profession at all periods of history.

Temple Medicine   From the fifth century B.C. onward, sanctuaries of the healing god Asklepios, such as that of Epidauros in the northeast Peloponnese, functioned as both religious and medical centers. This is demonstrated by the fact that surgical instruments and votive offerings in the form of parts of the body are commonly found together. Votive offerings were dedicated in the hope of securing the god's intervention on behalf of the part of the body so represented. Even if physicians were exclusively scientific in their approach to healing, many of their patients would have regarded their expertise as an "art" which was, at root, a gift of the god. The fact that Hippokratic physicians took their oath in the name of Asklepios and other healing deities affords further proof of the complementarity of the two approaches.

The healing that was practiced at the sanctuaries of Asklepios is likely to have been a potent mixture of medicine, auto-suggestion, faith healing, and divine intervention. While at night the sick slept within the temple precincts waiting for a vision from the god to reveal the source of their cure, by day they entrusted their aches and pains to human physicians. Grateful patients who were cured by Asklepios were encouraged to erect monuments commemorating the god's intervention. A characteristic feature of these inscriptions is their emphasis upon the incredulity that preceded the miraculous cure, as we see in the following example:

> A man came to the god as a suppliant who was so blind in one eye that all he had was an eyebrow with an empty eyesocket. Some of the people in the temple laughed at him for his stupidity in thinking that he would be able to see when the eyesocket was empty and contained nothing but a depression. When the man slept, however, a vision appeared to him. The god was seen to be preparing some medicine. He then opened the man's eyes and poured it over them. When day came, he could see with both eyes and departed. (Inscription)

Incidentally, the coexistence of religious alongside scientific healing need hardly surprise us, given the current level of interest in the subject. A 1995 study carried out at the Dartmouth-Hitchcock Medical Center determined that those with religious faith were more than three times as likely to survive heart surgery than those without faith.

Though relations between the advocates of faith healing and scientific medicine seem to have been essentially benign, some   **Epilepsy** rivalry did nonetheless exist. The Hippokratic author of the celebrated treatise entitled *On the Sacred Disease* (2–5), for instance, vehemently opposed the prevailing orthodoxy that epilepsy was an affliction caused by the gods. Castigating "witch doctors, faith-healers, quacks, and charlatans" for seeking to alleviate the symptoms "by prescribing purifications and incantations along with abstinence from baths," he boldly asserted that epilepsy "is not more divine than any other disease." The author concludes with the claim that any skilled practitioner could cure the disease "provided that he could distinguish the right moment for the application of the remedies."

Physicians   Basic first aid was practiced on the Greek battlefield from earliest times. Homer tells us that the Greek army at Troy relied on the services of two physician brothers named Machaon and Podaleirios, sons of Asklepios, who came from Thessaly, the original home of the healing god. Machaon extracted an arrow from Menelaos' midriff, sucked the blood from his wound, and then applied "healing medicines that Chiron [a centaur] had once generously given to his father" (*Iliad* 4.219). Homeric physicians were not employed full-time but practiced medicine in a secondary capacity; Machaon had to be summoned from the battlefield to attend Menelaos.

Not until the late sixth or early fifth century B.C. do we hear of professional physicians in the Greek world. One of the most famous was Demokedes of Krotona, whose impressive career is reported at length by Herodotos (3. 129–37). Demokedes, having cured Dareios, king of Persia, was subsequently employed first by the Aiginetans, then by the Athenians, and finally by Polykrates, tyrant of Samos. His salary increased in line with his growing reputation. The Aiginetans offered him 60 minai for his services, the Athenians 100, and Polykrates 120. (1 mina was equivalent to 100 drach-

Marble disk commemorating a physician.

mas, and 1 drachma was the equivalent of a day's pay). Demokedes' career indicates that there were several physicians with international reputations who were prepared to move from place to place in response to local demand. The Hippokratic treatise entitled *Airs, Waters, and Places,* whose topic is the effect of climate, water supply, and location on the general health of a population, was probably written to assist itinerant physicians. It is extremely unlikely, however, that any Greek state provided free public health service to its citizens. Public physicians probably received a retainer requiring them to reside within the state's territory for a fixed period of time but were free to charge for their services.

The principal centers of medical learning and research were Krotona in southern Italy, Kyrene in Libya, the island of Kos, and Knidos on the west coast of Turkey. These were not medical institutions in the modern sense of the word. Physicians did not have to undergo any formal training. Nor did they possess anything resembling a medical license. Medical students attached themselves to established practitioners on a purely informal basis. Once they had acquired sufficient knowledge, they discharged themselves and were free to practice independently. The success of their careers henceforth depended on their reputations. Given the absence of any objective criteria for determining standards of medical competence, it is hardly surprising that allegations of charlatanism and quackery are commonplace in medical texts.

Although anyone could claim to possess healing skills, some physicians organized themselves into guilds and agreed to abide by prescribed rules of medical conduct. The most important evidence for this is the famous Hippokratic Oath, which is attributed to Hippokrates himself

The Hippokratic Oath

and which remained the cornerstone of medical ethics in the West until recently. Though we do not know what proportion of the medical profession observed it, those who took it constituted a "closed shop" since they swore to divulge their professional knowledge only to a select few. The oath reads as follows:

I swear by Apollo the healer and Asklepios and Hygieia [wife of Asklepios, the personification of health] and Panakeia [daughter of Asklepios, personification of recovery from sickness] and all the gods and goddesses, who are my witnesses, that I will keep this oath and this promise to the best of my ability and judgement.

I will regard the person who taught me this art in equal honor to my parents and I will share my livelihood with him and make him a partner in my wealth when he is in financial need. I will esteem his family as I do my own brothers and I will teach them this art if they so desire to learn it, without accepting any fee or contract. I will pass on precepts, lectures, and all other instruction to my sons and to the sons of my teacher, as well as to apprenticed pupils who have taken the physician's oath, and to no others.

I will employ treatments for the relief of suffering to the best of my ability and judgement, but I will abstain from using them for the purpose of causing injury or harm. I will not give lethal poison to anyone who requests it, nor will I suggest such a course. Similarly I will not give a pessary to a woman that would induce an abortion. I will keep my life and my art pure and holy. I will not use surgery even on those who suffer from stone but I will make way for those who are adept in that procedure. Whatever houses I enter, I will do so in order to relieve sickness. I will refrain from all manner of intentional injury or harm. In particular I will not sexually abuse women or men, whether servile or free.

Whatsoever I see or hear in the course of my duties, or outside the course of my duties in my dealings with my fellow men, I will not divulge if it be matters that should not be gossiped abroad, but I will regard such matters as not to be spoken of. If I keep this oath and do not break it, may I prosper both in regard to my life and my art for all time. But if I violate it and break my oath, may the opposite fate befall me.

Diseases   Thanks chiefly to the Hippokratic writers and to a medical writer called Galen, we know a great deal about diseases in antiquity. Among the most common were malaria and tuberculosis. Given the extremely high incidence of infant mortality, childhood diseases, including rickets and anemia, must have been widespread. We also hear of diphtheria, chickenpox, mumps, and whooping cough, but there is no evidence for either cholera or measles. Venereal diseases such as syphilis and gonorrhea do not seem to have existed. Leprosy did not reach Greece until the Hellenistic Period.

Paleopathology, the study of disease in earlier populations, provides evidence for arteriosclerosis, which in some regions affected as much as 80 percent of the population. Poor sanitation, the lack of a hygienic water supply, and malnutrition were probably the major killers. Though diagnosis was of a high quality, there was very little understanding about how diseases were transmitted since there was no notion of germs. Drugs, surgery, purges, and bleeding were the most common forms of treatment.

Epidemics   The most famous epidemic in Greek history was the plague that afflicted Athens from 430 to 426 B.C. Brought about by Perikles' decision to crowd the entire population of Athens within the city walls, the plague carried off perhaps as much as one third of the entire population. Though its identity continues to be disputed by scholars, typhus and smallpox are the most likely candidates. Thukydides, who was himself afflicted by it, has left us a description of its effects upon the body that is a masterpiece of succinct clinical analysis:

> People who were quite healthy for no particular reason suddenly began to experience violent fevers in the head together with redness and inflammation of the eyes. The throat and the tongue became bloody, and they emitted a breath that was foul and unnatural. After these symptoms came sneezing and hoarseness. Soon afterwards the disease descended to the chest with violent coughing fits. Once it reached the stomach that too became upset. Vomitings of every kind of bile that has been identified by the medical profession ensued, accompanied by great pain and distress. The majority were afflicted with ineffectual retching, which produced violent convulsions. In some cases the convulsions ceased at this point, but in others they continued afterwards. Externally the body did not feel very hot nor was it pale. Rather it was reddish, livid, and breaking out into blisters and ulcers. Internally, however, there was a burn-

ing sensation so that sufferers could not endure to be covered by even fine linen but merely wanted to be naked. What they liked to do most of all was to plunge themselves into cold water. In fact many who received no attention threw themselves into cisterns, consumed by an unquenchable thirst. They were in the same state whether they drank a lot or a little. Restlessness and insomnia afflicted them throughout.

So long as the disease was at its height the body was not enfeebled but resisted the misery to a remarkable degree, so that the majority of people either perished on the seventh or eighth day as a result of internal burning while still having some strength left. Or, if they pulled through, once the sickness descended to the bowels and caused violent ulceration and watery diarrhoea, most of them perished subsequently as a result of the ensuing weakness. For beginning at the top, in the head, the disease made its way down through the whole body and if anyone survived the worst of its effects, yet it still left traces by seizing onto the extremities. It made its way to the genitals, the fingers and the toes, and many who lost the use of these parts still survived, while there were others who lost the use of their eyes. (2.49.2–8)

The majority of patients who received medical attention were those who suffered from curable illnesses and injuries. **Chronic** Probably the chronically sick, those suffering from degenera- **Illness** tive diseases, and the aged would have had little reason to avail themselves of the services of the medical profession. None of the Hippokratic case histories describes patients with chronic illness. This is further corroborated by an observation made by Sokrates in Plato's *Republic* that Asklepios revealed the art of medicine only on behalf of those who "by nature and way of life are healthy but have some hidden illness in them" (407de). Sokrates continues:

However, in the case of those whose bodies are inwardly diseased through and through, the god did not attempt ... to prolong an already wretched existence for the individual concerned, who in all probability would foster other offspring like himself. If a man is incapable of living a normal existence he did not think it right to treat him, since such a person is of use neither to himself nor to the state.

Despite the keen interest in medicine, knowledge of the internal workings of the human body was extremely rudi- **Dissection** mentary because dissection was not employed in the study of anatomy before the Hellenistic Period. Even then it was practiced perhaps only in Alexandria, Egypt, where it became common. In all the works ascribed to Hippokrates not one is devoted to the study of anatomy or physiology. Aristotle, writing at the close of the fourth century B.C., frankly states: "The internal parts of the body, especially those belonging to humans, are unknown. We must therefore refer to the parts of other creatures that resemble humans" (*History of Animals* 494b). This refusal, or at least reluctance, to perform dissection was due largely to religious scruples, since the Greeks believed that the procedure could prevent the deceased from entering Hades.

Women's Bodies   Ignorance of dissection did not prevent physicians and scientists from inventing elaborate theories about the internal workings of the human body, particularly the female body.

From Aristotle's perspective, women were failed males. It was their lack of heat that made them more "formless." Aristotle went so far as to propound the notion of a zoological hierarchy with men at the pinnacle and women one evolutionary step below. This one step nonetheless represented, in his telling phrase, "the first step along the road to deformity" (*Generation of Animals* 4.767b 7f.). Similarly Galen stated that if it were not for the fact that the menses were needed to contain the hot male seed, we might suppose that "the creator had purposely made one half of the whole race imperfect, and, as it were, mutilated" (*On the Use of Parts* 14.6).

The fact that women needed to menstruate was proof in Aristotle's eyes that they could not burn up the residue that coagulated inside them. They were judged to be particularly susceptible to what we would call today hysteria, a word which is derived from the Greek for "womb" (*hystera*), meaning literally "the lower parts," though the symptoms were rather different from the illness we identify by the name today. The Hippokratic school believed that the womb wandered around the body if the menses were suppressed or if women did not engage in intercourse.

Mental Disturbances   Though the Greeks lacked the modern scientific terminology to systematize and explain pathological states of consciousness, they were nonetheless capable of subjecting the individual to close psychological scrutiny. Greek tragedy manifests a keen fascination with mental abnormality, as the following outline of the plot of Sophokles' *Ajax* indicates.

After being defeated in his bid to win the prize for being the foremost soldier in the Greek army, Ajax goes completely berserk and slaughters cattle. He does this in the belief that he is murdering Agamemnon and Menelaos, the war leaders who awarded the prize to his rival. This delusional stage is followed by one of depression. When he returns to his senses, Ajax is overcome with intense shame—not because he tried to assassinate his superior officers but because he tried and so conspicuously failed. The hero now sees the world with unbearable clarity and

realizes that he has no place in it. The nineteenth-century French soci-
ologist Emile Durkheim identified three principal categories of suicide:
egoistic, altruistic, and anomic. Sophokles' depiction of Ajax's suicide is
so complex that it contains elements of all three.

It is not just in the realm of myth that we find incontrovertible evidence for major psychological disturbances. The madness of the Spartan
king Kleomenes, as reported by Herodotos, has been cited as a classic
instance of paranoid schizophrenia. The king's illness, which provoked
him to strike anyone whom he met in the face with his staff, was vari-
ously explained either as a punishment brought on by the gods for
having burnt down a sacred grove or as a consequence of his fondness
for unmixed wine, the consumption of which was believed to result in
madness. Kleomenes ultimately became so violent that his relatives had
him placed in the stocks. While in prison, he managed to intimidate his
jailer into giving him a knife, whereupon, as Herodotos relates, "He
began to mutilate himself, beginning with his shins. Cutting the flesh up
into strips, he proceeded from his ankles to his thighs, and from his
thighs to his hips and sides, until he reached his stomach, and while
cutting that up he died" (6.75.3).

It seems that no one tried to cure Kleomenes of his psychosis by medical means. Perhaps the Spartans were particularly unenlightened in such
matters. In Greek tragedy attempts are made to talk those who have
become temporarily deranged back to sanity, possibly reflecting the more
advanced attitude toward the mentally sick that prevailed in Athens. At
the end of Euripides' *Bacchai* Kadmos gently coaxes his daughter into
the realization that she has dismembered her son under the influence of
religious ecstasy. Despite the horror of her act, he treats her state of mind
as curable.

Though the references are few, it is not unlikely that paranoid schizophrenics and others who were judged to be a   **Plato's**
danger to the rest of society were kept in confinement for   **Madhouse**
short periods of time. The local jail probably did double
duty for criminals and the criminally insane. In a passage in *Laws*
(11.908c–909d), which anticipates the use of asylums for the incarceration
of political prisoners in the former Soviet Union, Plato refers darkly to
a *sophronistêrion* or "house of correction," where he proposes that those
professing atheism should be imprisoned for five years at a stretch.
While serving out their time, they should be permitted to consort only
with the members of the so-called nocturnal council, and then exclusively
about matters connected with their moral welfare.

There is no external evidence for the kind of institution to which Plato
alludes. It is, moreover, frankly inconceivable that the Greeks would
have possessed the resources to provide long-term professional care for
the mentally sick, any more than they had the resources to care for the

elderly or the chronically sick. Probably the mentally sick were in some cases subjected to a type of treatment based on the principle of the short, sharp shock, as has been recommended in recent times for certain types of violent criminals.

SEXUAL MORES

The function of marital sex was procreation. So important was procreation that in Sparta it was acceptable for a husband to lend out his wife to another man for the purpose of making her pregnant. In addition, most adult males, both married and unmarried, engaged in sex with prostitutes or slaves. Given the extreme emphasis that was placed on virginity and fidelity in women, it would have required much ingenuity and not a little luck to conduct a sexual liaison with a well-bred woman. For this reason, the image of a Don Juan is alien to Greek culture. In myth even the Trojan prince Paris, the most notorious of all philanderers, remained faithful to the woman he seduced. The exception that proves the rule is Alkibiades, who was much admired by men and women, and who numbered among his conquests a Spartan queen.

Nakedness It is sometimes suggested that the Greeks were more liberated in sexual matters than we are. The truth simply is that they were different. They were remarkably unabashed about the depiction of male genitals in art, images of which, both erect and unerect, were ubiquitous. Statues of naked youths in the guise of Apollo served as funerary markers. Herms, stone pillars with carved heads and penises, marked the boundaries of properties. Giant penises were borne aloft by Athenian virgins in Dionysiac processions. In the performance of comic plays actors wore oversize penises made out of padding in order to draw attention to their sexual organs.

Artistic representations are one thing. Reality is another. In everyday life the Greeks may well have been prudish. Though males appeared naked before other males in the gymnasium and in competitive athletics, women were not allowed to approach the sanctuary of Olympian Zeus during the Olympic Games, evidently to prevent them from spying upon the naked bodies of male athletes. In certain Spartan rituals, however, girls were encouraged to appear naked before Spartan youths in what appears to have been a kind of civic-sponsored incentive to marriage.

Male and Female Sexuality The famous myth of Pandora ("All-gifted"), told by Hesiod in *Theogony*, defines women as "a beautiful evil" which men cannot resist, evidently because of their sexual appetites and vulnerability to female charms. These characteristics are made comic sport of in Aristophanes' masterpiece *Lysistrata*, which presupposes that an international sex strike by women will bring about peace, by reducing all the combatants to another kind of impotence. The popular notion that men were slaves to their sexual appetites was balanced by the medical belief that women needed to have sexual intercourse for their physical and mental well-being (see section on Health and Sickness in this chapter).

The Greeks did not identify themselves as either homosexual or heterosexual. They did not, as we do, perceive sexual orientation in terms of a life choice. A **Homosexuality** homosexual union between males was acceptable only when asymmetrical, to use the modern jargon; that is to say, when it involved a younger and an older man and when it had a pedagogical as well as sexual dimension. Such associations provided the basis of aristocratic education in the Archaic Period and were institutionalized by the symposium. In later times they seem to have been regarded less favorably. Whereas earlier, black-figure vases exhibit a preponderance of homosexual lovemaking, the red-figure vases that had become popular by the end of the sixth century onward more frequently depict heterosexual activity. Plato's *Symposion*, which elevates homosexual above heterosexual love, thus provides a rather misleading picture of Athenian sexual mores at the turn of the fourth century B.C.

Any Athenian who practiced homosexuality exclusively was likely to become a target of abuse, as we see from contemptuous references in Aristophanic comedy. The most famous homoerotic relationship is that of Achilles and Patroklos in the *Iliad*, although Homer scrupulously avoids suggesting that it has a sexual basis. Homosexual depictions on vases are remarkably restrained. Anal and oral intercourse are never shown, whereas these acts appear frequently in a heterosexual context.

Male prostitution, though regarded with severe disfavor, was an ineradicable feature of Greek society. Athenians **Male** over the age of eighteen who entered the profession were **Prostitution** debarred from holding any executive or religious office and from addressing the assembly or council, although the law stopped short of depriving them of their citizenship. If a boy under the age of eighteen engaged in prostitution, his father or legal guardian was liable for prosecution. The boy in question was also released from the obligation to support his father in old age, as the law otherwise enjoined on him (Aischines 1.13–20). Intercourse between slaves and their masters and mistresses probably was commonplace. (Female prostitution has already been discussed in Chapter 4 in the section "The Working Woman.")

Adultery was punished more severely than rape because rape was regarded as "merely" an act of violence; adultery, **Adultery** however, required the transfer of a woman's affections and **and Rape** made it difficult to determine whether her offspring were legitimate. Whereas rapists were required to pay recompense to the husband, convicted adulterists faced the death penalty. If a husband discovered his wife in bed with her lover, he was permitted to take the lover's life with impunity. The husband of an adulterous woman was required by law to divorce his wife. If he failed to do so, he could be deprived of his citizenship. Adulterous women were not permitted to attend religious rites conducted by the citizen body. If they attempted to do so, the public was free to do to them any form of physical violence short of killing them.

Pornography   Pornography, a made-up word of Greek root which literally means a writer about or painter of whores or *pornai*, seems not to have been regarded as a corrupting influence. Occasionally it even attained the status of high art. One of the most striking depictions of women undergoing sexual abuse is the battle between the Lapiths and Centaurs depicted on the west pediment of the temple of Zeus at Olympia. To the right of the figure of Apollo, who stands in the center of the composition, we see the Centaur Eurytion intent on raping the bride Deidameia. To the left of Apollo another Centaur is about to kick in the groin a Lapith woman who is scratching his cheek.

Naked bathing women appear on the interior of red-figure cups of the late sixth and early fifth century B.C. The bather was revealed as the (male) drinker drained the cup. Pornographic literature existed in the Hellenistic period but seems to have been limited to sex manuals enumerating the positions of heterosexual intercourse. There was no genre devoted to sexual fantasy, although fantasy is not absent from the Hellenistic Greek novel. A prime example is Longus' *Daphnis and Chloe*, which carries strong undertones of sexual violence.

DEATH

The treatment of death and the dead divides us sharply from the mentality of the Greeks. In the modern industrialized world most people die in hospitals. If they happen to have relatives beside them when they pass away, they may count themselves lucky. As soon as they have drawn their final breath, the nurse arrives to cover up the body and pull across the plastic curtains. Most relatives and friends forego visiting the corpse in the hospital if they have not been at the bedside earlier. Very few have any physical contact with the corpse. The hospital authorities then transfer the corpse into the hands of professional undertakers. In Britain the deceased will never be seen again, since open caskets are extremely rare. In the United States the deceased, thanks to the fashioning hands of the undertaker, will reappear in a completely transformed state when it goes on view in the so-called funeral home.

In the Greek world death was prevalent among persons of all age groups, whether as a result of warfare, accident, or illness, or, in the case of women, as a consequence of giving birth. It was incorporated into the life of the community to a degree that would strike many people today as morbid. In modern Greece, too, the business of the undertaker is not conducted behind heavily shrouded windows in subdued surroundings but under the full glare of arc lighting.

Different cultures permit different degrees of physical contact with their dead. Some accept the physical aspect of death as a natural and intimate fact of life. Others are deeply troubled by the idea of a "rotting" corpse. Many people today regard the corpse as an object to shun and avoid.

Physical Contact with the Dead

Since there were no hospitals in Greece, most people died either at home or on the battlefield. If death occurred at home, it was the duty of the relatives to prepare the body for burial. Fondling and kissing the corpse were acceptable and customary practices. The Greeks were hardly more intimate with their deceased than their modern counterparts. At a Greek Orthodox funeral such practices also occur. Significantly, *kêdeia*, the Greek word for funeral, which literally means a "caring for," is still in regular use.

Though we occasionally hear of undertakers, known as *klimakophoroi* or "ladder bearers," *nekrophoroi* or "corpse-bearers," and *tapheis* or "buriers," the duty of these hired hands consisted merely in transporting the corpse from the house to the grave and preparing the ground for burial. They were not for the most part specialists but merely odd-job men. Nor did they attend to the corpse's needs prior to its departure from the house, as modern undertakers do. Everything suggests that the Greeks would have regarded the idea of handing over the corpse of a dead relative to strangers as offensive and incomprehensible.

This attitude had much to do with the belief that in the period between death and burial the deceased are in need of the solicitous attention of their relatives. Until inhumation or cremation has taken place, they were thought to be in what anthropologists describe as a "lim-

Helping the Dead to Reach Hades

inal" stage—a word which derives from the Latin for "threshold." They were between two worlds, having not yet fully disengaged from this world and awaiting incorporation into the next. Entry to Hades, the world of the dead, did not occur automatically but only as the consequence of strenuous activity on the part of the living. This betwixt and between status was regarded as extremely perilous, for which reason the unburied dead were believed to be at considerable risk. The primary obligation upon the living was thus to perform the burial as expeditiously and efficiently as possible. To fail in this sacred duty was to condemn the dead to wander up and down the banks of the River Styx, which surrounded Hades, for thousands of years. Thus when Achilles delays burying Patroklos' corpse because of his overwhelming grief, his ghost appears to Achilles and urgently requests that he bury him "as soon as possible, so that I can enter the gates of Hades" (*Iliad* 23.71ff.).

Displays of Grief

Unlike our culture, which encourages us to present a stiff upper lip in the face of loss, Greek culture not only tolerated but also expected highly demonstrative manifestations of grief. There are frequent references in literature to men and women tearing out their hair, rending their garments, beating and lacerating their breasts, rolling on the ground and wallowing in the dust, and going without food or drink for several days. This kind of behavior was prompted in part by a desire to honor the deceased, believed to take pleasure in witnessing the exaggerated displays of grief that their death occasioned. Homer tells us that when the Greeks were cremating the body of Patroklos, not everyone was grieving for the deceased. Some were using his death as a pretext to bewail their own private losses and griefs. To a Greek there was nothing hypocritical or insincere in such outpourings. The loss of a loved one is common to all human experience and Greek mourners brought to the funeral their own personal sense of life's pain.

Exeunt the Gods

Among persons of most faiths the death of a loved one is an occasion to seek the consolation of religion, irrespective of the extent of one's involvement with religion at other times. The Greeks, by contrast, knew better than to approach their gods in the hope that they could assuage their grief or assist the deceased. At the grave, as in the home, death was a domestic affair. Though the Olympian gods occasionally mourn the passing of their favorites, as Zeus mourns the death of his son Sarpedon, this was the exception rather than the rule. For the most part, they give the impression of being indifferent to the experience of human loss. To do the gods justice, we might argue that their own immortality shielded them from a comprehensive understanding of the finite nature of human life.

No less important was the fact that proximity to the dead and dying put the gods severely at risk from the contamination caused by death. When in Euripides' play *Hippolytos* (1437f.) Artemis' favorite Hippolytos is dying in agony after having been hurled from his chariot, the goddess swiftly takes her leave of him before he expires, since, as she explains to him, it is not permitted by divine law for a god or goddess "either to look at the dead or to sully their eyes with the expirations of the dying." For the same reason no priest or priestess was permitted to enter the house of the deceased or attend a burial. Just as the gods needed to preserve their purity, so, too, did those who ministered to their needs.

The Funeral

The Greek funeral, like our own, was a three-act drama. This comprised the laying out of the body in the home (*prothesis*), the funeral cortege from the home to the place of burial (*ekphora*), and the burial. The *prothesis* was performed by the female relatives of the dead. At the moment of death the deceased's eyes and mouth were closed. A chin strap was commonly tied around the head and chin to prevent the unsightly sagging of the jaw. The body was washed, anointed in olive oil, clothed, and wrapped in a winding sheet. Finally it was laid out on a couch with its head propped up on a pillow and its feet facing the door. This last-mentioned practice, which seems to be nearly universal, has given rise to the expression "to carry so-and-so out feet first." From the fourth century B.C. onward, there developed a tendency to dress the dead more ornately, sometimes even to place a crown made out of gold foil on the head. When the body had been laid out, relatives were permitted to view the deceased and dirges were sung.

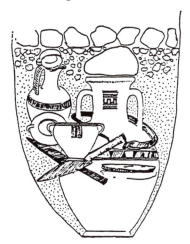

Cremation burial in Athenian Agora. Note sword wrapped around the neck of urn for use by the deceased. From D. Kurtz and J. Boardman, *Greek Burial Customs* (London: Thames and Hudson, 1971). Courtesy of University of Oxford.

On the day of the funeral, which in Athens had to take place at the latest within three days of the death, the mourners accompanied the corpse to the place of burial. Some corpses were laid in a simple wooden coffin, though because of the scarcity of wood many had to make do with only a winding sheet, strewn with a few branches. The corpse was either borne by pallbearers or transported in a cart to the grave. Solon regulated that it had to be transported from the house before sunrise in order to avoid unseemly displays of grief that could cause a public nuisance and draw too much attention to the family.

The burial was performed by the relatives of the deceased. Little is known about the details. The service, such as it was, probably consisted mainly of ritualized laments. If a prayer was delivered at the moment of interment, we know nothing of it. Though both inhumation and cremation were practiced with differing degrees of popularity at different times, cremation was regarded as the more prestigious, since this is how the dead are disposed of in the Homeric poems. After cremation the ashes were gathered up and placed in an urn, which was then buried. Once the grave had been filled in, a grave marker was erected. The mourners then returned to the house of the deceased for a commemorative meal.

Because a dead body constituted a strong source of pollution, relatives were required to take elaborate precautions to prevent its contagiousness from seeping out into the community. Such was the degree of public concern that many states passed detailed laws to ensure that the polluting effect of a corpse did not extend beyond the members of the immediate family. For this reason, too, Solon allowed only close family

Keeping Pollution at Bay

members and women over the age of sixty to enter the house of the deceased and take part in the funeral. Measures to contain the polluting effect of the dead included the following: placing a bowl of water brought from outside the house so that visitors could purify themselves upon entering and leaving; hanging a cypress branch on the door (a custom which may have served to warn passersby of the presence of a corpse within); placing oil flasks containing olive oil around the couch on which the dead was laid out; and, most important of all, bathing the corpse. Once the dead had been disposed of, the house was ritually cleaned. Inscriptions from different parts of the Greek world indicate that it was customary to debar relatives from participating in the life of the community for several weeks after the funeral.

Burial Grounds   The Greeks had no conception of a necropolis in the literal meaning of that word (though "necropolis" is, of course, a Greek word)—a city of the dead that is separate from the living. Those who dwelled in the country buried their dead on their estates, while city dwellers buried them beside the main roads. The highways leading out of Athens were lined with tombs, in much the

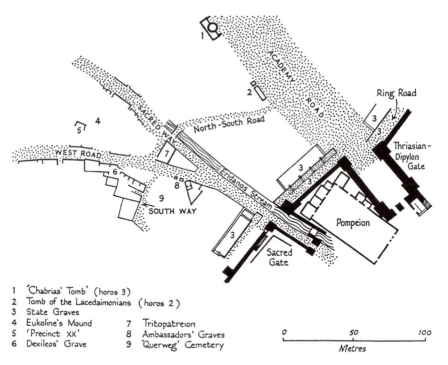

1 'Chabrias' Tomb' (horos 3)
2 Tomb of the Lacedaimonians (horos 2)
3 State Graves
4 Eukoline's Mound
5 'Precinct XX'
6 Dexileos' Grave
7 Tritopatreion
8 Ambassadors' Graves
9 'Querweg' Cemetery

0   50   100
Metres

Plan of the Kerameikos cemetery in Athens. From D. Kurtz and J. Boardman, *Greek Burial Customs* (London: Thames and Hudson, 1971). Courtesy of University of Oxford.

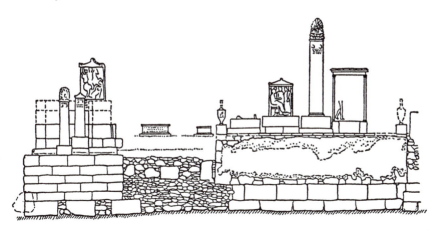

Family plot in the Kerameikos. From D. Kurtz and J. Boardman, *Greek Burial Customs* (London: Thames and Hudson, 1971). Courtesy of University of Oxford.

same way as advertising billboards clutter our major highways today. The most frequented roads provided the most favored burial spots for wealthy families, as indicated by the number of tombs located on the west side of the city in the area known as the Kerameikos or Potters' Quarter. The Kerameikos lay outside the Dipylon Gate and the Sacred Gate. The roads that passed through these gates led to the port of Piraeus and the deme of Eleusis, home of the Eleusinian Mysteries.

This practice of roadside burial was partly due to a ban on burials within the city because of the fear of the polluting effect of the dead. It may also have been occasioned by the need to conserve as much space as possible, given the fact that Athens was surrounded by a wall. Roadside burial also provided the family of the deceased with an opportunity to advertise its wealth and prestige in a permanent manner, since tombs so located were viewed constantly. For this reason, gravestones invariably face the passerby, their sculptured adornments often looking down from an imposing height several meters above the ground. Sepulchral epigrams frequently took the form of an address to the wayfarer, as in the case of a celebrated epigram by Simonides, which was inscribed on the tomb of the three hundred Spartans who died at Thermopylai in 480 B.C.:

> Tell them in Lakedaimon, passerby,
> That here obedient to their word we lie.

In Classical Athens there seems to have been a belief that the family would be able to reunite in the hereafter if its members were buried in the same place. This explains the popularity of the family plot, a large rectangular space walled on the front and at the sides, to which access could be gained only from the rear. Family plots, which had become popular by the end of the fifth century B.C., contained grave monuments commemorating all the family dead, including household slaves.

Expenditure on the dead came very high on the list of a rich citizen's financial priorities. We hear, for instance, of one family tomb erected in the final decade of the fifth century B.C. which cost at least 2,500 drachmas, although the defendant actually claims that the true figure was twice that amount (Lysias 32.1). This was at a time when a rower in Athens' navy earned merely one drachma per day. Grave monuments increased in elaboration as the fourth century progressed and remained in vogue until a lawgiver called Demetrios of Phaleron introduced legislation severely limiting their costliness. Henceforth they were simple, inexpensive, and uniform in style. The great age of honoring the dead with sumptuous monuments was over.

Looking After the Dead

Bereaved relatives continued to maintain a close attachment to the deceased long after death had occurred, since their welfare in Hades was thought to be dependent upon the attention that they received from the living. Women were expected to pay regular visits to the grave, particularly on the anniversary of the day of death but also at other intervals throughout the year. As the dead were believed either to dwell in the proximity of their grave or at least to be capable of visiting it, a variety of gifts judged necessary for their physical welfare were deposited on the steps of the tomb. These included jars of olive oil, branches of myrtle, wreaths, cakes, and drink. It was also customary to anoint gravestones with olive oil and wind colored sashes around their shafts.

Funerary Art

Images of death and the dead serve many different purposes, and understanding how these images function helps us to elucidate a society's attitude toward death. The Assyrians adorned the walls of their palaces with skull pyramids in order to magnify their achievements and intimidate their enemies. The Greeks, however, were extremely reserved in their depictions of death. By and large, emotions such as sentimentality, fear, horror, disgust, and guilt played little part in the visual imagery they employed. In fact, Greek funerary art virtually excludes overt demonstrations of emotion altogether, preferring in-

Hellenistic grave marker from Athens. The raised band facilitated the placing of a fillet around the marker as a sign of respect for the dead. From D. Kurtz and J. Boardman, *Greek BurialCustoms* (London: Thames and Hudson, 1971). Courtesy of University of Oxford.

stead to situate grief in a timeless world where death becomes a subject for detached, philosophical contemplation.

A frequent image is that of two persons, either seated or standing, shaking hands. In most cases, it is impossible to determine which is intended to represent the deceased and which the living. So we are left wondering whether the handshake signifies a farewell between the living and the dead or a reunion in the world to come. The motif of the handshake may have been deliberately chosen in order to blur the distinction between "here" and "there," as the Greeks termed the two worlds, in acknowledgment of the belief that those who part from one another in this world will soon be reunited in the next.

Despite or perhaps because of its frequency, the Greeks were profoundly moved by the pathos of premature death. **Whom** In the Archaic Period this was evoked by the statue of a na- **the Gods** ked youth at the peak of his physical fitness, striding pur- **Love ...** posefully forward. Such statues, which historians have dubbed *kouroi* or "youths," frequently commemorated those who died on the battlefield. Their aesthetic beauty speaks keenly to the sacrifice made by the dead youth on behalf of the state. It is important to note, however, that *kouroi* depended upon context and provenance for interpretation. Identical statues have also been found in sanctuaries of Apollo, the god who is eternally poised upon the threshold to adulthood. In other words, it is impossible to tell whether a *kouros* is intended to depict a dead youth or Apollo, other than by its provenance or inscription. This ambiguity tells us much about the way in which the Greeks sought to idealize death. By being assimilated to a god, the deceased becomes ageless and perfect for all eternity.

Most of our evidence about the handling of death relates to Athens; attitudes toward the dead surely varied mark- **Conclusions** edly from one Greek community to another. The Spartans, for instance, were far less circumspect in their dealings with the dead than the Athenians. Legislation attributed to the lawgiver Lykourgos attempted to reduce the fears associated with death by permitting burial within the precincts of the city and even in proximity to sacred places (Plutarch, *Life of Lykourgos* 27.1).

Let us take our leave of the dead by considering a *lêkythos*, or olive oil container, on which is depicted a particularly charming female moribund who is adjusting her coiffure in the presence of Hermes, the messenger and escort of the dead. Hermes is evidently waiting to escort the woman to Hades, while she for her part dallies over her preparations for her final journey. We are struck by the unearthly patience of Hermes, which is reminiscent of the patience of a devoted if long-suffering husband. Is the scene intended to mock a woman's concern for her appearance at a time when she might be expected to have more pressing concerns? Or is the artist sending us a message about how to confront our own exit from life—with equanimity, poise, and above all a sense of style?

AFTERLIFE

It is notoriously difficult to determine accurately the kind of life that people expect to encounter in the world to come because beliefs about the afterlife constitute a highly private and personal area of human reflection. They also tend to be self-contradictory, even where a strongly centralized religious authority like, say, the Roman Catholic Church provides certain guidelines. A fortiori in ancient Greece, where no centralized religious authority existed, even within the same community, differences in belief are likely to have been extreme. It has been claimed, and with good reason, that no two Greeks shared exactly the same idea about the afterlife. If we knew more about Greek eschatology, the picture would doubtless be even more baffling.

Almost all our information derives from highly wrought literary descriptions supplemented by chance references. These descriptions may or may not be representative of popular belief, though they were almost certainly influential in giving it a basic outline. This is particularly true in the case of Homer, who, in addition to bequeathing to the Greeks their image of the gods, may well have bequeathed their prevailing image of Hades. After Homer, no detailed description of Hades has survived before the one provided by Aristophanes in his play *Frogs*, performed in 405 B.C. What modifications popular belief underwent in the intervening three hundred years is virtually impossible to determine.

The Topography of Hades

Hades could be approached both by land and by sea. Homer gives its location as "at the bounds of Okeanos," the river that was believed to circle the inhabited earth, and "beneath the depths of the earth." In other words, it could be reached by sailing to the far west or by entering certain caves. In Book 10 of the *Odyssey*, the witch Kirke informs Odysseus, who is eager to consult the dead, that he must sail across Okeanos until he comes to the wild coast and groves of Persephone "where the tall poplars grow and willows that quickly shed their seeds" (508ff.). After beaching his ship, he is to seek the rock where the rivers Pyriphlegethon ("Blazing-like-fire") and Kokytos ("Wailing") flow into a river called Acheron. Perhaps Odysseus is instructed to take this route because he is a seasoned seafarer or perhaps it is simply less unpleasant than the land route.

In Book 24 of the *Odyssey*, Hermes, the escort of the dead, leads his charge by the land route. This traverses "the dark, mouldy ways"—a fitting path, we might say, for rotting cadavers. Hermes and his crew of gibbering dead then pass Okeanos, the White Rock, the gates of the sun god Helios, and the realm of dreams. Eventually they reach the asphodel meadow, so named for a type of wild flower that grows there. They are now officially in the realm of Hades, where "the spirits of the dead dwell, the phantoms of men who are worn out," as Homer puts it. And it is here, too, so to speak, that Homer's description peters out. We learn nothing about the appearance of Hades, its size, its notable landmarks, or its divisions. All that we know is that it was dark and windy. Perhaps Homer's imagination failed him or perhaps he thought it ill-omened to say more. It is possible, too, that the featurelessness of Hades may have something to do with its impenetrable darkness. The word "Hades," which denotes both the god of the underworld and the underworld itself, means literally "that which is unseen." Not the least forbidding aspect of the kingdom is its essential unknowability.

It may strike us as something of a paradox that the Greeks had such an elaborate ritual for dealing with death and burial when their ideas about the afterlife were apparently so indistinct and colorless. Their pictorial imagination also seems to have stopped dead at the entrance to Hades. Vase paintings rarely provide us with more than a glimpse of what lies beyond.

Everything that Homer tells us about the dead sug-   **The Miserable**
gests that their condition was lamentable in the extreme.   **Homeric Dead**
The quality of life in Hades is well summed up by Achil-
les' observation in the *Odyssey*, Book 11 that he would
rather work as a day laborer for a man who had little property than be lord of all the spirits of the dead (lines 489–91). Since the dead have been worn out by their earthly existence, it is not surprising that they are described as "strengthless" and bereft of their physical powers.

Worse than that, they are condemned to experience for all eternity the mental anguish to which they were subjected when alive. The shade of Agamemnon, the leader of the Greek forces at Troy, can do nothing but eternally lament the untrustworthiness of women—a subject particularly dear to his heart in view of the fact that he was murdered by his wife Klytaimnestra on his return from the war. Similarly, the Greek hero Ajax is unable to forget the rancor that he feels toward Odysseus, who was judged more worthy than himself in the contest for Achilles' gold armor. Though we cannot know whether the Greeks would have drawn any moral from such memorable images of unresolved mental torment, they serve as chilling reminders of the pain that awaits those in Hades who have left unfinished business up on earth. Equally pathetic is the preoccupation of the dead with the life that they have left behind. When summoned from below, they are eager, indeed greedy, for news of their relatives. Shorn of existence, however, they have nothing to report in return. All in all, it is as if the Homeric dead are caught in a time warp, unable to move beyond the recollection of their last moments on earth.

They remain, too, in the same physical condition as in the moment of their death. In the *Odyssey* we hear that the shades include "marriageable virgins and much-enduring old men . . . and many who had been wounded with bronze spears and war-killed men holding their bloodied armor" (24.38–41). Similarly, in Sophokles' *Oedipus the King*, the king informs the citizens of Thebes that the reason why he blinded himself after discovering that he had killed his father and married his mother was so that he would not have to look upon their faces in Hades (lines 1371–73).

The Perpetually Damned Deep in the bowels of Hades was a windy region called Tartaros, to which were consigned all the most miserable sinners. This did not include serial killers and rapists—they would almost certainly have ended up among the general mass of mankind—but those who had outraged and insulted the majesty of the gods. Such was Tantalos, who served his son Pelops to the gods to test whether they had the wit to distinguish human from animal flesh. Tantalos was condemned to stand in a pool of water with fruit trees overhead. He is, to use the word that derives from his particular form of punishment, eternally "tantalized," because whenever he bends to drink water it recedes and whenever he stretches for the fruit overhead the boughs sway out of reach. The overwhelming majority of the dead were spared the ordeal of having to go through any post-mortem judgement. Although we hear of a judge called Minos in the *Odyssey*, his task appears to have been confined to settling disputes between the litigious dead, rather than determining their moral culpability or distinguishing between the saved and the damned.

The Privileged Few In any system there exists a privileged minority who do not endure the same miserable lot as the rest of humanity, and Hades was no different from anywhere else. In the *Odyssey*, the old man of the sea, called Proteus, delivers the following prophecy:

In your case, Zeus-born Menelaos, it is not fated that you should die and meet your doom in horse-rearing Argos [where Menelaos ruled as king]. Instead the immortals will convey you to the Elysian plain and to the bounds of the earth, where fair-haired Rhadaman-thys [presumably the king of this region] dwells, and where life is easiest for men. There is no snow, nor heavy storm, nor rain, but Okeanos always sends the breezes of soft-blowing Zephyros [the west wind] to refresh men. (4.561–68)

Menelaos is accorded this privileged status not because he has distinguished himself during his lifetime, but because he married one of Zeus' daughters. What kind of existence awaited those who dwelt in the Elysian fields is unclear. Apart from the extremely favorable climatic conditions, which would surely pall after a while, the environment appears to have been unstimulating in the extreme.

Charon, the ferryman who transported the dead across the River Styx or Acheron, was elderly, unkempt, and disagreeable. It was certainly advisable to pay him for his services. A small coin called an obol was therefore placed in the deceased's mouth by caring relatives. Protecting the entrance to Hades was the two-, three-, or fifty-headed dog Kerberos. (Reports differ as to the exact number of his heads.) It was Kerberos' duty to fawn hypocritically on those who entered the region but devour them if they sought to leave. Hades, the lord of the dead and king of the entire region, the brother of Zeus and Poseidon, has few known physical traits, apart from dark hair. He is "monstrous" and "strong," "implacable" and "relentless"—no doubt because of the absolute finality of death itself. For obvious reasons he is also referred to as "all-receiving" and "ruling over many." We know little else about him, apart from the sinister fact that he abducted his wife Persephone when she was innocently plucking flowers. His palace and its domestic arrangements are never described. But though the image of the god is not exactly attractive, he never assumes the role of tormentor of the dead. On the contrary, he seems to have been content to leave the denizens of his realm alone so that they could lead their miserable existences unimpeded.

Hadean Bureaucracy

The realm of Hades also housed the three Furies, known as Alekto, Megaira, and Tisiphone, who sprang from the drops of blood caused by Kronos' castration of his father. The Furies were avengers of crimes, especially those committed within the family. They pursued their victims with torches, snakes, or whips. They seem to have directed their enmity wholly against the living; we never hear of them taking vengeance against the dead.

By and large those who ran Hades were inoffensive, if not wholly innocuous. It was the sheer boredom and dreariness of Hades that made it so awful. To be there for the duration must be hell indeed.

Though the Homeric image of Hades probably continued to exert a powerful hold over the imagination throughout antiquity, as time passed the Greeks became increasingly uncomfortable with the idea of equal misery for all. Accordingly, from the sixth century B.C. onward, they came to believe that those who had been exceptionally virtuous or those who belonged to certain closed sects could expect a more cheerful existence in the hereafter. Notable among these sects were the Pythagoreans and Orphics. Pythagoreanism was allegedly founded by the astronomer and mathematician Pythagoras of Samos, and Orphism by the mythic poet and musician Orpheus. Both advocated the belief that the soul did not perish along with the body.

Toward the Hope of Something Better

Charon, ferryman of the dead (from O. M. von Stackelberg's *Die Gräber der Hellenen* [Berlin: G. Reimer, 1837]).

Exactly what Pythagoreans and Orphics had in mind by the notion of "soul" is unclear, though it was certainly a more distinctive and conscious entity than a disembodied Homeric shade. They also maintained a belief in an underworld judgement involving rewards and punishments. Abstinence from eating meat and self-discipline were important requirements. Regrettably we have no means of knowing how widespread such beliefs were or whether they made any significant impact on popular belief.

Pythagoreanism also promoted belief in the transmigration of the soul at the moment of death. Securing a blessed lot in the hereafter could take several incarnations to achieve. Pythagoras claimed to have been so illuminated that he could even remember his previous incarnations, which laid him open to much mockery. In a lost work the philosopher Xenophanes, who came from Kolophon in Ionia, tells the following facetious anecdote about the sage: "They say that Pythagoras was passing by one day when a puppy was being whipped. Taking pity on the animal, he said, 'Stop don't beat it. It's the soul of my friend. I recognize him by his bark.' "

The Greeks lacked a clear idea about the type of existence that was reserved for those who finally reached moral perfection. Even the Homeric *Hymn to Demeter*, which incorporates the founding charter of the Eleusinian Mysteries, merely states that those who have been initiated into the mysteries will become "blessed" (lines 480–82).

A series of Classical reliefs depict the dead savoring the delights of this world with no evidence of wasting or physical decay, as if taking their ease at the symposium. Though we do not know for certain whether this scene is situated in the hereafter, this cannot be ruled out, since the symposium was the nearest earthly equivalent to a sensual paradise that the Greeks ever devised. All this does not add up to much, however, and we are left with the impression that the Greeks found it as difficult to envisage paradise as most people have throughout history.

The afterlife is a subject that is extremely resistant to clear and unambiguous conclusions. Ideas about it are in- **Conclusions** evitably a hotchpotch of contradictory and ill-thought-out hopes, fears, and fantasies. Our own beliefs and practices are no less conflictive than those of the Greeks. Few people are able to dispose of the belongings of a dead relative immediately after decease, and sometimes it takes years to do so, whether due to sentiment or some vague notion that the dead are still present. Even the passing of a cherished household pet provokes confused ideas.

At the beginning of the *Republic*, Plato puts the following pronouncement into the mouth of the elderly Kephalos:

> When a man gets to the end of his life he becomes subject to fear and anxiety about what lies ahead. The stories told about people in Hades, that if you commit crimes on earth you must pay for them down below, although they were ridiculed for a while, now begin to disturb a man's soul with the possibility that they might be true. (1.330de)

Kephalos' observation may serve as a fitting epitaph to the instability of beliefs concerning the afterlife within the same individual at different periods of his life.

MAGIC

Magic is a difficult concept to identify in ancient Greece since there was no category exactly equivalent to our notion. (The word *magos*, from which our word "magic" derives, referred to a Persian shaman.) It is likely that the use of magical practices was widespread in all places and at all times. Though a number of Greek philosophers, including Plato and Aristotle, as well as members of the medical profession, tended to equate magic with fraud, there was never any systematic persecution of its practitioners, as there was of witches in Medieval Europe and later.

This is all the more surprising in view of the negative image of witches that we receive from Greek mythology. A particularly chilling example is Medea, who in Euripides' play uses her dark skills to fashion a deadly wedding dress for her ex-husband's bride and also murders her own children. As today, witchcraft seems to have been associated primarily with women, especially foreigners.

The Hellenistic writer Theophrastos provides a compelling portrait of an individual who is weighed down by a dread of both religious and magical taboos:

> The superstitious man is the kind of person who ... if a weasel crosses his path will not walk on until someone else has passed him or until he has thrown three stones across the road. ... When he encounters smooth stones at the crossroads, he will pour oil from his oil flask upon them and go down on his knees and perform obeisance in order to be released from their power. And if a mouse gnaws a hole in a sack of barley, he goes to an expert in order to find out what to do. And if the expert tells him to go to a cobbler and have it stitched up, he won't pay any attention. Instead he'll go away and perform a sacrifice. (*Characters* 16.3–6)

There are numerous references to magic in Greek literature. The earliest is in Book 10 of Homer's *Odyssey* where we encounter the witch Kirke, who uses a variety of magical devices, including salves, potions, and a magic wand, and who is capable of transforming Odysseus' companions into swine. Odysseus defends himself against her by means of a magical herb called *moly* which was provided for him by the god Hermes. When Kirke has been subdued, she proceeds to instruct Odysseus in the art of summoning up the spirits of the dead, a magical practice commonly described in later Greek literature.

From the late fifth century B.C. onward, individuals who wished to evoke the dark powers beneath the earth commonly used the dead as their go-betweens. Favored messengers were those who died young and those who died violently, particularly suicides and murder victims. A popular custom was to inscribe a lead tablet with the names of the persons to be cursed and then place the tablet in the grave alongside the gifts that were intended for use by the deceased in the world to come. In some cases, as many as fifteen names are mentioned on a single tablet. Many tablets allude to the parts of a person's body that are to be cursed—the tongue, the eyes, the soul, the mind, the mouth, the arms, the legs, and so forth. Various underworld powers are invoked, including Persephone and Hermes. To reach the other world, the lead tablet had to be "canceled" for use by the living. For this reason, tablets are often found with a nail driven through them. A variant on this device

Drawing of Hekate, goddess of sorcery, on a lead curse tablet. Courtesy of the American School of Classical Studies at Athens.

was a kind of antique "voodoo doll"—a miniature figure made of lead whose arms were bound behind its back. The doll was sometimes transfixed through the breast with a needle. One of the most common reasons for cursing in litigious Athens was a lawsuit, as we know from the discovery of tablets that curse individuals who have allegedly given false testimony. Magic also played an important part in religious rituals, notably in regard to birth. The midwife, who in the absence of male physicians presided unaided in the birthing room, possessed a variety of skills of a magical, religious, and quasi-medical nature.

As a protection against curses, bad luck, and the evil eye, amulets were often worn around the body, particularly in the case of young children. Many of these were made of cheap materials, though precious stones were believed to have special efficacy. Plutarch (*Life of Perikles* 38.2) tells us that when Perikles fell ill of the plague he tied an amulet around his neck. This was taken as proof that the statesman, an avowed rationalist, really must be in a bad way "if he was prepared to put up with such nonsense." Herbs and plants were believed to possess magical healing properties. In addition, foreign and nonsense words were credited with magical powers.

6

The Public Sphere

RELIGION

Religion was something for which the Greeks, who had a word for most things, did not have a word. What we identify as religion was not regarded by them as something distinct and separate from other departments of life. On the contrary, the secular and the profane were constantly overlapping and intersecting with one another. The gods were everywhere and in all things. They were in the home, in the crops, in the city, on the battlefield, in the body, in the birthing room, in the weather, and in the mind. There was hardly any human activity or undertaking that was not susceptible to divine influence. The Greek gods, however, were not mind readers. They were not, therefore, the least interested in whether their worshipers were, to use a Christian expression, "pure of heart." Much of what we know about the practice of Greek religion comes to us from highly unrepresentative authors, including Homer, Hesiod, Aeschylus, Sophokles, and Euripides.

Since most Greeks took the existence of their gods for granted, they had no use for any creed or dogma, which is why they have not bequeathed to us any sacred literature comparable to the Bible or the Koran. The focus of their devotion was not upon belief but upon action. What mattered to them principally was securing the goodwill of their gods, and what mattered in turn to the gods was what they received from mortals. Piety consisted mainly in giving the gods what they wanted. In practice, this took much the same form as giving presents to a spoiled child.

The main objective behind Greek religion was to secure advancement in this life, rather than any imagined state of blessedness in the life to come. To come to terms with it, we have to step outside the assumptions of a monotheistic worldview and conceive of a universe not ruled by a single beneficent deity but by a host of warring deities whose interests frequently conflicted and who were only marginally concerned with the good of mankind. Greek religion was an inclusive and, by and large, essentially tolerant system, which operated from the following basic principles:

1. There are many gods.
2. Any community is necessarily eclectic in its choice of which gods to worship.
3. There will always be genuine gods who are left out of the community's pantheon.

Polytheism did not have to wage war against would-be intruders, unless the would-be intruder happened to come in the form of an exclusive monotheistic religion that challenged its fundamental belief in the plurality of the divine.

Invoking the Gods In order to invoke the power of the gods it was necessary to attract their attention, since only fitfully did they take an interest in human affairs. Their general attitude toward the human race is indicated by the following words addressed by Apollo to Hephaistos on the battlefield outside Troy:

Earthshaker, you would think I was out of my mind if I were to fight with you for the sake of wretched mortals, who are like leaves, now flourishing and growing warm with life . . . but then fading away and dying. So let us give up this quarrel at once and let mortals fight their own battles. (*Iliad* 21.462–67)

This being the prevailing attitude of the gods, it follows that it was something of an uphill battle to enlist their support. Their attention had to be first attracted by a prayer in which the petitioner reminded the deity of his or her preexisting relationship with the petitioner. This was accompanied by sacrifice, libation (drink offering), votive offering, or a combination of these. A votive offering was a gift which was "vowed" or promised to the deity in recompense for his or her assistance. Sacrifices consisted of first fruits, grain, beans, cakes, wine, or milk. The most powerful sacrificial offering involved the spilling of animal blood, pref-

Roasting meat on an altar. The bearded man on the left performs a libation. To right of center is a herm. From *Religion and the Greeks* by Robert Garland (Bristol, U.K.: Bristol Classical Press, 1994). Reprinted by permission of Duckworth Publishers.

erably in large quantities, since the gods were thought to derive both pleasure and sustenance from the smoke of the sacrificial victim that wafted up from the altar and entered their nostrils. The most common victims were goats, sheep, and oxen.

The largest sacrifices were performed annually in honor of the deities who were worshiped by the state as a whole. At the Great Dionysia held in Athens in honor of Dionysos in 333 B.C. no fewer than 240 bulls were slaughtered. Just before the axe fell, barley grains were sprinkled on the victim's head to induce the animal to nod in assent at its own killing. It was then flayed, chopped up, and roasted on top of the altar. Public sacrifices afforded one of the few occasions when the entire citizen body had an opportunity to eat meat, since all of the victim, except the thigh pieces, was later distributed among the priests and the celebrants.

Votive offerings took many forms. They could be either as small as a cheap terra-cotta figurine or as large as a miniature temple. It was customary to offer a tenth-part of the spoils captured from the enemy after a victory in fulfillment of a vow made to the gods who were believed to have guaranteed it. The sanctuary of Apollo at Delphi was crammed full of miniature temples, called "treasuries," erected by victorious Greek states from the spoils filched from vanquished Greek states, since Apollo was invoked as a god of victory whenever states entered the fray.

The Olympians   The Greeks worshiped a pantheon consisting of Zeus and eleven other deities who were thought to inhabit the peaks of Olympos, a mountain in central Greece perpetually shrouded in cloud. The eleven were all siblings or offspring of Zeus. The Olympian gods were not, however, identical everywhere in the Greek world, nor indeed were they held in equal honor. In addition, some major gods, such as Asklepios, the god of healing, never joined their ranks. Arrogant, fickle, cruel, and treacherous, the Olympians have been aptly described as superhuman in power and subhuman in morality. Neither good nor evil in themselves, they were a combination of both.

What human beings had to avoid most of all was the sin of *hybris* or overweening pride, since this made the gods jealous. Those who exhibited *hybris* were punished with *nemesis* or vengeful destruction. Herodotos depicts a Persian noble giving this warning to Xerxes as he is contemplating invading Greece (7.10e): "It is always the biggest buildings and the tallest trees that are struck by lightning. The gods are accustomed to throw down whatever is too high." Mercifully, however, there was no Prince of Darkness to prey on people's fears.

The difference between the Olympian deities and, in particular, the Christian God, who has been likened to an inoffensive celestial social worker of indeterminate gender, could hardly be more extreme. The Olympians cared little for the great mass of mankind, with whom their relations were for the most part distant and somewhat strained. An exception is the bond that existed between Athena and Odysseus as depicted in the *Odyssey*. Though the gods were anthropomorphic—having the same physical shape as human beings—in origin they embodied aspects of the natural world and the human psyche. Apart from Hera, the first generation of Olympians—Zeus, Poseidon, Demeter, Hestia, and Hades—all personified natural forces, whereas the second generation— Hephaistos, Athena, Ares, Apollo, Artemis, Hermes, and Aphrodite— were representative of human accomplishments or attributes.

The Olympians did not create the world. They were not the first dynasty of gods to rule over it nor was there any guarantee that they would go on ruling it forever. Kronos, who came to power by castrating his father Ouranos, sought to preserve his rule by swallowing his children alive. Likewise his son Zeus, who acquired power by overthrowing his father in turn, took active steps to circumvent the prophecy that he

Zeus. From Thomas Hope, *Costumes of the Greeks and Romans* (New York: Dover, 1962). Reprinted by permission of Dover Publications.

would sire a son more powerful than himself. The following paragraphs describe the major deities and their spheres of influence.

Zeus. Though Zeus, "the father of gods and men" as Homer describes him, was supreme among the Olympians, his authority did not go unchallenged. Hera, his current wife, constantly sought to thwart his will. (Hesiod tells us that he had been married seven times previously.) Zeus alone of the gods concerned himself with justice, though he was far from consistent in his pursuit of that aim. Moreover, his own behavior fell lamentably short of setting a standard of morality for human beings. His sexual appetite was insatiable and later tradition credits him with having adulterous relations with no fewer than 115 women, both mortal and immortal. In many cases Zeus adopted a disguise, perhaps in order to try, unsuccessfully for the most part, to evade the watchful eyes of Hera. He turned into a bull to pursue Europa, a shower of rain to seduce Danaë, and a swan to entice Leda.

There were more aspects to Zeus than to any other deity. He was the god of rain, hospitality, justice, and persuasion. There was even a Zeus who was the averter of flies. Though in theory above Fate, Zeus nonetheless followed its dictates. A notable demonstration takes place in the *Iliad* when, on the advice of Hera, he reluctantly decides not to save his son Sarpedon from his predestined death. Zeus' weapon was the thunderbolt, which he wielded with deadly effect against perjurors. The greatest temple built in his honor was located at Olympia, where the Olympic Games were celebrated every four years. The statue of the seated god in the temple, which was made by the Athenian sculptor Pheidias, was regarded as one of the seven wonders of the world. His biggest temple was erected in Athens. Begun in c. 520 B.C., it took about 650 years to complete—"a great victory of time," as one ancient writer aptly put it.

Hera. Hera, Zeus' wife and eldest sister, was the guardian of marriage and queen of Olympos. Her symbol was the peacock, the eyes of whose tail feathers were believed to be the eyes of Argos, her hundred-eyed spy. In the *Iliad* Homer depicts Hera as a nagging wife, ever suspicious that her husband is conniving behind her back but fully capable of paying him back. As indicated above, she had good reason to be suspicious of his philandering. Hera's temple at Olympia was older than that of Zeus, which has suggested to some scholars that her worship on the Greek mainland predated that of Zeus. Another venerable shrine in her honor was erected at Argos. There was no significant temple in Athens dedicated to her.

Poseidon. Poseidon, Zeus' brother, was god of the sea. His symbol was the trident, which he used to spear fish and stir up tempests. By taking the form of a colossal bull, he became the Earthshaker, capable of making the earth rumble and quake. It was Poseidon's animosity, aroused by the blinding of his son the Cyclops Polyphemos, that caused the detention of Odysseus on the island of Kalypso for seven years. Poseidon was defeated by Athena in the contest for the guardianship of Athens. His gift to Athens was a saltwater spring that he miraculously caused to spurt up out of the Acropolis, symbolizing Athens' mastery of the sea.

Aphrodite. Aphrodite, the goddess of love and beauty, personified male sexual desire. The scene of her being awarded the golden apple in the divine beauty contest by the Trojan prince Paris is one of the most popular mythological subjects in Western art. Aphrodite won the contest over her rivals Hera and Athena by promising to bestow upon the judge the most beautiful woman in the world. This promise directly caused the Trojan War since Helen, the woman in question, was married and Greek. According to Hesiod, Aphrodite was born from the semen of Ouranos' castrated genitals, which his son Kronos threw into the sea. Homer, however, makes her the daughter of Zeus and Dione. According to some accounts she was the mother of Eros, the winged boy who shoots arrows of desire into humans and gods.

Phoibos Apollo. Phoibos Apollo was the god of such varied activities as music, healing, plague, purification, and sunlight. In wartime he carried a bow, in peace a lyre. It was he who sent a plague upon the Greek army encamped outside the walls of Troy in response to a prayer from his insulted priest at the beginning of Homer's *Iliad*. He also afflicted Thebes with plague when its people unknowingly harbored the parricide Oedipus. Apollo's two foremost sanctuaries were located on the tiny island of Delos, where he was born, and at Delphi, where he established his oracle. In art he is depicted as a beautiful youth eternally poised on the threshold between adolescence and manhood. Despite his good looks, Apollo was consistently unlucky in love, often choosing partners who resisted his advances. One was Daphne, who prayed to Zeus to preserve her virginity and was transformed into a bay tree in consequence. Apollo is often regarded as the incarnation of the Hellenic spirit and embodiment of spiritual and intellectual enlightenment. This simplistic view ignores the darker side of his personality as the god of plague and unrequited love.

Artemis. Artemis, Apollo's twin sister, was both huntress and protectress of wild animals. She was also identified with the moon. Being a confirmed virgin, she was bitterly opposed to sexual intercourse. Women in childbirth were well advised to placate her fury by presenting her with offerings in advance of and after delivery. When the hunter Aktaion inadvertently observed her bathing, the goddess turned him into a stag and set his own dogs upon him. Artemis' temple at Ephesos on the coast of Asia Minor was one of the seven wonders of the world.

Athena. Athena, the daughter of Zeus and Metis, was born from her father's head when he was struck by Hephaistos' hammer during a quarrel. She emerged fully adult and dressed as a warrior. She was the goddess of women's crafts and of defensive war. She became the patron deity of Athens by causing an olive tree to spring up on the Acropolis. This was symbolic of the fact that Athens' economic prosperity was based on the olive. The most sublime of all Greek temples, the Parthenon, which dominates the Acropolis, was dedicated to Athena in her capacity as a virgin or *parthenos*. It contained a statue sculpted by Pheidias that was over thirty-six feet high and covered in gold and ivory.

Hades. Hades, the brother of Zeus, was the god of the underworld. Together with his wife Persephone, he ruled over the dead.

Demeter. Demeter was the goddess of vegetation and the harvest. Her grief for her lost daughter Persephone, who was abducted by Hades to be his bride, was believed to cause the "death" of the vegetative cycle in winter. Conversely, her yearly reunion with Persephone was thought to usher in the spring. In the outpouring of her grief for her daughter, we see her touched by genuine emotion to a greater degree than any other Olympian deity. Almost uniquely Demeter does not seem to have had a shadow side, although she played a prominent part in rituals per-

Dionysos. From *Religion and the Greeks* by Robert Garland (Bristol, U.K.: Bristol Classical Press, 1994). Reprinted by permission of Duckworth Publishers.

taining to death and the afterlife, notably the Eleusinian Mysteries, which were celebrated at Eleusis in Attica. These mysteries were open to all Greek speakers, men as well as women, slave as well as free man.

Dionysos. Dionysos, the son of Zeus and Semele, was the god of wine, fertility, nature in the raw, liberation, irrationality, and drama. Semele was incinerated when Zeus manifested himself to her in his full glory as a thunderbolt. The god managed to rescue the embryo, which he sewed into his thigh. In due course he gave birth to his infant. According to another myth, Dionysos was killed and eaten by the Titans, who were subsequently destroyed by Zeus' thunderbolt. Out of their ashes arose the human race, part human and part divine. Dionysos was a iatecomer to Olympos. His origins seem to lie in Thrace, although he is also connected with Asia Minor. His entry into Greece, and the opposition that he had to overcome, is the subject of Euripides' *Bacchai.*

Hephaistos. Hephaistos, the god of the forge, was the patron god of metalworkers. Being lame, he was the only deity who was not physically perfect. According to one version of his birth, his mother Hera bore him by parthenogenesis in order to spite Zeus. Oddly he was married to the beautiful Aphrodite, who not unsurprisingly found the nimble-footed Ares a more agreeable partner. In the *Odyssey* we learn that when the pair began an adulterous affair, Hephaistos fashioned a miraculous net that locked them in an inextricable embrace. He then invited all the gods to come and witness the spectacle. An important temple to Hephaistos overlooked the Agora in Athens. In its vicinity much evidence of bronze working has been found.

Hermes. Hermes, the son of Zeus and Maia, was the god of trade, commerce, and thieves. He also served as messenger of the gods and guide of the dead to the underworld. For this reason he is usually depicted wearing a traveling hat and winged sandals, and carrying a herald's staff known as a *kêrykeion*. Statues of the god in the form of an upright pillar with sculpted head and erect phallus stood at street corners throughout Athens. These figures, known as herms, safeguarded gates and doorways.

Ares. Ares, the god of war, was the son of Zeus and Hera. Despite his importance, he was little venerated by the Greeks, perhaps because of his bloodthirsty nature. Even in the *Iliad* he is treated with scant respect. When he is wounded and comes sniveling to Zeus, the latter describes him as a two-faced liar and sends him packing (5.889f.). Ares received little attention in Athens despite the fact that the most venerable council, known as the Areopagos or Hill of Ares, bore his name.

Hestia. Hestia, guardian of the Olympian hearth, was the most neglected of the Olympian deities. She features in no myths and no temples were erected in her honor. Both the family hearth and the hearth that symbolized the city were sacred to her.

Other important gods who did not reside on Olympos include Pan and Asklepios, both of whom gained entry into Athens in the fifth century B.C.

Pan. Pan, who resembled a goat from the waist down, personified the natural world. He was worshiped in caves throughout Attica, the most prominent of which was situated on the north side of the Acropolis. The seven-reed syrinx or panpipe was his invention. He was capable of causing panic both in individuals and in armies. His cult was officially introduced to Athens after the Battle of Marathon in 490 B.C.

Asklepios. The healing god Asklepios, who began his life as a hero, was later awarded divine status. His shrine at Epidauros in the northeast Peloponnese was the foremost healing sanctuary in the Greek world.

There were also a number of minor deities who were believed to reside in streams, rivers, and lakes (naiads), on mountains (oreads), and in trees (dryads).

Gods of the Earth

All the deities whom we have discussed so far dwelt in the sky, on the earth, or underwater. There was, however, another powerful group of divine beings, thought to reside underground. They are called chthonic deities, after the Greek word *chthôn*, meaning "earth." Chthonic deities were worshiped in caves and subterranean passages. We know much less about them because they have left little trace upon the archaeological record. In ad-

dition, few Greek writers make reference to them. There can be no
doubt, however, that chthonic deities
constituted an important aspect of
Greek religion, even though the state
did not expend much money on their
worship. Many individuals privately
carried out rituals in order to appease
their anger or invoke their assistance.
They were believed to exert a profound influence on human affairs, notably in regard to fertility and food
production. They were also invoked
in order to bring evil and destruction
upon one's enemy. The most persist-
ent motif of chthonic religion is the
snake, since snakes were thought to
be generated spontaneously inside
the earth.

Whereas the Olympian deities, except for the lame metalworking god
Hephaistos, were physically perfect,
chthonic deities tended to be loath-
some and repulsive. At the opening
of the *Eumenides*, the third play in
Aeschylus' *Oresteia*, chthonic deities
known as the Furies, who pursue
Orestes to Delphi for the crime of
murdering his mother, are described

as follows: "They are women—no,
not women but Gorgons rather. And
yet they are not quite Gorgons either.
... They are wingless, black and they
snore. Evil puss oozes from their
eyes" (lines 48–54).

Asklepios. From Thomas Hope,
Costumes of the Greeks and Romans
(New York: Dover, 1962). Reprinted
by permission of Dover Publications.

Later Apollo orders them from his sanctuary with the following menacing words: "Go to where heads are chopped off and eyes gouged out,
to justice and slaughterings, to destruction of seed and of young men's
pride, to mutilations and stonings, and to the lamentations of people
being impaled" (lines 186–90).

Household Religion   Minor deities were believed to safeguard the security and
prosperity of the home. Chief among these were Zeus Kte-
sios, or Zeus in his capacity as protector of property; Zeus
Herkeios, or Zeus in his capacity as protector of boundaries;
and Apollo Patroös, or Apollo in his capacity as divine ancestor of the

Athenian race. In addition, each home possessed a hearth that was sacred to the goddess Hestia. Worship at these shrines, supervised by the head of the household, probably took place on a daily basis. Since the welfare of the entire household was placed under the protection of these gods, slaves as well as those who were free were required to participate.

The Greek word *hiereus*, which is roughly translated as "priest," denotes an official who supervised the *hiera* (i.e., **Priests and** sacred objects) stored within a sanctuary and who con- **Priestesses** ducted sacred rites connected with the cult. The chief of these was the supervision of the sacrifices. In general, male deities were attended by priests and female deities by priestesses. Eligibility to a priesthood was based on external qualifications rather than intellectual or moral attributes, though it is no surprise to learn that prostitutes, army deserters, and debtors were forbidden to hold this office. The principal qualification seems to have been the absence of any deformity or disability, since the possession of a physical blemish was thought to constitute proof of divine disfavor. As far as we know, priests did not have to undergo any formal training. Nor were they ordained before assuming office. In the majority of cases, holding a priesthood was probably a part-time occupation. In democratic Athens, the newer priesthoods were annual appointments to which all members of the citizen body were eligible, whereas the older cults, such as that of Athena Polias (Of the city), were reserved for members of a particular noble kin group or *genos* and held for life.

Priests received only a modest fee for their services, though they were entitled to a choice piece of the sacrificial meat. Their duties were primarily of a liturgical and administrative nature. They were not expected to administer to the spiritual needs of worshipers, nor did they take any part in ceremonies that had to do with birth, marriage, and death. The Stranger in Plato's *Statesman* (290c) aptly defines priests as persons who "know how to offer our gifts to the gods in sacrifices in a manner that is pleasing to them, and who know, too, the right forms of prayer for petitioning the gods to bestow blessings on worshipers." Since there was no centralized religious authority either in Athens or anywhere else in the Greek world, priests were not able to exercise any influence over the political process, other than by virtue of their personalities.

One of the most terrifying inventions of the Greek mind was the belief in *miasma* or pollution. *Miasma*, whose work- **Pollution** ings were invisible, was analogous to a virus and capable of infecting a whole community if its course went unchecked. The belief in pollution may well owe its origins in part to the experience of contagious diseases such as plague or typhus, for which no medical explanation was available. However, *miasma* was not exclusively a physiological phenomenon. It had a religious dimension as well. In ascending order of magnitude, the principal causes of pollution were childbirth, death by natural causes, accidental homicide, and murder. The presence of an undiscovered murderer in a community was believed, at least in early times, to be capable of causing barrenness and blight among humans, livestock, and crops alike, as we see from the following description of the city of Thebes at the beginning of Sophokles' *Oedipus the King*:

> A blight is upon the fruitful plants of the earth, a blight is upon cattle among the pastures, and upon the barren labor pangs of women. A god who carries fire, a deadly pestilence, swoops down upon our city and ravages it, emptying the house of Kadmos [its founder]. Black Hades grows rich with groans and lamentations. (lines 25–30)

In order to prevent *miasma* from seeping into the community, elaborate rites of purification were conducted by priests in consultation with religious experts. The most common purifying agents were saltwater, fire, sulphur, and blood. The most effective agent was the blood of a pig.

Foretelling the Future   Not the least important reason for worshiping the gods was the fact that they had knowledge of the future, even though they did not control human destiny. Consultations mainly took place at oracles, where the gods often dispensed their knowledge through a medium who served as their mouthpiece. Ten oracular shrines are known to us. The most prestigious was at Delphi, where Pythian Apollo presided. No question was too important or too trivial to put to the oracle. Individuals might inquire, "Should I get married?," "Should I go on a sea voyage?," or "Should I adopt an heir?" States might ask, "Should we go to war?," Should we make peace?," or "Should we make a treaty?" Most answers came in the form of a simple affirmative or negative, but occasionally the petitioner received a more detailed and complicated response. In many cases, one suspects, he or she came to the oracle primarily in order to seek divine sanction for a decision that had already been reached.

An oracular response did not remove the responsibility of decision making from the petitioner, as the following anecdote told by Herodotos (1.53) clearly indicates. When Kroisos, king of Lydia, consulted Delphi about the advisability of declaring war on the neighboring kingdom of Persia, he was informed that if he did so he would destroy a large empire. Emboldened by this response, Kroisos duly declared war on Persia and fulfilled the prophecy—by destroying his own empire. What this cautionary tale reveals is that Delphi was not a place to get a "quick fix" on life's problems. On the contrary, the value of its utterances was nil if the petitioner did not interpret them with a proper sense of his own limitations. Not for nothing was the injunction "Know yourself" engraved on the sanctuary wall.

Other means of foretelling the future included examining the entrails of sacrificial victims, observing the flights of birds, and interpreting the significance of dreams. Natural phenomena such as eclipses and earthquakes were also thought to presage the future. The reading of these signs was in the hands of seers, who hired out their services to individuals as well as states. Seers played a particularly important role on the battlefield, being required to supervise the sacrifices that preceded any decision to join or delay battle. It was on the advice of a seer that the Athenian general Nikias took the fatal decision to delay withdrawing his forces from Sicily after an eclipse of the moon had taken place in 413 B.C. This decision led to the complete destruction of his army.

Mainstream Greek religion offered a wide choice of deities from which individuals were free to choose on the basis **Breakaway** of a variety of criteria. These included family tradition, so- **Sects** cial status, personal preference, and last, but not least, ease of access to the deity's shrine. In addition to the worship of individual deities, there was also a type of religion that demanded unwavering and exclusive devotion by its adherents. Two such groups, as noted earlier, were Orphism and Pythagoreanism, both of which rejected state religion and sought to establish separate communities of worshipers.

The fortunes of individual deities ebbed and flowed, according to necessity and need. Cults came and went, and **Conclusions** in extreme cases sanctuaries were leased out to new gods— or sold altogether, just as today the Anglican church in the town where I grew up, St. Barnabas, in northwest London, has been converted into a synagogue and the Ebenezer Baptist Chapel in the same neighborhood into a Moslem mosque. A new cult was accepted into the city's pantheon typically when the Greeks won a spectacular military victory, experienced a natural disaster such as drought, famine, or plague, or redefined their social and political identity. In other words, war, catastrophe, and social or political unrest were the main catalysts of change within a system of belief that was constantly in flux.

Greek polytheism endured long after the rise of Christianity. The Delphic Oracle was still issuing pronouncements in A.D. 267 when it was finally destroyed by a barbarous people called the Heruli. As late as A.D. 395 Athens was saved from Alaric and the Visigoths by an epiphany of Athena and Achilles, who appeared, fully armed, astride the city walls. Not until A.D. 529 were the old gods finally laid to rest, when the Emperor Justinian forbade any pagan to teach philosophy in Athens.

ECONOMY AND TRADE

Although our word "economy" derives directly from *oikonomia*, which means literally "regulation of the household," the Greeks did not have a concept of economics in the modern sense of the word. There is no evidence to suggest that their behavior was determined by economic considerations of the kind that influence modern nation-states. More fundamentally, they did not regard the economy as an autonomous category over which the state might exercise control. There was no such thing as a budget. Except in extreme circumstances, it is doubtful whether they had any way of determining what we would call today the health of their economy.

So far as there was anything resembling economic policy, this was generally limited to the supply of necessities. Clearly prices fluctuated according to the law of supply and demand, and clearly as well these fluctuations affected the standard of living. The Peloponnesian War had a profound effect upon wealthy and poor Athenians alike, as a result of the devastation of the countryside by the enemy and the heavy burden of taxation. Similarly, at the end of the Social War in 355 B.C., Athens was practically bankrupt. Her need to recoup her losses is evident in the subsequent reluctance of her citizens to engage in hostilities. Because Greeks, unlike ourselves, had no expectation that their standard of living would increase over the course of their lifetime, they were doubtless more accepting of this eventuality than we would be.

Coinage   Coinage first appeared in western Anatolia (modern Turkey) in around 600 B.C. Legend also connects the origins of coinage with this region through Midas, the legendary king of Phrygia, whose touch turned everything to gold. Prior to the invention of coinage, most transactions were conducted in kind. At the beginning of the *Odyssey*, Athena in the guise of Mentes declares that she has a cargo of iron which she is going to exchange for bronze (1.182–84). This was no doubt how many exchanges continued to take place throughout antiquity.

The first kingdom to mint coins was Lydia, whose king's name, Croesus, has become a byword for wealth ("as rich as Croesus"). The earliest productions were made of electrum, an alloy of gold and silver found in the waters of the River Paktolos near the Lydian capital of Sardis. Later, the Lydians struck coins of pure gold and silver. Coinage was introduced to the Greek mainland in the first half of the sixth century B.C. The leader was the island of Aigina, which began minting silver coins in c. 570 B.C. Aiginetan coins were stamped with a sea tortoise, the island's emblem, on the obverse (i.e., principal face of a coin). In time all cities identified their coins by stamping them with an emblem. Corinthian coins are identified by the figure of Pegasos, the winged horse, whereas Athenian coins bear an owl, the symbol of Athena. In all, some 1,500 mints have been identified. A notable absentee is Sparta, which used iron spits known as obols as currency. These ranged from twelve to eighteen inches in length. This cumbersome system seems to have been intentionally designed to discourage the flow of trade across her borders. Not until the third century B.C. did Sparta begin to mint coins. Arguably the most beautiful coins were minted by Syracuse and Akragas, two Sicilian cities. Their die cutters took such pride in their work that they even signed the dies.

Athens first began minting her famous owls during the Peisistratid tyranny. These were so named because they bore the image of an owl, the symbol of wisdom, on the reverse. On the obverse they bore the helmeted head of the goddess Athena. Beside the head of Athena were written the letters "AΘE" (ATHE), an abbreviation for the name of the city. The principal units of Athenian currency were the following:

6 obols = 1 drachma

100 drachmas = 1 mina

60 minas = 1 talent.

One drachma was the equivalent of a day's pay in the second half of the fifth century B.C. The commonest unit was the tetradrachm or four-drachma piece.

To cope with the increasing complexity of financial transactions, money changers, known as *trapezitai*, set up tables in public places and operated a system based on letters of credit that anticipated the use of checks. In the Hellenistic Period, Egypt developed a centralized banking system with numerous local branches and a head bank in Alexandria. In the same period, coins bearing the heads of rulers became common. Particularly noteworthy are those issued by Alexander the Great in order to pay his soldiers. These depict the king in the guise of Herakles wearing the skin of the Nemean lion. On the obverse, Zeus is seated on his throne. The coins of Alexander performed an important propagandist function. By illustrating the king's claim to be the descendant of Herakles, the son of Zeus, they reinforced the view that the Macedonians were genuine Greeks.

From the middle of the fifth century B.C. onward, Athens was dependent on imported corn, most of which came from the Black Sea area, particularly the Bosphoros. Other major sources of supply included Egypt, Libya, Cyprus, Sicily, and Italy. **Imports and Exports** This dependency was a leading factor in Athens' decision to develop the Piraeus, which became the foremost commercial port in the eastern Mediterranean. So vital was corn to Athens' survival that the *dêmos* made it a capital offense to ship it to ports other than the Piraeus. It was also illegal to extend a maritime loan other than to a merchant who agreed to convey corn to the Piraeus. In the high season a minimum of six grain ships had to dock at the port each day in order to meet Athens' huge requirement.

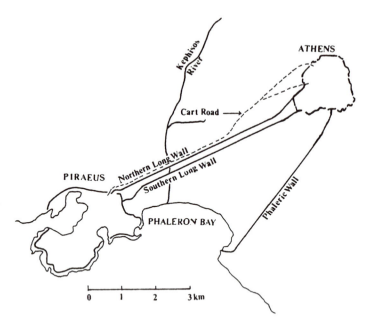

The port of Piraeus, with the Long Walls linking it to Athens. From *The Piraeus* by Robert Garland (London: Duckworth, 1987). Reprinted by permission of Duckworth Publishers.

Athens also had to import virtually all her shipbuilding supplies. These included timber, sailcloth, and ruddle, which was used for the painting of triremes. The chief supplier of timber was Macedon, supplemented by Thrace and southern Italy. Athens also imported slaves, particularly from Thrace, the Black Sea region, and Asia Minor. In the fourth century B.C. she needed to import approximately 6,000 per annum in order to maintain her force at full strength. Other imports included tin, iron, and copper.

Athens' essential imports were not her only ones. Perikles boasted with justification that "all the produce of every land comes to Athens" (Thukydides 2.38). An impressive list of the exotic commodities for sale in Athenian markets is provided by a comic writer called Hermippos in a play dated c. 420 B.C. It includes silphion (a plant used in medicine or as a condiment) and ox hides from Cyrene in Libya; mackerel and salt fish from the Hellespont; pork and cheese from Syracuse; sailcloth, rigging, and papyrus from Egypt; cypress wood from Crete; ivory from Libya; raisins and dried figs from Rhodes; pears and apples from Euboia; slaves from Phrygia; mercenaries from Arcadia; tattooed and untattooed slaves from Pagasai; acorns and almonds from Paphlagonia; dates and wheat flour from Phoenicia; and, finally, rugs and cushions from Carthage.

The most valuable Athenian export was silver, which is discussed in the next section. Other exports included olives, olive oil, wine, marble, and honey. The only manufactured goods that were exported were pottery and armor.

In the *Politics* Aristotle claims that economic *autarkia*, or self-sufficiency, was the goal to which each state should aspire. It is abundantly clear that, by the middle of the fifth century B.C., Athens had long since rejected that ideal. When the Athenians took the decision to abandon the Attic countryside at the outbreak of the Peloponnesian War and live off the revenue and trade from their empire, they were tacitly acknowledging the extent to which they had shifted from a land-based to a maritime economy. No doubt the abandonment of the countryside caused a great deal of economic hardship to many people; however, the fact that such a move was possible is a measure of the degree to which Athens was no longer dependent on her agriculture. And this in turn indicates that she had a very different kind of economy from that of any other Greek state.

Athens was fortunate in possessing rich deposits of silver. Her mines were located at Lavrion in southeast Attica. Mining concessions were auctioned off annually by state officials to private individuals. They were purchased by both indigent and wealthy lessees. Each successful bidder was free to extract as much silver from his concession as he could for the duration of his lease. The monies accruing to the Athenian state from her silver mines was considerable. A strike made in 483 B.C. yielded a revenue of 100 talents. On the recommendation of Themistokles, this sum was devoted to the building of a fleet of 100 triremes or warships. When mining activity reached its peak in the middle of the fourth century B.C., production stood at around 1,000 talents per year. Mining was very much subject to external pressures, and in time of war it was sometimes suspended altogether.

The Silver Mines

Although the Athenians were incapable of planning an economic strategy, they did possess a public exchequer. In Thukydides' *History*, Perikles informs them on the eve of the outbreak of the Peloponnesian War that the state possessed 6,000 talents of coined silver, stored for safekeeping on the Acropolis (2.13.3–6). In addition, the gold that covered the statue of Athena Parthenos was worth 40 talents. This, he suggested, could be melted down and used in the war effort, so long as it was replaced afterward. It became commonplace in the following century to plunder temple treasures in order to finance war efforts. Those that suffered the most included the sanctuaries at Delphi and Olympia.

The State Exchequer

The acquisition of her maritime empire greatly increased Athens' wealth. Though ostensibly the tribute exacted from the allies financed their fleet, the Athenians were in no doubt that they were the beneficiaries of an imperialist enterprise. This is evident from their custom of parading their tribute in the theater of Dionysos at the City Dionysia. In Aristophanes' *Knights,* a character called Demos, who is an unflattering personification of the Athenian people, dotes idiotically on a diet of tribute, flattery, gifts, feasts, and festivals.

Taxation Lower- and middle-income Athenians did not pay taxes. Only the wealthy were required to make a contribution to the state.

The first instance of direct taxation occurred during the Peloponnesian War, when the state exacted a special levy called an *eisphora* or "contribution" to meet the cost of soldiers' pay. In the fourth century B.C., the 300 wealthiest citizens were required to pay an annual *eisphora.* Wealthy Athenians were also required to subsidize important and costly public programs called liturgies. Those selected to be gymnasiarchs had to bear the cost of maintaining a public gymnasium, whereas *chorêgoi* had to pay all the expenses involved in training the chorus for a tragic or comic production. The largest group of all, the trierarchs, had the burden of equipping and maintaining a trireme. No fixed sum of money was laid down for any of these duties because it was confidently expected that gymnasiarchs, *chorêgoi,* and trierarchs would compete with one another for the reputation of financing the best gymnasium, the best production or the best trireme. It is unclear how Athenians in this supertax bracket were identified. As a safeguard against abuse, however, any Athenian who was called upon to perform a liturgy and who believed that he had been wrongly identified had the right to issue a challenge to any other Athenian whom he considered to be wealthier than himself. The person so challenged was then under an obligation either to undertake the liturgy himself or to swap properties with the person who had challenged him.

Conclusions Greeks tended to be either wealthy or poor. There is little evidence for the existence of a middle class. Inevitably we hear most about the wealthy. The aristocrat Alkibiades led a life of decadence, frittering away his fortune on the training of expensive race horses. As today, there was a sort of lurid interest in his antics on the part of his fellow citizens. Most Athenians, however, lived a life of bare subsistence.

With so much surplus wealth in the Athenian economy in the second half of the fifth century as a result of the empire, we might expect that the standard of living would have risen. Archaeological evidence, however, suggests no such thing. As we have seen, the residential quarters of Athens were extremely modest. Evidently the attainment of private wealth was not seen as a necessary goal. If it had been, the Athenians would not have spent 2,000 talents on one of the most ambitious building programs ever conceived. In sum, though a few wealthy citizens became more wealthy, most of the poor tended to remain poor. What Athens' increased wealth did provide, however, was the means whereby a majority of her citizens could combine leisure with frugality.

LAW AND ORDER

Our knowledge of crime is meager. We know much more about legal procedure than about criminals. Although we hear about burglary, theft, mugging, rape, and murder, we know only of isolated cases. We are unable to compare the prevalence of such crimes in antiquity with their occurrence today. Most of our evidence comes from law-court speeches that were written on behalf of well-to-do clients embroiled in cases of disputed adoption, inheritance, and the like. What follows, therefore, inevitably reflects the limitations of our sources.

No Greek community had a police force in the modern sense of the term. The Skythian archers whom Athens possessed had the primary task of keeping the peace. In the absence of any state-run means of law enforcement, it was up to the injured party to arrest any criminal caught in the act and to bring him (or her) before the magistrates. This must have been extremely difficult in the case of victims of violent crime, especially if they happened to be elderly or female. If the injured party was incapable of arresting the criminal, he could summon the magistrate, who would then make an arrest on his behalf. In the case of a wrongful arrest, a fine of 1,000 drachmas was imposed. Other than in cases involving theft, murder, rape, and adultery, the accused received a written summons naming the day that he or she was required to appear before a magistrate.

Athenian law was divided into public and private actions. Public actions involved the community as a whole, whereas private actions concerned individuals. There was no public prosecutor. Though in practice many cases would have been **Bringing an Action** brought to the courts by magistrates or other officials, Solon legislated that "anyone who wishes" was free to initiate prosecution in a public action or *graphê*. In the case of a private suit or *dikê*, it was the responsibility of the injured party to bring the action. In cases of homicide, the relatives of the victim were required to prosecute the killer.

A preliminary hearing called an *anakrisis* took place before a magistrate. Oaths were exchanged by the plaintiff and the defendant, the former swearing that his accusation was genuine, the latter either admitting guilt or swearing that he was innocent. The defendant was free at this time to enter a counterplea. The case was then assigned to a particular court on a particular date. All trials, irrespective of the severity of the charges, were confined in scope to the space of a single day. Only a limited amount of cross-examination took place. The testimony of slaves could be obtained only under torture.

Trial Procedure

Though magistrates presided over trials, they did not serve as judges in the modern sense of the term. They gave neither advice nor directions to the jury nor did they sentence those who were found guilty. They merely supervised the proceedings in a general way. Juries, composed of citizens over thirty years of age, were often extremely large because it was believed that this reduced the likelihood of bribery. Exceptionally the jury might even include 600 members. After the speeches had been delivered by the prosecution and defense, the jurors voted without deliberation. In the fifth century B.C., jurors cast their votes in secret. Each juror was provided with two tokens, one for conviction and the other for acquittal. The juror deposited one of these in a wooden urn whose tokens were disregarded, and the other in a "valid" bronze urn whose votes were counted. Judgement was passed on a majority verdict. In the fifth century B.C., a tie meant an acquittal. In the following century, odd-numbered juries were the norm.

Sokrates on Trial

Athens' most celebrated trial took place in 399 B.C., just after the restoration of democracy at the end of the Peloponnesian War. The defendant was the seventy-year-old philosopher Sokrates, who was accused of corrupting the youth, of introducing new gods (the technical term was "new daimonic beings," or divine beings who were not quite on the level of gods), and failing to worship "the gods whom the city worshiped." This last charge seems to have rested on the claim that Sokrates did not participate in the state festivals held regularly throughout the year, attendance at which was regarded as the mark of a good citizen.

The underlying charge, however, was that Sokrates had consorted with certain aristocrats who had suspended the Athenian constitution in 404 B.C. and had set up a very repressive government known as the Thirty Tyrants. On a more general level many Athenians probably found Sokrates insufferable and self-righteous, since he never tired of pointing out other people's faults and adopted a somewhat supercilious and patronizing tone that became characteristic of his style of teaching. He also manifested a barely disguised contempt for democracy. In other words, it is fair to say that Sokrates' character was on trial as well. Sokrates himself says this in Plato's *Apology*, when he claims that his accusers include not only the three men who have brought charges against him but also all those who hold a negative opinion of him (18b).

Plato's *Apology* purports to be a record of what Sokrates said in his defense. (The Greek word *apologia* does not carry the same connotation of guilt as it does in English. On the contrary, it is the technical term for any speech delivered by the defense.) Plato, who idolized Sokrates, was equally contemptuous of democracy. For a variety of reasons, we therefore need to be wary of treating his *Apology* as a transcript of what Sokrates actually said.

Instead of trying to win over the hearts of the jurors, Sokrates went out of his way to dare them to pronounce him guilty. He even had the temerity to summon the Delphic Oracle, which had declared him to be the most intelligent of all Athenians, as a defense witness. He likened himself to a gadfly that flutters around an indolent horse. The image was hardly calculated to make the jury feel well-disposed toward the accused, not least because Athenians prided themselves on their energy and intelligence. Hardly surprisingly, a majority of sixty found him guilty.

Sentencing

For certain crimes, statutory punishments were laid down by law. In private actions damages were often agreed in advance, dependent upon a conviction. In the absence of any agreement, one third of the trial day was put aside to determine the penalty. After a verdict of guilty had been pronounced, the prosecutor rose to propose a penalty, followed by the defendant, who would obviously propose a more lenient penalty. The jury then voted again. Fines, exile, partial or complete loss of citizen rights, and execution were customary punishments. Imprisonment was rarely used, other than as a temporary expedient. In civil cases, if the plaintiff failed to secure one fifth of the votes or if he failed to put in an appearance at the court, the standard fine was one sixth of the damages that he was claiming.

At Sokrates' trial the prosecution demanded the death penalty. To show his contempt for this suggestion, Sokrates recommended that he be given free meals in the Prytaneion or City Hall for the rest of his life—a privilege that was reserved for public benefactors. This so infuriated the jury that they voted by a margin of eighty more votes in favor of his execution. In other words, eighty jurymen voted to execute a man whom they had previously found innocent. Something obviously was wrong with the system, but we never hear of any attempts to reform it.

Imprisonment

Imprisonment was applied only on a short-term basis to those awaiting trial or execution. Prisoners were supervised by a group of junior magistrates known as the Eleven, who also had the task of supervising the execution of condemned criminals. Sokrates was detained in the state prison for several days while awaiting his execution. (His execution was delayed because his trial and condemnation coincided with an important religious festival.) Athens' state prison has tentatively been identified with a building located in the southwest corner of the Agora. It consisted of twelve small rooms that possibly served as cells. The identification is strengthened by

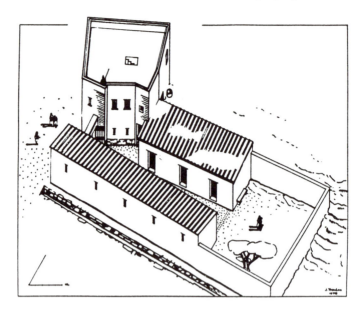

The state prison in the Athenian Agora. Courtesy of the American School of Classical Studies at Athens.

the discovery of thirteen miniature bottles. These may have contained the hemlock that condemned prisoners such as Sokrates were required to drink.

Execution Execution was mainly reserved for crimes such as murder, larceny, theft, picking pockets, housebreaking, kidnaping, and temple robbing. As Sokrates' trial indicates, however, any serious offense was punishable by death if the prosecution saw fit to demand it. In extreme cases such as treason and tomb robbery, the condemned was denied the rite of burial. After being hurled off a rock, he was left to rot in the *barathron* or pit, a rocky gully which probably lay a short distance west of the Acropolis. In Sparta a similar practice took place at a site called the Kaiades. This practice ensured that the dead would never be granted access to Hades but wander disconsolately up and down the banks of the River Styx for all eternity. In Macedon hanging was the preferred form of execution. There is little evidence to suggest that decapitation was ever practiced.

Conclusions There were several weaknesses in the Athenian legal system, excellent though it was by the standards of the day.

In the first place, a trial resembled a public spectacle, with skillful oratory playing a disproportionate part in the outcome. In addition, the large size of many juries increased the possibility of a verdict being subject to crowd hysteria. We know of at least one instance in which the citizen body, sitting in assembly, made a decision in the heat of the moment and reversed it the next day; it is likely that comparable changes of heart among jurors occurred from time to time. As there was no procedure for lodging an appeal, however, only exceptionally was a verdict overturned.

Though the legal system was intended to uphold the rule of law, in practice it continued to countenance, if not actively encourage, the pursuit of a family vendetta. This was particularly true in cases of homicide, where it was the duty of the relatives of the murdered victim to prosecute the killer. Many actions of lesser import are also likely to have been motivated by revenge. In one a prosecutor admitted as much, confident that his honesty would not count against him in the eyes of the jury.

WORK

Because of the importance attached to land ownership, the most respected occupation was farming. Even in the late **Agriculture** fifth century B.C., at least half the population of Athens was still engaged in agriculture. The overwhelming majority were smallholders, who owned no more than two or three acres of land. Only a small minority were wealthy landowners, whose estates occupied several hundred acres. We learn most about farming from Hesiod, whose *Works and Days* provides us with a vivid account of the agricultural year. As the poet emphasizes, it was an extremely hard occupation even at the best of times, owing to the poor quality of the soil. The fact that land had to be left fallow for a year after each season's cultivation in order not to exhaust its goodness made agriculture even more laborious.

From the fifth century B.C. onward, crops were rotated and manure was used. As a general rule, the cultivation of olives and grapes, along with animal husbandry, was more profitable than that of corn and vegetables. To economize on space, vines, planted in rows, were interspersed with vegetables and fruit trees. Ploughing took place twice a year, in spring and in autumn. Wooden ploughs, sometimes tipped with iron, were pulled by teams of oxen. Behind them walked the farmer (or one of his slaves), breaking up the clods with a hoe and covering the seeds with earth. In the harvest season, in May, all available hands gathered in the ripe grain. The grain was threshed on a stone threshing floor by driving oxen around in a circle to separate the wheat from the chaff. Each procedure was accompanied by religious ceremonies to ensure the favor of the gods. Few small farms were entirely self-sufficient. Most farmers had to travel to market in order to exchange their produce. In the Hellenistic Period Egypt became the most intensively cultivated region in the Greek world.

Commerce
Already in Homer's *Odyssey* we can detect a marked disdain for those who made their livelihood by commerce. When the Phaeacians ask Odysseus whether he is a trader, the question comes across as something of an insult. Even in the Classical Period much of Athens' trade was conducted by her metic population rather than by her citizenry, which reflects this age-old prejudice. Yet despite their low status, traders played a vital role in the exchange of corn, wine, salted fish, and luxury goods.

Part of the odium that attached to those who made their living by commerce was due to the fact that there was no clear distinction between trading and piracy in early Greece. Pirates frequently pillaged coastal communities. Because of the risk of seaborne raids, cities like Athens were founded some distance from the coast. When Athens took control of the Aegean in the fifth century B.C., piracy had virtually been eliminated. With the decline of Athenian naval power in the fourth century, it correspondingly enjoyed a resurgence. So serious was the problem in the Hellenistic Period that several Greek islands passed laws requiring women to stay indoors, for fear that they might be snatched by pirates.

Manufacture and Retailing
Most manufacturing enterprises were extremely small. The largest Athenian *ergastêrion* or workshop of which we have record belonged to Kephalos, a metic who employed 120 slaves in his shield factory. The father of Demosthenes employed over fifty slaves in his knife factory. The majority of enterprises were probably much smaller. It is estimated that Athens' entire force of potters in the fifth century B.C. numbered no more than 500, most of whom worked in groups of about six.

Specific cities specialized in the production of specific products. Athens was noted for her painted pottery, Corinth for her metalwork, Megara for her cloaks. Most citizens whose livelihood derived from manufactured goods were content to leave their businesses in the hands of trusted slaves, rather than devote the time and energy to expanding them themselves. Many more products were produced in the home than is the case today. Spinning, weaving, and baking were done almost exclusively by women.

The evidence for retailing is very meager. Most establishments took the form of temporary booths set up in the marketplace on specific days each month, since the retailer was in many cases the producer or manufacturer. Only a few permanent establishments have come to light. A notable example is a shoe shop in the Athenian Agora, which was identified by the discovery of leather thongs for sandals and boots, bone eyelets, and hobnails among its ruins. Though Athens and the Piraeus were the principal markets for the exchange of imported goods, each deme possessed its own agora.

The Greeks regarded the condition of working for some- **Employment** one else as worse than that of being a slave; slaves at least enjoyed some security. Temporary employees, in addition to being laid off at a moment's notice, had to endure the indignity of taking orders from a fellow citizen. Inimical though employment was, however, it is likely to have been fairly widespread. In Athens those who wished to hire themselves out as wage laborers gathered each day on a hill overlooking the Agora.

The most acceptable type of employment was as an employee of the state, since this did not entail subjection to a fellow citizen. In the second half of the fifth century B.C. the livelihoods of an increasing number of Athenians were made possible by the imperial tribute. Even when Athens had lost her empire, the state continued to be a major employer. Though Aristotle's claim that state pay supported "over twenty thousand men" in the fourth century B.C. is an exaggeration (*Constitution of Athens* 24.3), there can be little doubt that it enabled the poor to participate in democracy.

Most of the revenue received from the empire went to pay the rowers of Athens' fleet. Sailors' rate of pay reflected Athens' changing economic fortunes. When her naval expedition was dispatched to Sicily in 415 B.C., it stood at one drachma per day. At the end of the Peloponnesian War, when Athens' reserves were well-nigh exhausted, that figure was cut by half. Unlike hoplites, whose service was intermittent, rowers were a full-time professional body. Since Athens generally maintained at least 100 ships on active service during the fifth and fourth centuries B.C., the fleet must have provided employment for some 20,000 men. Because her rowers were mostly drawn from the poorest class of citizens, the growth in Athenian naval power coincided with a growth in the political importance of the lowest social group, known as the *thêtes*. Maintaining the fleet in a seaworthy condition required the services of a large and highly specialized workforce of joiners, fitters, rope makers, painters, and sailcloth makers. Many of these were probably also rowers, who worked in these capacities when the fleet was laid up.

Since the size of her tribute exceeded the cost of maintaining her fleet, Athens was also able to support other programs that paid the wages of state employees. The most costly was the Periklean building program, instituted in 447 B.C. The building accounts for the Erechtheion indicate that citizens, slaves, and metics worked alongside one another on this project. Skilled workers, like rowers, were paid one drachma per day.

The allied tribute also funded Athens' jury service, which consisted of a pool of 6,000 citizens. The pay of jurors amounted to only two obols per day in court, which was increased to three obols after c. 425 B.C. Since most jurors were elderly, this served as a kind of old-age pension. Although being a state employee was decidedly preferable to being in the employ of another citizen, any Athenian who had to work for his living was regarded as socially inferior to those whose livelihood and leisure were guaranteed by landed wealth.

Conclusions
Lacking any notion of job satisfaction, the Greeks were not much in favor of hard work. Nor were they burdened with anything comparable to the Protestant work ethic. Aristotle was of the opinion that leisure was the precondition of civilized life, and no doubt the majority of Greeks would have agreed. Just as they did not believe in the virtues of work for work's sake, so, too, they hardly had any notion of the concept of wasting time. Loafing was thus an essential part of every citizen's life. It was by loafing in the Agora each day that Athenians learned the latest gossip, exchanged ideas about the burning political issues of the day, and discussed informally the proposals that were tabled for the next meeting of the assembly. As we have already noted, Athenians also used their time in the Agora to make their daily purchases, since respectable women were expected to stay at home.

TRAVEL AND TRANSPORTATION

Travel was widespread in all periods. From the eighth century B.C. onward, traders had regular contacts with non-Greeks such as Phoenicians and Egyptians. Already in the *Odyssey* we encounter itinerant experts, including bards, physicians, builders, and seers, known collectively as "those who serve the community," who, as Homer tells us (17.386), were "invited from the ends of the earth." To this group in later times should be added the sophists, or teachers of rhetoric, who were much in demand in the fifth century B.C., and—a much larger group— the mercenaries. In addition, many Greeks made long journeys at some point in their lives, to either attend a panhellenic festival, consult an oracle, or visit a healing sanctuary.

Land Travel
Horses were a luxury confined to the very rich. As they were unshod, they were incapable of traveling long distances or negotiating the steep mountain paths that dotted the Greek landscape. Stirrups and saddles were unknown, which made horseback riding extremely uncomfortable. Chariots and other wheeled vehicles were useful only over short distances. Most Greeks would therefore have been accustomed to walking considerable distances. In Xenophon's *Memorabilia* (3.13.5), Sokrates talks nonchalantly of the journey from Athens to Olympia as a five- to six-day walk. The going was tough, not to mention dangerous. That is why a favorite theme of Greek

myth is the "culture hero," who cleared the roads of brigands and ma-
rauders, as Theseus did for the stretch between Megara and Athens.

Road-building techniques were by no means unsophisticated. There is
evidence of ramps, switchbacks, and pull-offs even in the Archaic Period.
All roads, however, were local; they did not join one community to another. In Athens the principal paved road was the Panathenaic Way,
which began at the Dipylon Gate and ended up on the Acropolis. It
served primarily as a processional way. More functional was the paved
road to Athens from the marble quarries on Mount Pentelikon. Goods
were conveyed to and from the port of Piraeus along a cart road which
began on the west side of the city. During the Peloponnesian War, when
it was no longer safe to travel outside the city walls, a road running the
entire length of the Long Walls that joined Athens to its port served in
its place.

The most impressive road-building project in Greece was the *diolkos*
or slipway, built by the Corinthians around 600 B.C. The *diolkos* enabled
ships to be towed across the isthmus of Corinth, rather than having to
circumnavigate the Peloponnese. It remained in use until the ninth century A.D.

The most common means of long-distance travel was by sea,
though this was dangerous due both to weather conditions and   **Sea**
to piracy. The sea god Poseidon's enmity to Odysseus, which   **Travel**
delays the hero's homecoming and causes him the loss of all his
ships, reflects a genuine paranoia about sea travel, notwithstanding its
importance to Greek culture.

Since the terrain was unsuitable for wheeled traffic and since there are
no navigable rivers in Greece, most goods had to be conveyed by sea.
No part of Greece is more than sixty miles from the sea, and safe harbors
are numerous around the entire coastline. Goods were conveyed loose,
in sacks, or in earthenware jars known as amphorae.

The busiest commercial port in the Greek world was the Piraeus, situated about five miles southwest of Athens. The Piraeus functioned not
only as a center for the export of Athenian merchandise and the import
of goods destined for Athens, but also as an entrepôt or place of redis-
tribution and transshipment for traders who found it more convenient
to use its unrivaled facilities than deal directly with the source of supply.
Given the unpredictability of the Aegean during the winter months, the
commercial port, which was known as the *emporion*, hummed and
buzzed with frenetic activity for half the year and was practically idle
for the rest.

The volume of traffic that passed through the Piraeus required an extremely efficient system of loading and unloading to prevent a backlog
of ships from clogging up the harbor with spoiled cargoes. After un-

loading their wares, merchants were under considerable pressure from the harbor authorities to sell their cargoes and depart as quickly as possible. The majority of dockers were slaves, hired out to shipowners on a contractual basis. Smaller merchant vessels unloaded from the stern, whereas larger vessels remained at anchor in the harbor basin while their merchandise was transferred onto barges. From the sixth century B.C. onward, cranes were used to unload the heaviest commodities such as marble and timber; pulleys were not in use until the fourth century. Loose merchandise was removed from the hold by means of a swing-beam with a weight attached to one end and a bucket to the other. Amphorae had to be removed singly with the assistance of a wooden pole supported at either end. Most cargoes were probably mixed. A duty was levied on all cargoes entering or leaving the Piraeus, which in 399 B.C. amounted to more than 18,000 talents.

Inns and Hostelries   As early Greece knew nothing of inns, an institution known as "guest-friendship" or *xenia* developed. This meant that aristocrats offered board and lodging to other aristocrats when they were on the road. Zeus Xenios protected the rights and responsibilities of guests and hosts alike. Inns are not heard of until the early fifth century B.C. At the end of the century panhellenic shrines were offering public accommodation for visitors, with separate quarters for foreign dignitaries (Thukydides 3.68.3).

Even in a major commercial and tourist center like the Piraeus, the standard of accommodation was deplorably low. Aristophanes implies that its inns had a reputation for discomfort, prostitution, and bedbugs (*Frogs*, lines 112–15). By the middle of the fourth century B.C., the lack of decent facilities led Xenophon in *Revenues* (3.12) to recommend "the construction of more hotels for shipowners . . . around the harbors . . . as well as public hostels for visitors." Whether his advice was followed is not known. By the Roman period the situation had deteriorated even more. Cicero, in *Letters to Friends* (4.12.3), tells us that when a certain Servius Sulpicius journeyed to the Piraeus to collect the body of a friend who had died there, he found the latter stretched out under a tent. Evidently his friend had been unable to find any other accommodation in the port.

WARFARE

Homeric Warfare   Homeric warfare, which probably resembled the style of fighting that was actually current in Homer's day, was highly ritualistic. Though mass engagements are occasionally described, it is the individual encounters between heroes such as Achilles and Hektor that account for most of the action and ultimately determine

Homeric warrior. From Thomas Hope, *Costumes of the Greeks and Romans* (New York: Dover, 1962). Reprinted by permission of Dover Publications.

the course of the war. The plot of the *Iliad* rests upon the pretension that the prowess of a single warrior is such that his withdrawal from the battlefield causes a complete reversal in the fortunes of the two sides. Likewise the death of Hektor at the end of the poem portends the destruction of Troy, since Hektor was Troy's most valiant defender.

Heroes only did battle with warriors of comparable rank and fighting ability. They were seemingly oblivious to the possibility of being struck by a stray arrow or a rock hurled by one of the mob. Though usually conveyed to the battlefield in chariots, they fought almost exclusively on foot. Their chariots remained parked while the encounter was taking place, ready to provide a means of escape if their owners were forced to retreat or when they went in search of a new opponent. Having found a suitable opponent, heroes revealed their identity and issued a challenge. Ritual insults often preceded the exchange of blows. On rare occasions combatants might have declined to fight with one another if they discovered that there existed a long-standing tie of friendship between their families. This happened in the case of the Greek Diomedes and the Trojan Glaukos in *Iliad* Book 6. After learning of each other's pedigree, the two men actually exchanged armor with each other "so that everyone will realize that our families have provided hospitality for one another in days of yore" (230f.).

The armor described in the Homeric poems was made of bronze, as is consistent with the Bronze Age context of the Trojan War. It consisted of greaves (i.e., leg guards), a corselet, and a helmet with a crest of horsehair. There was also a special kind of helmet worn by a few warriors made out of ox hide, to which were attached plates made out of boar's tusk. Shields were made of ox hide stretched over a wooden frame. The most common type of shield was small and round. Ajax, however, who was the tallest of the Greek warriors, had a rectangular shield with a rising curve on its top edge. Heroes fought mainly with a pair of throwing spears or a single thrusting spear, though at close quarters they also used the sword, frequently described as "silver-studded." The bow and arrow were chiefly limited to the common soldiery and a very few heroes, including Paris and Odysseus.

The vanquished warrior, if not killed outright, typically offered the victor a ransom in order to spare his life. If the victor rejected his appeal, he might follow up the killing with an attempt to strip his victim's corpse of its armor. Where particular animosity existed, the victor might even have despoiled the corpse. Achilles engaged in this barbaric practice when he attached Hektor's corpse to his chariot and then dragged it around the walls of Troy under full view of his victim's parents. The death of a major hero on either side caused such disruption that it interrupted the whole war. Even on the battlefield, the aristocratic hero required a full-scale aristocratic funeral. Seventeen days were devoted to the obsequies of Achilles, nine for Hektor, and two for Patroklos. The extent of funeral rites conducted on behalf of any individual reflected his social standing and value to the army. Ordinary soldiers received only minimal rites of burial. The only method of disposing of the dead was cremation.

The primary objective of the Homeric hero was to win "imperishable glory" so that his deeds of prowess would be celebrated forever in epic verse of the kind written by Homer himself. His goal was "always to excel in battle and to outstrip others," as Peleus explained to his son Achilles (11.784). The value of the prize or *geras* that he received when the spoils of war were distributed to the army reflected his individual worth and thus symbolized the honor in which he was held. Only marginally was the hero concerned with the collective good of the whole army. Warfare, in other words, primarily presented an opportunity for status enhancement and personal enrichment. At the beginning of the *Iliad*, Achilles, after being insulted by his commander in chief Agamemnon, withdraws to his tent, secure in the knowledge that this decision will cause the deaths of many of his comrades. What matters to him foremost is the public recognition of his own worth. Although he is criticized by his peers for his lack of judgement, none of them ever suggests that his behavior is selfish or immoral.

Even though Homeric warfare was highly ritualistic, the poet's description of what Achilles calls "blood and slaughter and the choking groans of men" (*Iliad* 19.214) is virtually unsurpassed for its realistic evocation of the brutality of the battlefield. It provides an unforgettable picture of the type of warfare that depended primarily on a thrust of the spear. Homer describes the deaths of 240 warriors in the *Iliad*, of whom 188 are Trojan and 52 Greek. An almost infinite variety of wounds are described, not all of which are anatomically possible. We are told, for instance, that "the brain ran along the socket of the spear-head in blood-spurts" (17.297f.) and in another that "the point of the spear shattered the collarbone, tore through it, and stuck out by the base of the shoulder" (17.309–10).

Hektor arms for battle. On the left is his aged father Priam, on the right the god Apollo. From *Homer* by Martin Thorpe (Bristol, U.K.: Bristol Classical Press, 1973). Reprinted by permission of Duckworth Publishers.

Yet despite the poet's evident fascination with war, the *Iliad* is by no means a glorification of war. Brutality is constantly exposed for what it is, while the achievements of the heroes are evocatively contrasted with the plight of the innocent, including women, children, and the elderly. In the following passage, Hektor poignantly describes the envisioned fate of Troy as he takes his leave of his wife before going into battle, profoundly aware that her welfare is dependent upon his survival:

I know in my heart and soul
that there will come a day
when sacred Ilion and
Priam and the subjects of

Priam of the strong ash will perish. But my grief is not so much for the Trojans nor for Hecuba nor for king Priam nor for my brothers, who in large numbers will fall beneath the spears of their enemies, as it is for you when some bronze-corseleted Achaean will lead you away to slavery. Then in Argos you will work at the loom of a foreign woman and carry water from the spring Messeis or Hypereia much against your will, and the heavy yoke of necessity will be upon you. Then one day someone observing you weeping will remark, "This is the wife of Hector, who was foremost among the horse-taming Trojans when they fought at Troy." (6.447–61)

The most passionate denunciation of the futility of war in the entire poem is put into the mouth of the warlike Achilles:

A man suffers the same fate whether he holds back or if he goes into battle. The coward and the brave man are held in equal honor. I have achieved nothing with all the sufferings I have endured, forever risking my life in the line of battle. (9.318–22)

Hoplite Warfare

In c. 700 B.C. a new style of warfare called hoplite was introduced, named for the *hoplon* or round bronze shield with which soldiers were equipped. The *hoplon*, which was made of wood or stiffened leather with a bronze covering, was about three feet in diameter and designed to cover half the entire body. It had a double grip and could be rested against the right shoulder, since it was concave on the inside. It was intended to protect not only its bearer but also in part the man standing to his left. For this reason hoplite armies showed a tendency to drift to the right while they were advancing, as each hoplite sought protection on his exposed side from the shield of his companion on the right. Like Homeric heroes, hoplites wore helmets, corselets and greaves made of bronze to a thickness of about half an inch. The principal weapon of attack was the thrusting spear, which was eight feet in length and tipped with iron. As the unit advanced, the spears held by the hoplites standing in the first five ranks all projected beyond the front line. If a spear broke, it could be turned around, since the reverse end possessed an iron spike. Hoplites also carried a short sword, which they could use if they lost their spears. Hoplite gear, though essentially uniform, is likely to have been highly individual in appearance. As there was no government issue of arms or armor, individuals were at liberty to request from the armorer whatever modifications to the basic design they desired.

Service in a hoplite army was regarded as a privilege rather than an obligation, since only citizens were eligible. It is not accidental, therefore, that the introduction of hoplite warfare coincided with the rise of the city-state. Success in battle now depended not on individual deeds of prowess but on the collective discipline of the whole army, whose members were rewarded for their services by being given a role in the politics of the community they defended. However, because armor was expensive to purchase, service remained confined to the well-to-do.

Before a general gave orders for his army to engage in battle, a seer took the omens in order to determine whether they were favorable. Sacrificial victims were then slaughtered to the gods in the hope of securing their goodwill. The Spartans drove whole herds of goats onto the battlefield for sacrifice. Armies advanced singing a *paean* or hymn in honor of Apollo. As they often closed in on each other at a trot and as each hoplite was carrying approximately seventy pounds of bronze, the initial engagement must have resembled a head-on collision between two heavy vehicles. When the Athenians advanced against the Persians at the battle of Marathon, they did so, Herodotos tells us, at a run. This tactic so unnerved the Persians that, although they heavily outnumbered the Athenians, they were instantly thrown into a panic. After the battle the Athenians established a cult in honor of Pan, the god of panic.

The unit in which hoplites fought was known as a phalanx. This was a rectangular formation with a long battlefront usually eight ranks deep. Most hoplite battles took place on level terrain, since only thus could a phalanx maintain its cohesion. The objective was to break through the enemy ranks en masse. Most battles resembled a kind of tug-of-war, with both sides evenly balanced for some time, while much pushing and shoving took place. Complicated maneuvers were rarely attempted, as these made it difficult for a phalanx to retain its formation. Since hoplite helmets had only small eye slots and no piercings for the ears, it was practically impossible for generals to give precise orders. Once battle had commenced, they could do little more than bark out words of encouragement.

When one army finally began to yield, a swift outcome generally ensued, since it would have been practically impossible for a broken phalanx to regroup. However, because the victorious side also put itself at risk if it broke rank and began pursuing a fleeing army, it was usually content merely to occupy the field. Thus most hoplite battles ended in a tactical victory. The victors rarely sought to annihilate the enemy or render him incapable of waging further war. For this reason, often the only tangible consequence was the setting up of a trophy or *tropaion* at the spot where the keenest fighting had taken place. A *tropaion* was the trunk of an oak tree decorated with the spoils of victory. These consisted mainly of the weapons and armor that had been taken from the losing side.

Disposal of the Dead

It was a universally upheld law throughout the Greek world to allow the defeated side to return to the battlefield to retrieve its dead. Only very rarely was this law violated since sensibilities touching burial ran extremely high. During their retreat from Syracuse, the demoralization of the Athenians was greatly increased by the fact that they were unable to care for their dead and wounded (Thukydides 7.75.3). The dead were usually cremated on the field of battle. Their ashes were then placed in individual cinerary urns identified by name tags and brought home. The Athenians arranged their dead in ten piles according to their ten tribes and publicly interred their remains at the end of each campaigning season. Only rarely, as in the case of the 192 Athenians who died fighting the Persians at Marathon, did they accord the war dead the honor of burial on the battlefield. Likewise the Spartans buried the 300 who died with their king Leonidas, while guarding the pass of Thermopylai, where they fell.

Siegecraft

Legend reports that the Greeks besieged Troy for ten years and succeeded in taking it only by using the device of a wooden horse which they left outside the city, ostensibly as a peace offering. Though this story may well be pure fantasy, the supposition that Troy was able to resist for a whole decade the entire military capability of the Greek world is by no means inconsistent with what we know about the ineffectual nature of Greek siegecraft, which even in the fifth century B.C. remained rudimentary. Virtually the only way to achieve success was by starving a city into submission, which was why Perikles was so confident that the Peloponnesians would never be able to defeat Athens if her population withdrew within the walls, because her navy could guarantee her supply routes. In the fourth century B.C. siegecraft became more sophisticated with the development of catapults and mobile towers. In response to these improved techniques, walls and towers became thicker and higher. Curtain walls, ditches, and postern gates were also introduced. At the conclusion of a successful siege, the defeated population tended to be treated much more harshly than when hostilities were confined to the battlefield. This was no doubt partly due to the protracted nature of siege warfare, and partly to the fact that besieging armies often suffered great hardship, notably from plague and other diseases.

Athenian Military Service

When Athenian youths reached the age of eighteen, they were required to serve for two years in the army as ephebes in the company of other members of their tribes (*ephêbos* means "poised at the moment of youth"). Their first year was devoted to training in hoplite and light-armed warfare. Light-armed warfare included the use of the bow, the javelin, and the catapult. At the end of the year a review was held, at which each ephebe was presented with a shield and spear. During their second year, ephebes

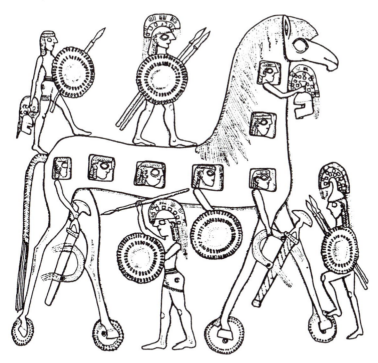

The earliest depiction of the Trojan Horse in Greek art. From *Homer* by Martin Thorpe (Bristol, U.K.: Bristol Classical Press, 1973). Reprinted by permission of Duckworth Publishers.

served as patrolmen at forts situated along the borders of Attica. Then, probably at the end of their second year, they were required to take the following oath of loyalty to the Athenian state:

> I shall not disgrace my sacred weapons nor shall I desert my comrade at my side whenever I stand in the rank. I shall fight in defense of both sacred and secular things and I shall not hand down a fatherland that is reduced in size but one that is larger and stronger. . . . I shall be obedient to the laws that are established and to any that in the future may be wisely established. . . . I shall honor the sacred rites that are ancestral. (Inscription)

Having completed their two years of military service, ephebes became full citizens. They remained eligible for service until the age of fifty-nine, though it was between the ages of twenty and thirty that they were most liable to be called up. Though proficiency in warfare was an essential attribute of any state, Athens did not let it dominate her entire existence. As we see from the speech delivered by Perikles in honor of the dead

Graphic reconstruction of fortification wall. From F. Krischnen, *Die Befestigungen von Herakleia am Latmos* (Berlin, 1922), Miletus III/2.

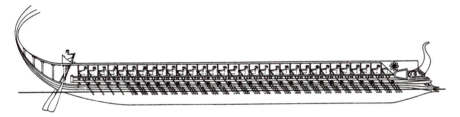

Graphic reconstruction of a trireme. From J. S. Morrison, *Greek Oared Ships* (Cambridge, U.K.: Cambridge University Press, 1968), p. 184. Courtesy of Cambridge University Press.

who fell during the first year of the Peloponnesian War, Athenians took considerable pride in the fact that, whereas their enemies submitted themselves to a rigorous system of military training, they by contrast "pass the time without such restrictions but are still just as ready to face the same dangers as the Spartans" (Thukydides 2.39.4).

In 483 B.C. Athens made the historic decision to build a fleet and become a naval power. Prior to that date, she possessed only a skeletal navy of about fifty ships. It was with her navy that she helped the Greek alliance to defeat the Persian invasion two years later and that she subsequently acquired a maritime empire. Athens achieved her naval supremacy with the aid of a new battleship known as a trireme. The word "trireme" is derived from the Greek *trierês*, meaning "three-fitted," a reference to its three banks of oars. Two banks of rowers sat in the hold of the ship and one on the crossbeams. The trireme was designed to achieve maximum speed and maneuverability with minimum weight. Its hull was about 170 feet in length and its width a mere 15 feet, giving it a ratio of 9 to 1. It provided accommodation for 170 rowers, with ten hoplites, four archers, and sixteen crew members, making a complement of 200. Its objective was to ram the enemy by means of an iron ram mounted on its prow. It is estimated that a trireme could maintain an average speed of about eight knots and ram at twelve knots. In the Hellenistic Period much larger warships, such as quadriremes (four-bankers) and quinqueremes (five-bankers), became common throughout the Greek world.

The headquarters of the Athenian navy was in the Piraeus, whose three harbors were equipped with over 370 shipsheds. The discovery of a circuit wall marking off the naval zone from the rest of the port suggests that entry was reserved for naval personnel. Aristophanes evocatively tells us that when an expedition was about to set sail the Piraeus reverberated with the sound of "oars being planed, pegs hammered, and rowlocks banged into place, and all to the accompaniment of shouting, flutes and whistles of boatswains' orders" (*Acharnians*, lines 552–54). At the outbreak of the Peloponnesian War, Athens possessed 300 seaworthy

Trireme Warfare

triremes. By the terms of her defeat in 404 B.C. she was required to surrender all but twelve. The size of her fleet increased during the fourth
century, reaching an all-time peak of over 400 in 322 B.C.—ironically just
before her sea power suffered a fatal reverse at the hands of the Macedonians.

Mercenaries   From the end of the fifth century B.C. onward, Greek states
increasingly relied on the services of mercenaries, particularly in specialist capacities as light-armed troops or as
archers. This development first came about during the Peloponnesian
War, whose duration caused a shortage of manpower on both sides.
Many of those who enlisted as mercenaries came from such poverty-
stricken regions as Arkadia. Others came from outside the Greek world
proper, like the Thracians who were hired by the Athenians in order to
assist their expedition to Sicily. Although it was economic hardship that
primarily drove increasing numbers of men to seek mercenary service,
new modes of fighting were now rendering hoplite warfare increasingly
obsolete, since many engagements took place in rough terrain where
hoplites were virtually useless. As a result the previously indissoluble
bond between service in the army and citizenship was undermined for
all time.

In the fourth century B.C., Greek mercenaries came to enlist in the
armies of both Greeks and non-Greeks. Theoretically, therefore, Athenians could find themselves fighting in the same battle against other Athenians, though whether this actually ever happened is not known.
Because they had an excellent reputation for discipline, Greek mercenaries were in considerable demand. In 397 B.C. a Persian prince called
Cyrus hired 10,000 mercenaries from the Greek mainland in his bid to
seize the throne from his brother. When Cyrus was killed in battle, the
mercenaries succeeded in making their way from the Persian heartland
back to friendly territory without suffering serious losses. The march,
which is stirringly described by Xenophon in a work called *Anabasis* or
The March Up-Country, demonstrated the military superiority of Greeks
over barbarians. This was to be proven even more dramatically when
Alexander the Great invaded Persia in the 330s B.C. at the head of an
army which consisted largely of mercenaries attracted by the promise of
rich rewards.

Reliance on mercenaries from the end of the fifth century B.C. onward
was not a completely new departure in the history of Greek warfare,
however, as is illustrated by the following fragmentary poem written by
the seventh-century B.C. poet Alkaios in celebration of his brother's
homecoming from the wars:

> You have come from the ends of the earth, Antimenidas, my be-
> loved brother, clasping your sword with its gold and ivory handle.

You served alongside the Babylonians and you took on a mighty challenge when you rescued them by slaying a warrior who was all but a finger shy of eight foot in height.

With the exception of siegecraft, which had its own rules, warfare tended to adhere to fairly civilized standards of be- **Rules of** havior. Unlike their Homeric counterparts, hoplites did not **Warfare** make a habit of stripping their opponents' bodies or mutilating them in the way that Achilles mutilated Hektor's body. Nor was it their practice to despoil temples, sanctuaries, or tombs, which were regarded as sacrosanct. The destruction of property, whether public or private, was extremely rare, in part because warfare was confined largely to the battlefield. A notable exception was the Persians' destruction of the temples and statues that stood on the Athenian Acropolis in 480 B.C. The Athenians were so outraged by this act of vandalism that they left their temples in their ruined condition for thirty years as a living testimony to barbarian savagery.

Hostilities between Greek states were suspended for the duration of the Olympic Games in accordance with a sacred truce known as the *ekecheiria*, which means literally "a restraining of hands." Ambassadors were placed under the protection of the gods, and their persons were regarded as inviolate. Though local squabbles leading to bloodshed were endemic, wars tended to be short in duration. The campaign season began in the spring and ended in the fall. In Athens its conclusion was marked by the mass burial of all those who had died in the preceding season.

Not until the Peloponnesian War did the Greek world experience anything akin to the modern notion of total war. Thukydides constantly emphasizes the decline in moral standards that this brought about. In 413 B.C. a contingent of Thracian mercenaries, who had been hired by the Athenians, ran amok and killed all the inhabitants of the town of Mykalessos in Boiotia, slaughtering "even the livestock and whatever other living creatures they saw," including all the pupils at a boys' school (7.29.4).

It was not only the barbarians who practiced such savagery, however. When the town of Mytilene on the island of Lesbos revolted from the Athenian Confederacy and was forced to surrender in 427 B.C., the Athenians decided to execute all the men and enslave the women and children. The next day, however, they revoked their decision and opted instead to execute only the ring leaders, one thousand in number (3.50). Just over ten years later the island of Melos, which was neutral, declined to join Athens' alliance. After a short siege the Athenians did not think twice about carrying out the punishment that they had originally reserved for the Mytileneans. They slaughtered the men, enslaved the

women, and repopulated the island with five hundred of their own citizens (5.116).

Conclusions   Greek warfare was conducted on a miniscule scale in com-
parison with its modern counterpart. It has been estimated
that at no time in history were the Greeks able to put more
than 50,000 soldiers into the field. Another major difference is that it was
not conducted under the glare of publicity as it is today. Once an expedition had departed only general reports of its fortunes reached home.
Aeschylus in *Agamemnon* (lines 437ff.) memorably describes Ares, god of
war, as the "gold-broker of corpses," who accepted soldiers in exchange
for the ashes that were brought back from the battlefield in cinerary urns.
Just as relatives waved goodbye on the quayside as the fleet set sail at
the beginning of a campaign, so, too, they awaited the arrival of "urns
in place of men" announcing the death of a husband, brother, or son.

7

Pleasure and Leisure

ATHLETICS AND THE CULT OF PHYSICAL FITNESS

Few peoples have attached so much significance to the cult of physical fitness as the Greeks. The notion of physical perfection was so central to their sense of selfhood that they seem to have been almost incapable of conceiving of themselves in any other terms. Greek art is saturated with images of perfectly formed men and women—so much so that it is tempting at first sight to conclude that the people who produced such impressive works were physically superior not only to their contemporaries but to every other race that has ever existed. It hardly needs to be pointed out that this was far from being the case. To comprehend their deeply ingrained narcissism, it may be instructive to remember that theirs was a culture which saw no daylight between what was *kalos* (beautiful) on the one hand and *agathos* (good) on the other.

The adoration of the human body found many outlets. Greek art, especially sculpture, gave it uninhibited expression. It was the Greeks who first identified the naked human body as the primary object of artistic attention. No less important, physical perfection was exemplified through competitive athletics, which occupied a central place in a number of major festivals. The apparent assumption was that the gods, who themselves exemplified physical perfection on the divine plane, took delight in observing their human counterparts.

Keeping Fit

Athletic training was a vital part of education for boys from wealthy families. As soon as they began school at about the age of seven, Athenian boys were entrusted to a professional trainer known as a *paidotribês*, who worked in a *palaistra* or "wrestling school." Athens contained many *palaistrai*, but none has been fully excavated. Their general layout was similar to that of a Greek house. The training ground was probably enclosed by a wall with a verandah to provide shelter from the rain and sun. Most *palaistrai* possessed a changing room, a bathroom, and a place to store equipment.

Maturer athletes exercised naked in the gymnasium, a Greek word whose root is the adjective *gymnos* ("naked" or "lightly clad"). Though many gymnasia were equipped with changing rooms and other facilities, the basic requisite was a piece of level, open terrain, where athletes could practice javelin- and discus-throwing, as well as running. Gymnasia tended to be located near a river, enabling athletes to refresh themselves and bathe after exercising. Though only their foundations have survived, they were probably verdant oases with well-shaded walks. By the end of the sixth century B.C., Athens had acquired three principal gymnasia—the Academy, the Lyceum, and the Kynosarges—all situated outside the city. These were used by Athens' ephebes, as well as by her hoplites.

Socializing also went on in the gymnasium. Not only aspiring athletes but also older men would gather there to converse, gossip, and argue, while sitting in the

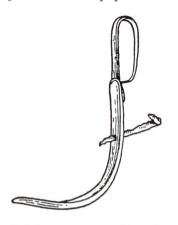

Strigil or scraper used by athletes. (It has been pierced by an iron nail to "cancel" it, or reserve it for use by the dead.) From D. Kurtz and J. Boardman, *Greek Burial Customs* (London: Thames and Hudson, 1971). Courtesy of University of Oxford.

shade beside running water. Here, too, itinerant professors, known as sophists, would talk and give lectures. In the fourth century B.C., the gymnasia of Athens came to acquire a new identity as centers for philosophical discussion. Plato established his school in the vicinity of the Academy. The name, which derives from a local hero called Akademos, is the origin of our word "academic." Half a century later his pupil Aristotle established a rival philosophical school in the Lyceum. Aristotle's followers were dubbed peripatetics (from the verb *peripateô*, "to walk up and down") because of their habit of pacing up and down as they pursued their philosophical inquiries. The geographical coincidence between intellectual and athletic excellence testifies to the Greek conviction that the two aspirations are complementary.

Competitive athletics was one of the principal means by which the Greeks promoted a sense of cultural unity. Though there were probably hundreds of local athletic festivals, four panhellenic, or "all-Greek," games attracted athletes from all over the Greek world. These were the Olympic and Nemean Games, both held in honor of Zeus; the Pythian Games, held in honor of Apollo; and the Isthmian Games, held in honor of Poseidon. The most prestigious of these were the Olympic Games, held every four years from 776 B.C. to A.D. 261. It is a remarkable testimony to the Greek ability to rise above politics at least on a temporary basis that in the course of this thousand-year period never once, so far as we know, were they canceled. By contrast, our modern series, which was first held in 1896, has already been canceled three times, quite aside from being regularly exploited for propagandist or commercial advantage.

The Olympic Spirit

There were a number of reasons why the ancient Olympic Games were successful in promoting the spirit of panhellenism. In the first place, Olympia, due to its location in a politically unimportant region of Greece, never fell prey to the ambitions of any neighboring power. For most of its history, the sanctuary was controlled by the neighboring city of Elis. Consequently the games were never used for self-promotion by the host country, in the way that the Nazis used the Munich games in 1936 to promote an image of racial superiority. The ancient Olympics did, however, occasionally serve the propagandist aims of individuals, notably in A.D. 69 when they were postponed for two years to enable the Roman Emperor Nero to compete. To the credit of the Olympic authorities, his victories in the chariot race and musical contest were later expunged from the record books.

Another reason why the Olympic Games genuinely embodied the Olympic ideal is that they formed part of a religious festival held in honor of Zeus Olympios. Olympia was the chief sanctuary of Zeus on the mainland. The religious component, which accounted for two and a half out of the five days devoted to the festival, was never overshadowed by the kind of hoopla that characterizes the modern series. A sacred truce, known as the *ekecheiria*, which remained in effect for one month, was observed to allow spectators and competitors to travel to and from Olympia in safety. In later times this was extended to two months, and finally to three months. Only once was the truce broken, by Sparta in 420 B.C. As a punishment, her athletes were prohibited from participation in the games that year.

All Greek speakers were eligible to participate, and there was virtually no distinction between professionals and amateurs. Most cities subsidized the training of their athletes. Participants had to spend the entire month preceding the games training at Olympia under the supervision of the *Hellênodikai* or "Judges of the Greeks."

The sanctuary of Zeus at Olympia (reconstruction by F. Adler [1894]).

The
Olympic
Program

The first day of the Olympic Games was devoted to oath taking, checking the qualifications of the competitors, sacrifices, and prayers. So important was winning that competitors prayed "either for the wreath or for death." All contestants participated naked and barefoot. The origin of this practice is attributed to a certain Orsippos, who was in the lead in a footrace when his loincloth fell off. Orsippos tripped and lost the race.

On the second day of the festival the chariot race took place in the hippodrome. This was the most spectacular as well as the most dangerous event. It consisted of twelve laps up and down a straight track. The chariots had two wheels and were drawn by a team of four horses. As there was no dividing barrier between the up and down track, and as charioteers were required to perform 180-degree turns when they reached the end of each lap, head-on collisions were frequent. What increased the likelihood of serious injury was the fact that charioteers tied their horses' reins around their bodies, so that if they fell they were dragged along the ground. Pindar, who wrote many odes commemorating victors in the games, claims that in one race at Delphi "forty drivers were laid low" (*Pythian Ode* 5.49). The chariot race was followed by a horseback race without stirrups or saddles over the same course. The victor in both events was not the charioteer or the jockey, but the owner. As horses were extremely expensive, this was almost invariably a wealthy aristocrat or tyrant.

The remaining events took place in the Olympic stadium. This was named for the stade, a unit of measurement approximately 210 yards in length. The stadium consisted of a level piece of ground covered with sand. Spectators watched from a raised bank of earth on either side. Only the judges were provided with seating. The first event was the pentathlon, which took place on the afternoon of the second day. This consisted of five events: discus, long jump, javelin, footrace, and wrestling. The javelin was thrown with the aid of a thong to give it more momentum. For the long jump athletes carried weights, enabling them to lengthen their jump. On the morning of the third day more religious celebrations took place, culminating in the sacrifice of a hundred oxen on the great altar of Zeus. In the afternoon competitions between boys aged between twelve and eighteen took place. These consisted of a footrace, wrestling, and boxing. On the morning of the fourth day adult footraces were held over various distances, the longest being twelve laps. (There was no equivalent of a modern marathon.) The afternoon was given over to body-contact sports, including wrestling, boxing, and pankration. The pankration, which can be best translated as "all-in combat," was a combination of wrestling and boxing. There were no rules, and serious injuries, even deaths, were not uncommon. On one occasion the prize was awarded to a pankratiast called Arrachion, who was strangled to death. His opponent gave in just as Arrachion was expiring because the latter had broken his toe. The final event was a race over two laps by competitors dressed in full hoplite armor, helmets and greaves, and carrying large, round shields. Proficiency in this event may have contributed to the Athenian victory at the battle of Marathon, in which the heavily armed hoplites unnerved the Persians by charging from a distance.

The only competition for unmarried girls was a footrace in honor of Hera. It is described by Pausanias as follows:

> The competitors are divided into three age groups, and they run in this way: their hair hangs down, a tunic reaches a little way above the knee, and they bare the right shoulder down to the bosom. They have the Olympic stadium reserved for the games, but the course is shortened to about one sixth of its length. The winning girls are presented with crowns of olive and a portion of the cow that is sacrificed to Hera. (5.16.2–3)

On the fifth and final day prizes of olive wreaths were awarded to the victors. There were no prizes for those who finished second or third. Victors were permitted to erect statues in the sanctuary and were feted lavishly by their own cities when they returned home. Some were granted free meals at public expense for the rest of their lives. States whose athletes won prizes gained enormous prestige. Alkibiades boasted that "the Greeks believed that Athens had even greater power than was the case because of my success in the Olympic Games, although earlier they had thought they had entirely worn us out in the war" (Thukydides 6.16). The most suc-

Winners and Losers

cessful state was Elis, where Olympia was situated. Elis produced the first recorded Olympic victor, Koribos, in 776 B.C. Sparta was also prominent, whereas Athens, even at the height of her power in the mid-fifth century B.C., won far fewer victories. The most successful athlete was Milo of Kroton, who won the wrestling prize in five successive Olympiads between 536 and 520 B.C. Milo, a notorious show-off, used to challenge people to bend back his little finger—apparently no one could. He was also in the habit of tying a band around his head, taking a deep breath, and snapping the band with the aid of the veins of his head (Pausanias 6.14.7).

We should also spare a thought for the losers, whose plight is described by Pindar: "They, when their mothers meet them, have no sweet laughter around them, arousing delight. But in back streets they cower, out of their enemies' way, bitten by disaster" (*Pythian* 8.85–87).

Women were not permitted to enter the sanctuary of Zeus while the games were in progress. Pausanias (5.6.7) tells us that the ban was introduced after a woman called Kallipateira managed to disguise herself as an Olympic trainer in order to watch her son compete. She was exposed (literally) when she jumped over the trainers' enclosure. The judges decided not to punish her out of deference to her brothers, her father, and her son, all of whom had been Olympic victors. Though women could not watch the games in progress, handsome athletes had their "groupies," who hung about the entrance to the site, eager to catch a glimpse of their favorites. Pindar writes of one such favorite as follows:

On the many occasions that you won in the Panathenaia, Telesikrates, unmarried girls saw you and under their breath prayed that you might be their beloved husband or son, and they did the same at Olympia and Delphi, and at all the local festivals. (*Pythian* 9.97– 103)

Though only a minute proportion of the Greek population actually participated in the games, young men were inspired to train in the *palaistra* in the hope that they might one day have the distinction of representing their city. The games thus functioned as a general incentive to achieve physical excellence. Not everyone, however, approved of the adulation that victorious athletes received. A character in a lost play by Euripides inquires,

Who has ever assisted his city by winning a prize for wrestling or running fast or throwing the discus or striking someone full on the chin? Will they fight the enemy with a discus or kick them out of the country as if they were footballs? (*Autolykos* fr. 282)

The Greeks were not, of course, unique in their prejudice for physical perfection. The same prejudice was central to the Renaissance, as the numerous images of perfectly formed saints, the embodiments of physical and moral energy, by art- **The Bare Facts** ists such as Michelangelo and Raphael conclusively demonstrate. So far as the common man figured at all in Renaissance art, he did so primarily as an adjunct to the central biblical and mythological scenes that were enacted by the Renaissance equivalents of the Hollywood idols of today. This remained the case until the seventeenth century, when he finally became an object of artistic interest in his own right.

In crafting an image of themselves that was at such variance with physiological reality, the Greeks were not wholly different from us, although they have bequeathed to us almost exclusively this image of themselves. If by some quirk of history all that survived of contemporary Western "art" were copies of *GQ, Vogue,* or *Woman,* posterity might be equally intrigued by the disjunction between representational image and physiological fact. It is a disjunction that hardly diminishes as we become wealthier, more leisured, and better fed. The Third National Health and Nutrition Examination Survey (1995) revealed that 4.7 million American youths aged between six and seventeen are seriously overweight. Phys- iological perfection was even *less* attainable in antiquity than it is in the modern world.

FESTIVALS

Observances help to fill what Dr. Samuel Johnson, the great eighteenth-century man of letters, called "the great vacancies of life." Or, as a Greek proverb put it, "a life without festivals is like a road that has no inns." Festivals regulate the flow of life. Without them the passage of life is in constant danger of becoming monotonous and undifferen- tiated.

Yet today in both the United States and Britain festivals play only a minor part in the life of our community. This state of affairs is charac- teristic of societies that regard their holidays as peripheral, and whose members do not closely identify with one another through the collective memory of shared experience. The Greeks would not have understood how society can function without a sense of shared experience. Our lack of the celebratory would have struck them as uncongenial in the extreme. Since, moreover, they did not divide the year into periods of seven days with an appointed period of rest at the end of each week, festivals con- stituted the primary pretext for recreation. They also afforded the Greeks an opportunity to express their common identity as citizens, tribesmen, and demesmen, and to reinforce their sense of an inherited tradition. In

Athens more than sixty days of the year were devoted to festivals annually.

Greek festivals took many forms. At the lower end of the scale were the deme festivals. At the upper end were the civic festivals, in which the entire citizen body, including in some cases resident aliens, participated. The best attended were the prestigious panhellenic or all-Greek festivals, which attracted celebrants from all over the Greek world. In the Hellenistic Period kings founded festivals at their capitals with the object of impressing their subjects as well as their rivals. One such was the Ptolemaia, which was instituted by Ptolemy II in the early third century B.C. at Alexandria, Egypt, in honor of his deified father. The procession he arranged under its auspices in 270 B.C. was one of the grandest events ever celebrated in antiquity.

Each festival was a unique expression of worship, tailor-made to the deity in whose honor it was held. A number of features, however, were common to many: a procession to a deity's shrine with ritual stops along the way; the singing of hymns; the decorating of a wooden object that embodied the deity's power; athletic, musical, and dramatic contests; and, finally, the most essential feature of all, a blood sacrifice performed on an altar in front of the deity's shrine, followed by the distribution of meat among the priests and worshipers.

Agricultural Festivals
Our knowledge of Greek festivals is not sufficiently detailed to permit us to fathom the precise significance that they held for the people who celebrated them. In general, the impulses that propelled the Greeks to congregate and perform these elaborate rituals incorporated anxiety and fear on the one hand, relief and gratitude on the other. Festivals connected with the agricultural year were designed to secure a good harvest, though we never gain a detailed insight into why precisely the celebrants did what they did. One of the most puzzling was the Thesmophoria, a fall festival conducted exclusively by women. This was held all over the Greek world in honor of Demeter, goddess of the corn. The culminating ritual involved throwing the bodies of sacrificial pigs into snake-infested pits. Three days later women were lowered into the pits to retrieve their putrefied remains, which were then placed on an altar and mixed with seed grain. This bizarre rite, which was perhaps seen as a kind of enactment of Persephone's descent to Hades, was evidently intended to facilitate the germination of the grain, but why it took this precise form is a complete mystery.

Other agricultural festivals included the Oschophoria, in which two youths carried branches known as *ôschoi* laden with grapes; the Haloa, held in honor of Demeter in midwinter, when cakes in the form of phalluses were eaten; the Rural Dionysia, held in honor of Dionysos, during which a giant phallus was carried aloft; the Anthesteria, a flower festival held in early spring, when wine jars containing newly fermented wine were opened and blessed by Dionysos; the Thargelia, held in honor of Apollo, during which a pot of boiled vegetables called *thargela* was offered to the god and a human scapegoat, who perhaps personified hunger, was beaten and driven out of the city; and finally, the Pyanopsia, in which branches laden with wool, fruits, cakes, wine, and oil flasks were borne by children in procession and later hung on the front doors of every Athenian home.

Because the passage from one stage of life to another was thought to be fraught with danger, the Greeks paid very close attention to the junctures between these stages. The first rite of passage for an Athenian child took place on the second day of **Rites of Passage** the flower festival called Anthesteria, when infants aged between three and four would be given their first taste of wine. It seems probable that this ritual signaled the formal admission of the child into the Athenian religious community, since wine, the gift of Dionysos, was a feature of almost every religious rite. Rites of passage were also conducted at later moments in a person's life, notably at adolescence and adulthood, and of course at marriage and death.

Festivals in honor of the dead formed a major feature of the calendar. The most spectacular was the annual cere- **Festivals in** mony held in honor of the war dead. Known as the *taphai* **Honor of** or "burials," it took place at the end of the campaigning **the Dead** season in early winter. Thukydides describes it as follows:

> Three days before the ceremony the bones of the fallen are brought and put in a tent which has been erected, and people make whatever offerings they wish to their own dead. Then there is a funeral procession in which coffins of cypress wood are carried on wagons. There is one coffin for each tribe, which contains the bones of members of that tribe. One empty bier is decorated and carried in the procession. This is for the missing, whose bodies could not be recovered. Everyone who wishes, both citizens and foreigners, can join the procession, and the women who are related to the dead make their laments at the tomb. When the bones have been laid in the earth a man chosen for his intellectual gifts and general reputation makes an appropriate speech in praise of the dead and after the speech everyone departs. (2.34)

Other festivals in honor of the dead include the third day of the Anthesteria, or flower festival, known as the Chytroi or Pots, which was so named because pots of porridge were offered on that day. Chytroi, in other words, was the Athenian equivalent to All-Souls-Day, when the souls of the dead left their graves and wandered abroad. To counter their noxious presence, people would chew buckthorn and smear the doors of their houses with pitch. The dead were also celebrated at the Genesia and Nemeseia. The latter festival was held at night and, as its name (derived from *nemesis*, or "vengeance") suggests, it was intended to placate those who had come to a violent end.

The Panathenaia   The most prestigious Athenian festival was the Panathenaia or All-Athenian Festival, held annually on the birthday of Athena, the city's patron goddess. Once every four years the festival was celebrated with special grandeur. This occasion is the subject of the great frieze that ran around the outer wall of the Parthenon. The procession assembled outside the city at the Dipylon Gate and proceeded through the Agora along the ceremonial Panathenaic Way in the direction of the Acropolis, its final destination.

Groups representing the entire population of Athens participated, the largest of which was a military contingent. On the Parthenon frieze this takes the form of a cavalcade of naked horsemen. Young girls carried baskets containing barley meal to sprinkle on the heads of the sacrificial victims, as well as cushions for the gods to sit on. Youths carried water pitchers, old men brandished olive branches sacred to Athena, and metics bore offering trays. The central feature of the procession was a ship mounted on wheels with a woollen peplos rigged to its mast in place of a sail. The peplos, which was woven by Athenian maidens of noble birth who resided on the Acropolis, clothed an olive wood statue of Athena that was believed to have dropped onto the Acropolis out of the sky. The removal of the goddess' old peplos and its replacement by a new one evidently formed the climax to the entire Panathenaia, for this is the scene depicted on the portion of the frieze directly above the entrance to the Parthenon. A herd of cows was sacrificed to the goddess on the altar outside her temple, and the meat was then distributed to participants down at the Dipylon Gate, where the procession had begun.

The Panathenaia also featured competitions, including recitations of the works of Homer, contests on the flute and harp, athletic and equestrian events, dancing, and, in later times, a naval competition. Victors were awarded Panathenaic amphoras containing olive oil in commemoration of the fact that the olive tree was the goddess' gift to the state. These bore the simple inscription, "One of the prizes from Athens."

THEATRICAL PERFORMANCES

When we talk about Greek drama, we usually mean Athenian drama, both tragedy and comedy. Only a few non-Athenian playwrights are known to us by name and none of their plays has survived. Drama was both an invention and an integral aspect of Athenian democracy, so much so that it is quite impossible to talk about it other than as an expression of the distinctive political and civic realities of the Athenian state.

The origins of Greek drama are very imperfectly understood, but they probably derive from an opposition between the chorus and a single actor. From earliest times the Greeks held choral performances in honor of the gods, in commemoration of military and athletic victories, and in mourning for the dead. *Tragoidia*, the Greek word for tragedy, which derives from *tragos*, "goat," and *oidê*, "song," probably owes its origins either to the fact that choruses were originally dressed in the loinskins of goats or to the fact that the prize for the song was a goat. The Athenians attributed the invention of tragedy to a shadowy figure called Thespis, who is credited with having won first prize in the first contest for tragedy held in c. 534 B.C. *Kômoidia*, which gives us our word "comedy," means "*kômos*-singing." A *kômos* was a band of tipsy revelers who wandered about the town, crashing drinking parties.

The promotion of drama to the level of Athenian national pastime par excellence owed much to the tyrant Peisistratos, who accorded it a central position in a new festival instituted in honor of Dionysos, the patron god of drama. It was at this festival, known as the Great or City Dionysia, that plays were staged which rank today among the foremost achievements of Athenian culture, namely the tragedies of Aeschylus, Sophokles, and Euripides, and the comedies of Aristophanes. The Dionysia was a four-day festival held in March. In the opening ceremony a statue of the god was carried into the theater so that Dionysos could witness the performances. At the center of the playing area stood an altar. Both the statue and altar were reminders of the religious aspect of drama.

Since the Dionysia coincided with the beginning of the sailing season, many foreigners and tourists were able to attend, including Athens' allies. The annual tribute that they brought with them was displayed in the theater (Isokrates, *On the Peace* 82)—a curious mingling of the secular with the divine that is so characteristic of Greek culture. On this occasion, too, orphans of the war dead paraded in battle gear and received the blessings of the people. The Dionysia was largely devoted to tragedy, although from 486 B.C. comedies were performed as well. In c. 440 B.C. the Athenians established a separate festival devoted exclusively to comedy, known as the Lenaia, held around the end of January. Only citizens were permitted to attend the Lenaia.

Staging a Dramatic Performance

Each tragedian had to submit three tragedies to a magistrate known as the archon eponymos (i.e., the Athenian magistrate who gave his name to the year). He also had to write a satyr play, so named because of its chorus of half-animal, half-human creatures, whose drunken and licentious antics provided an uproarious coda to the serious business of tragedy. Comic poets submitted only one drama. It was the archon's duty to choose which plays should be performed. Once he had made his choice of three tragic and three comic productions, he allocated to each a *chorêgos* or chorus master, who was a wealthy Athenian or metic. It was the responsibility of the *chorêgos* to pay all the expenses of the production, chief of which was the training and costuming of the chorus. It is estimated that the services of some 1,500 persons were needed to stage all the plays produced at the City Dionysia each year. Plutarch actually claimed that the Athenians spent more money on dramatic productions than they did on their defense budget (*Moral Precepts* 349a).

If a play failed to attract state sponsorship, its chances of being performed in Athens or elsewhere were virtually nil. There was no equivalent to an off-Broadway theater devoted to experimental drama. Even so, so far as we know, no playwright ever questioned the conditions to which he was forced to submit in order to have his plays produced, nor did any ever complain that state funding inhibited the free expression of his ideas. In the first half of the fifth century B.C., playwrights were required to be composers, choreographers, designers, directors, and actors as well. Increasingly, however, these roles were taken over by specialists, though the playwrights still had to write the music for the chorus. Being a playwright hardly amounted to having a profession in the modern sense of the word because they received payment only if they won first prize. Some, however, may have earned a modest income from the sale of copies of their plays.

The Theater

A Greek theater consisted of a *theatron* or "seeing space," which was frequently cut into a hillside in the form of steeply raked tiers of seats, and a circular *orchêstra* or "dancing space" about twenty meters in diameter, almost entirely surrounded by the *theatron*. Seats were arranged in the form of wedges and divided from one another by vertical gangways. In the fifth century B.C., the seats were wooden, but in the next century stone became commonplace. The best surviving theater is at Epidauros in the northeast Peloponnese, whose acoustics are so refined that it is possible to hear a piece of paper being torn up in the center of the *orchêstra* from the back row of seats over fifty meters away. The raised stage was an invention of the fifth century B.C., as, too, was scenery. The Greek *skênê*, meaning "hut" or "tent," from which our word "scenery" derives, describes the actors' changing room, the outside of which could be painted to resemble the façade of a palace or temple and thus provide a sense of place. There was no other form of stage setting.

The Theater of Dionysos in Athens could probably accommodate about 20,000 spectators. (Plato mentions 30,000 in the *Symposium* but this is almost certainly an exaggeration.) Even if only 10,000 attended, this probably amounted to a quarter of the citizen body. The front rows were reserved for priests, magistrates, and distinguished visitors. In the center of the front row was the throne of the priest of Dionysos Eleuthereus ("Liberator"). Special areas were reserved for ephebes, members of the council, and metics. Probably the rest of the audience sat in blocks allocated to each of the ten tribes. Even prisoners were let out on bail so that they could attend performances. The price of admission was two obols, though from the fourth century B.C. onward and possibly earlier citizens were admitted free. We do not know for certain whether women or slaves were permitted to attend.

Going to the theater was hardly a relaxing experience in the modern sense of the word, since the audience was expected to sit through four plays a day at least, or five if the tragic plays performed in the morning were followed by a comedy in the afternoon. That amounts to about ten hours of uninterrupted performance per day. There were no intervals, except between plays. Not surprisingly, audiences became extremely restless if they were bored or displeased. We hear of several instances when a hostile crowd pelted the performers with stones and fruit. In the fifth century B.C., plays received only a single performance. The only exception was Aristophanes' *Frogs*, whose political message was judged to be so relevant that the play was put on a second time. In the fourth century, however, revivals became commonplace.

Since theatrical performances took place in broad daylight, there was no opportunity to focus on a particular spot through lighting effects. Only two items of stage equipment were in regular use. One was known as the *ekkyklêma*, or **Stage Equipment** "object that is rolled out." This low platform on wheels was projected into the *orchêstra* from the central doors of the scene building to reveal the interior of a place or temple. The *ekkyklêma* was undoubtedly used by Aeschylus in *Agamemnon* in order to display the bodies of Klytaimnestra and her lover Aigisthos after they had been murdered by Orestes. The other device was the *mêchanê*, a word which simply means "machine." The *mêchanê* was a kind of crane that enabled a character to be transported on or off stage by being swung through the air. The Latin phrase *deus ex machina*, literally "a god from a machine," which has entered into our language, is a reference to the overworking of this device by dramatists who used it to extricate their characters from an otherwise insoluble plot.

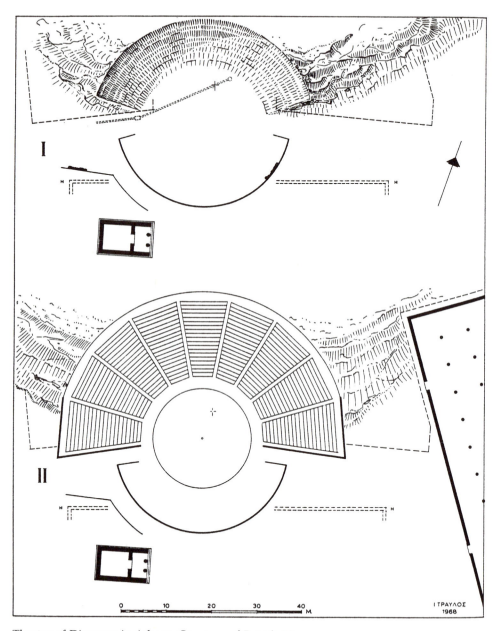

Theater of Dionysos in Athens. Courtesy of British Museum.

The Greek word "chorus," which to us suggests collective singing, literally means "dance" (as in our word "choreography"). Most Greek choruses were a combination of **The Chorus** music, dance, and song. Choral performances generally took place at religious festivals in honor of the gods, though some were secular. These include the encomium (*enkômion*), whose name derives from the fact that it was originally a song sung at a revel or *kômos*; the victory ode; and the dirge. The earliest surviving choral poetry was written by Alkman, who composed songs for choruses of Spartan girls in the seventh century B.C. Alkman's work provides us with a glimpse of a Sparta that is sensuous, delicate, and refined—very different from the militaristic state that it became in later times. Choral lyric reached its peak in the early fifth century B.C. Its chief exponent was Pindar, who wrote numerous odes celebrating victories in the Olympic, Pythian, and Nemean games.

The central importance of the chorus in Greek drama is indicated by the fact that it was the *orchêstra* that formed the focus for a theatrical production. In earlier times choruses numbered about fifty, but around the middle of the fifth century B.C. they were reduced in size to fifteen or twelve. The training of a chorus was a lengthy and expensive undertaking. Costumes were often costly and elaborate. We are told that when the chorus of Furies entered in Aeschylus' *Eumenides*, their appearance was so frightful that pregnant women miscarried on the spot. However, since we are not even sure that women attended the theater, the anecdote may be apocryphal. In comedy, the costumes worn by the chorus were often extremely exotic, as suggested by the names of some of Aristophanes' comedies, such as *Birds, Wasps, Clouds,* and *Frogs*.

The chorus entered the *orchêstra* at the end of the first scene and remained there throughout the whole performance. During the choral passages its members would sing and dance to the accompaniment of the *aulos*, a double-pipe with reeds. The chorus leader might converse with the actors from time to time. One of the primary functions of the chorus was to comment on the action and urge caution. Its reactions also helped the audience to reach its own verdict about events, though the chorus was not the mouthpiece of the poet. At a more mundane level, it enabled the actors to change costumes between scenes. Its significance declined over time, and in many of Euripides' late plays it is little more than an adjunct. The exception to this rule is *Bacchai*, where its role is central to the drama. Even Menander, however, writing in the late fourth century B.C., did not abolish the chorus altogether.

All the speaking parts in both comedy and tragedy were performed by a maximum of three male actors. Since there **The Actors** could be as many as eight different dramatis personae in a play, however, actors frequently had to change parts. They did this both by switching masks and costumes and by altering the pitch of their voices. Masks, which were probably made out of stiffened linen, were fairly naturalistic in the case of tragedy but grotesque caricatures in the case of comedy. Because actors could not rely on facial expressions to convey their emotions, they had to be far more expressive in both voice and gesture than their modern counterparts.

In keeping with the idea of a heroic age, tragic actors wore brightly colored robes decorated with elaborate patterns. They also wore a calf-length boot known as the *kothornos*, which was loose enough to fit on either foot. In later times the *kothornos* was fitted with a high heel in order to make actors look more impressive. Comic actors were heavily padded so as to make them look completely ridiculous. Beneath their short tunics they sported huge phalluses to depict the erect male organ, strapped around the waist by means of a belt. Actors were also provided with role-markers, such as a scepter in the case of a king or a club in the case of Herakles.

Initially the main character in the drama, known as the "protagonist," was played by the dramatist. By the end of the fifth century B.C., however, actors were professionals and allocated to each production by lot.

The Judges Drama was a highly competitive activity. The prizes for first, second, and third place were decided by panels of ten *kritai* or "judges." It is from *kritês* that "critic" is derived, although the English word is something of a misnomer since Athenian critics were elected by lot from the citizenry as a whole and in no sense constituted a panel of experts. Each of the judges wrote his decision on a tablet. The ten choices were then placed in an urn, from which the archon eponymos drew out only five. This system was intended to leave some part of the decision making to the gods. Regrettably there is no way of telling to what extent the judges' verdict was based on dramatic content and structure, and to what extent it was influenced by the quality of the production. Several of what today are regarded as the finest examples of Attic tragedy were not awarded first prize.

The victorious dramatist received a wreath and a small cash prize, and the winning *chorêgos* was permitted to erect a column in his own honor. Of the three tragedians whose works survive, the most successful was Sophokles who wrote 123 plays, won first prize 18 times, and never dropped lower than second place. From 449 B.C. the judges also awarded a prize to the best protagonist.

Tragedy We have complete plays of only three Attic tragedians. Of the works of Aeschylus (525–426 B.C.), the earliest of the three, we possess only seven. Aeschylus introduced the second actor, which enabled a dialogue between two actors to take place on stage. He described his work as "slices from the great banquet of Homer," though his earliest surviving play is the *Persians*, a historical drama which deals with the Persian naval defeat at Salamis in 480 B.C. Aeschylus' master-piece is the *Oresteia*, which was produced in 458 B.C. when he was sixty-seven years old. The *Oresteia*, the only complete trilogy that we possess, traces the fortunes of the house of Atreus from the murder of Agamemnon by his wife Klytaimnestra through to the acquittal of his son Orestes for avenging his father's death. Aeschylus, who fought at the battle of Marathon, allegedly met his death when an eagle dropped a tortoise on his bald head in the belief that it was a stone.

Aeschylus' successor Sophokles (495–406 B.C.) is also represented by only seven tragedies. His introduction of the third actor enabled more complicated dramatic interchanges between actors to take place. This also had the incidental consequence of reducing the chorus to the role of spectator. His most celebrated drama, *Oedipus the King*, traces Oedipus' discovery of the fact that he has inadvertently killed his father and married his mother. At the end of his life Sophokles is said to have been taken to court by one of his sons, who tried to have him declared insane. The poet successfully refuted the charge by reading out one of the choruses from the play that he was currently working upon. He then turned to the jury and inquired, "Do you consider that to be the work of a madman?" Despite the fact that his plays illustrate the inscrutable will of the gods, Sophokles was a humanist. The following lines, which are delivered by the Chorus in *Antigone*, seem to echo the poet's own judgement on human achievement:

Wonders are many, but none is more wonderful than man, who traverses the grey deep in wintery storms, making his way through waves that crash around him, wearing away the oldest of the gods, Earth, the indestructible, ploughing the soil year in and year out with his horses. . . . Only Death he has found no way to escape, though from irresistible sickness he has devised a way out. His ingeniousness and contriving are beyond everything. Now he makes his way to destruction, now to greatness. When he establishes laws and divine oaths and justice, his city rides high. (lines 332ff.)

Nineteen extant dramas written by Euripides (480–406 B.C.) survive. Euripides, Sophokles' younger contemporary, consistently depicted the gods as violent and inhumane. There is a tradition that he caused so much offense in Athens that he was prosecuted for atheism, though we do not know for certain whether this is true. In *Bacchai*, one of his last plays, the god Dionysos takes terrible revenge on the royal house of Thebes which has denied his divinity by causing a mother to tear her son limb from limb. The poet became so alienated and embittered at the end of his life that he abandoned Athens for Macedon, where *Bacchai* was performed. It is said that he met his death by being torn apart by hunting dogs—another tradition of dubious authenticity.

The majority of tragedies are set in Greece's heroic past and depict the fortunes of her royal houses. Only a minority are set in Athens, and none at all in contemporary Athens. This does not mean that they were devoted to the exploration of outworn themes. Rather, the heroic past served as a backdrop for the lively investigation of contemporary political, moral, and social issues. Aeschylus' *Eumenides*, for instance, which was produced in 458 B.C. as the third play in the *Oresteia*, contains a clear and ringing endorsement of the democratic revolution that took place in Athens four years earlier.

All tragedy, like comedy, is written in a variety of meters. The choral passages are punctuated by "episodes" that resemble the scenes of a modern play. A central feature of many plays is the *agôn*, which takes the form of a contest or dispute between two characters, each of whom seeks to defeat his opponent in argument. In Sophokles' *Antigone*, for instance, the *agôn* between Kreon and his son Haimon turns upon the justice of Kreon's decision to wall up Antigone alive in punishment for having given burial to her brother, who has been condemned as a traitor.

Although the majority of tragedies are concerned with violent and destructive actions, we never see any violence perpetrated on stage. Instead, it was common practice for a messenger to provide the audience with an extremely detailed description of a murder, suicide, self-mutilation, or other grisly occurrence that he has just witnessed off stage.

Most tragedies end with the chorus' muttering of a few platitudes along the lines of "What we expected to happen has not happened and what we expected not to happen has happened." The banality of such conclusions is due to the fact that the audience would have been heading for the exit by the time they were delivered. They should not be interpreted as the author's final judgement on the subject of the drama.

Comedy   Evidence for fifth-century comedy is even more meager than for tragedy. We possess only eleven plays by a single dramatist, Aristophanes (c. 450–c. 385 B.C.). Highly topical in subject matter, they contain plentiful references to events and personalities in contemporary Athens, many of which are lost on us. They are also extremely ribald and scatological. Frequently the plot turns upon a solution to a contemporary problem, such as how to end the Peloponnesian War. In *Acharnians*, for instance, the hero, who is a very average Athenian citizen called Dikaiopolis, achieves his goal by making a private peace with the Spartans. Similarly in *Lysistrata*, the women of Athens decide to jump-start the peace process by refusing to have sex with their husbands. Other plays are even more fantastic. *Birds*, for instance, is a fantasy about two Athenians who, fed up with all the pressures of modern life, attempt to set up a new city among the birds called Cloudcuckooland. In *Frogs* Dionysos descends to Hades in order to bring back Euripides from the dead, though in the end he decides instead to resurrect Aeschylus, since Euripides' poetry is partly responsible for Athens' current troubles.

In the fourth century a new style of comedy evolved that was almost entirely shorn of chorus and contained no contemporary allusions. Its greatest exponent was Menander (342–c. 293 B.C.). Only one of his plays, *The Ill-Tempered Man*, has survived in complete form. Most of his plots explored the theme of romantic love through a complex intermingling of improbable devices including identical twins, broken families, and abandoned children. The genre, which is known as New Comedy, was taken over and adapted by the Romans. New Comedy was destined to provide the basis for comic inventiveness for centuries to come, an obvious example being Shakespeare's *Comedy of Errors*.

Tragedy and comedy may be said to be two sides of the same coin. The principal difference was that whereas trag- **Conclusions** edy explored the tragic consequences of conflict, comedy envisioned the possibility of some kind of reconciliation or resolution, however far-fetched it might be. Between these extremes there was little place for melodrama or sentimentality.

Publicly funded, profoundly civic in orientation, and fundamentally sacred in character, Attic drama might at first sight strike us as a covert means of reinforcing social conformity. The truth was far different. Although drama took place in a religious context, the playwrights did not see it as their objective to offer pious platitudes or promote supine obedience to the will of the gods. On the contrary, they were anything but shy of depicting the Olympians as degenerate and even morally repellent, whenever it suited their purposes. Legend had it that after witnessing Thespis' first tragedy, the Athenian audience was so mystified by its lack of religious content that they angrily demanded, "What's this got to do with Dionysos?" The question is still posed by scholars to this day.

What drama chiefly did was to to provide a context in which issues of public and private concern could be literally aired in the open. Its purpose in other words was not to promote some kind of party line or function as a moral arbiter, but rather to give expression to the hard moral choices that define human existence, to explore the problematic nature of man's relationship with the gods, and to demonstrate the human (and divine) capacity for evil. As such it frequently served subversive rather than conformist ends.

There is no more eloquent proof of the central importance of drama in the life of the Athenian community than the fact that the hardline conservative Plato proposed expelling the playwrights, along with all poets, from his ideal city, being fearful of their influence upon the morals of his contemporaries. And there is no stronger proof of the relevance of Attic drama to the contemporary world than the fact that the Colonels, who suspended democracy and ruled Greece from 1967 to 1974 as an oligarchy, found it necessary in the interests of public order to ban the performance of Euripides' works.

MUSIC

The Greek word *mousikê* identified a much broader range of cultural activity than our word "music." It included all of the arts that came under the patronage of Apollo and the nine Muses; that is to say, singing and dancing, as well as philosophical discourse. The epithet *mousikos*, which means "muse-ish," was synonymous with good taste. Conversely, *amousikos* described a person who lacked refinement or education. In this section, however, we will consider the word music in its limited, modern sense.

Music was a central part of Greek daily life. It was a feature of all social gatherings, including births, weddings, and funerals. Songs were sung by laborers to lighten the workload, especially at harvest and vintage, and by women in the home while they were grinding the grain or weaving. Soldiers and athletes trained to the sound of pipes. Every religious event was marked by the singing of hymns. Nearly every genre of poetry, including epic, lyric, and dramatic, was written to be sung. Music was an essential accompaniment to the drinking party. The various modes of music were believed to exercise a profound impact upon the mind. The so-called Dorian mode, being solemn and martial, was thought to induce courage, whereas the Phrygian mode, which was wild and perhaps atonal, was thought to encourage impetuosity. In Classical Athens musical proficiency was a basic part of every boy's education. Philosophers were of the opinion that it contributed to a well-balanced and disciplined personality. Plato, however, was extremely sceptical of its influence and banished it from his ideal state. Greek vases depicting scenes at the tomb suggest that delight in music was not interrupted by death.

Professional musicians were commonly employed in the Greek world. The earliest were the itinerant bards, who traveled from one aristocratic house to another, reciting tales about heroes and gods which they improvised, relying heavily on the formulaic structure of epic verse. Demodokos, the blind seer whom we encounter at the court of the Phaiakians in *Odyssey*, Book 8, is often thought to be a self-portrait of Homer, who was himself in all probability a bard. Originally bards accompanied themselves on the lyre. Later they abandoned the lyre and carried a staff instead. Even after they ceased to accompany their recitations with the lyre, however, they probably continued to recite in a

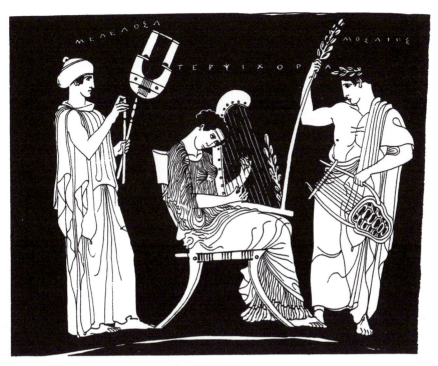

Red-figure amphora depicting from left to right: *auloi*, harp, and kithara. From I. Jenkins and S. Bird, *Greek Music* (London: British Museum Education Service, n.d.). Courtesy of British Museum.

rather singsong style. It was at the instigation of the Athenian tyrant Peisistratos that Homer's poems were standardized and written down. Recitation contests now became part of the Panathenaic festival. Festivals also provided an opportunity for new works to be heard.

The most popular instrument was the lyre or kithara, which resembled a modern guitar. Even Achilles, the most violent of Greek heroes, is depicted playing the lyre in *Iliad* Book 9 as a way of soothing his troubled feelings. In its simplest version the sound box is made out of a tortoise shell with a hide stretched over the hollow underside. The sound was produced by plucking the strings, usually seven in number, either with the fingers or with a plectrum. A variant on this instrument was the *barbiton*, which had longer strings. The *barbiton* was associated with scenes of revelry that were held in honor of Dionysos. Another stringed instrument was the harp, whose use seems to have been confined largely to professional musicians.

The most popular wind instrument was the *aulos*. This is often identified with the flute, although the sound it produced was actually closer to that of the oboe. The *aulos* consisted of a hollow pipe made out of wood, bronze, bone, or reed. It was pierced with holes for the fingers and fitted with a reed mouthpiece. *Auloi* were usually played in pairs. The chorus of Greek drama sang and danced to the accompaniment of an *aulos* player, who also piped soldiers into battle. Another wind instrument was the *syrinx*, which consisted of a number of pipes bound together. Variations in pitch were made by blocking the inside of the pipes with wax at different intervals. The *syrinx* was a somewhat crude instrument, whose invention was attributed to the goat god Pan. It was especially popular among shepherds.

The nearest approximation to a brass instrument was the *salpinx*, a long slender instrument terminating in a bell-shaped aperture. It was used primarily to herald the beginning and end of religious and other ceremonies. Several percussion instruments are known, including the *kymbala*, from which our word "cymbals" is derived, the *tympanon*, meaning a small drum, the *krotala* or castanets, and the *sistra* or rattles. These were used in ecstatic cults, notably those which were imported into Greece from the East.

Some forty-six musical scores, mostly fragmentary, have survived. Despite all the work that has been done by scholars, however, it would be overbold to suggest that we actually know what Greek music sounded like.

THE VISUAL ARTS

In our culture art carries a price tag and is often purchased either as an investment or as a status symbol. Most works of art are intended for private purchase. Art appreciation is a branch of connoisseurship that requires a highly trained, professional eye, not least in order to distinguish between an authentic work of art and a fake. While the public plays a minor role in the changing fortunes of an artist's reputation, this is determined largely by the expert. Though the artist may ultimately become something of a public institution, he or she ideally remains a fashionable outsider. Finally, although some artists receive state sponsorship in the form of grants from the National Endowment for the Arts in the United States or from the Arts Council of Great Britain, society is by no means in agreement that this is an appropriate or valuable use of public funds.

Greek art shared nothing in common with the picture drawn above. It was never purchased as an investment. Other than perhaps in the minor arts, the connoisseur had no equivalent. The only expert was the community as a whole. The Greeks did not regard costly works of art to be symbols of status and wealth. To our best knowledge not a single marble or bronze statue ever graced a private home until the Roman era, which witnessed a veritable craze for Greek statuary. Most major works of art were commissioned by the state and served a religious function, whether as temples, dedications to the gods, or monuments erected in commemoration of victorious athletes or the dead. The Greek artist often found himself in the pay of the state and had to work to a very strict set of specifications and guidelines. Greece never developed anything equivalent to the modern cult of the artist. We know the names of very few artists and virtually nothing about their private lives.

Greek sculpture originated around the middle of the seventh century B.C. Its initial inspiration owes much to Egypt. **Sculpture** Marble, limestone, bronze, terra-cotta, wood, or a combination of gold and ivory known as chryselephantine were the chief materials. The thirty-six-foot-high statue of Athena Parthenos, housed inside the Parthenon and designed by the sculptor Pheidias, was covered in ivory and gold to represent flesh and clothing. Stone statues were painted, which lent them a very vivid appearance. Accessories, including jewelry and even eyes, were often reproduced in a different material. Statues were not cheap to purchase. It is reckoned that a bronze statue would have cost 3,000 drachmas.

The Greeks did not make the same clear-cut distinction between reality and artistic illusion that we do, as the following anecdote makes plain. The statue of a famous athlete called Theagenes was erected in his honor on the island of Thasos. One of Theagenes' rivals was so incensed by this that he began to flog the statue at night. Eventually the statue toppled over and crushed him. The victim's sons now proceeded to prosecute the statue in the courts. The statue was convicted and drowned at sea. This sequence of events only makes sense if we accept the fact that the image of a person or a deity was thought to embody—in the literal sense—his or her essence.

The Greek sculptor did not see it as his goal to produce works of art that reflected the accidental and true-to-life deficiencies of authentic human anatomy. The chief artistic inspiration throughout antiquity was the physically perfect, primarily male body, as exemplified by the god Apollo, who is invariably depicted as a youth in peak physical condition. A superb example of this is the Apollo who presides over a battle between the civilized Lapiths and the half-human, half-animal Centaurs on the west pediment of the temple of Zeus at Olympia. Unperturbed and impassive, Apollo extends his right arm horizontally in a gesture that indicates his support for the Lapiths.

Portraiture inspired relatively few works of Greek art. Many sculptures that purport to be portraits were produced long after the subject's death. Their resemblance to the sitter is therefore questionable at best. A

Mythological scene depicting Athena visiting Hephaistos, at work in his bronze foundry.

notable exception are the portraits of Sokrates, which probably do convey an authentic likeness. Even in the Hellenistic era, which saw the birth of a more realistic tendency, the depictions of careworn philosophers, aging athletes, and old women are more stereotypical than naturalistic. Among sculptures, only those depicting the Hellenistic kings seem to have been accorded a truly individualistic identity, especially in the profiles on coins. One of the most memorable coin portraits is that of Euthydemos I of Bactria, dated c. 200 B.C., which gazes at us across the millennia with disillusionment and disarming candor.

From the very beginning of full-size Greek sculpture in c. 660 B.C., males were depicted naked. Statues, known as *kouroi* (i.e., "boys" or "youths"), stand frontally with one foot advanced, hands at side, fists clenched. The earliest examples are based on a sculptural formula that had been used by the Egyptians for two thousand years. Statues of women, called *korai* (i.e., "girls"), which have no antecedent in Egyptian art, are by contrast invariably clothed, albeit in diaphanous, clinging drapery that leaves little to the imagination. Since the proportions of

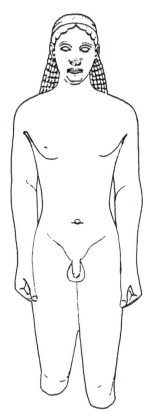

Kouros or standing male nude.

the *korai* are not noticeably different from those of males, they have been wittily described as "*kouroi* in drag." One of the reasons for their lack of naturalism is the fact that women's bodies were not available for detailed study.

It was not until the second half of the fourth century B.C. that female nudity became acceptable in statuary. Even then nudes are usually shown coyly covering the genital area with a hand or piece of drapery. A celebrated example is Praxiteles' sculpture of Aphrodite taking a bath, which was described by the Roman writer Pliny as "the finest statue in the whole world." Praxiteles actually carved two statues of Aphrodite, one clothed and the other nude. He then asked the inhabitants of the island of Kos which they preferred. They chose the clothed figure on the grounds that it was more chaste. The naked version of the goddess was subsequently purchased by the people of Knidos, a city which lies opposite Kos on the coast. Two hundred years later, when the Knidians were in dire financial straits, Nikomedes, king of Bithynia, offered to purchase the naked statue from them. The Knidians refused, claiming that it was the nude statue of Aphrodite for which their city was best known.

Architecture

The Greek temple afforded the primary context for the expression of Greek artistic excellence. It was also the artistic medium on which was expended the most effort and expenditure. Built primarily to house a cult statue, it provided a showcase for the finest achievements of Greek art. The temple was by no means intrinsic to worship, since all cultic activity took place in the open air, around the altar. Its primary religious function was to secure the goodwill of the deity to whom it was erected.

The basic layout of the temple was established around the end of the seventh century B.C. A *pronaos* or porch leads to a central room or *naos*. In some cases, there is a back porch or *opisthodomos* and a surrounding colonnade known as a peristyle. Temples were mostly aligned on an east-west axis, with the cult statue facing east so that it could witness the sacrifice being performed on the altar. At first only the stepped platform on which the temple stood was made of stone, but later stone replaced wood for both the columns and the superstructure. The first temple to be made entirely of stone was that of Artemis on the island of Corcyra (Corfu). The best preserved is the Second Temple of Hera at Poseidonia, which was built of limestone around the middle of the fifth century B.C. The crowning achievement of Greek architecture is the Parthenon, which uses a numerical ratio of 9:4 in all its proportions. Such are its stylistic refinements, which are intended to counteract the effects of optical illusion, that not a single line in the entire building is completely straight.

Greek temples are categorized according to the so-called orders of architecture. The principal orders are the Doric and Ionic, which both evolved in the fifth century B.C. A third, known as the Corinthian, came into being somewhat later. Doric columns, which are somewhat squat in appearance, rise from their platform without any base. They are decorated with twenty vertical grooves, known as flutes, in which shadows settle as the sky darkens, thereby lending a sense of drama and plasticity to the building. They are topped by capitals that resemble cushions. The Ionic column, which is considerably taller in proportion to its width, rises from a molded base and terminates in a capital that is surmounted by a pair of volutes. It has twenty-four flutes, separated from one another by a narrow band. The Corinthian capital also rises from a molded base but its capital resembles bands of acanthus leaves.

The differences in style extended up into the superstructure. A Doric frieze consists of rectangular blocks called metopes, interrupted by narrower rectangles with vertical grooves called triglyphs. By contrast, an Ionic frieze is continuous. The crowning member is a triangular gable known as a pediment, which is located at either end of the temple. A few temples, notably the Parthenon, combine elements of both the Doric and Ionic orders. Metopes, pediments, and friezes are frequently decorated with relief sculpture. Since these were painted, the overall effect would have been extremely colorful. Most large temples on the Greek mainland were built in the Doric style with a surrounding colonnade, whereas in Asia Minor (Turkey) the fashion was for massive temples in the Ionic style with double colonnades.

Much of the sculpture that decorated a temple was narrative. A masterly example is to be found on the east pediment of the temple of Zeus Olympios at Olympia. Its subject is the chariot race between Pelops and Oinomaos. Pelops, who wished to wed Oinomaos' daughter, Hippodameia, had to defeat him in order to secure her hand. To assure his victory, he bribed Oinomaos' charioteer to tamper with the king's chariot wheels so that they would fall off during the race. Instead of portraying the drama of the collision, however, the sculptor has chosen to depict the tense moment before the race begins. The composition, which is dominated by the commanding presence of Zeus flanked on either side by the contestants, purveys an unearthly stillness. What shatters this mood

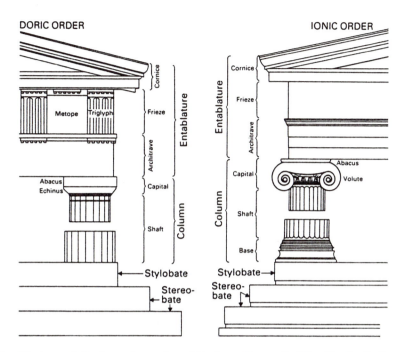

The Doric and Ionic orders of architecture. From S. Woodford, *Parthenon* (Cambridge, U.K.: Cambridge University Press, 1981). Courtesy of British Museum.

is the reclining seer who raises his clenched fist to his cheek in a gesture of alarm. We comprehend that the seer is gazing into the future and envisions the catastrophe ahead.

It is testimony to the extraordinary achievements of Greek architecture that no fewer than five of the Seven Wonders of the World listed in the second century B.C. by Antipater of Sidon for the benefit of tourists were Greek. They include the statue of Zeus at Olympia, the temple of Artemis at Ephesos, the Mausoleum at Halikarnassos, the Colossus of Rhodes, and the Pharos (or Lighthouse) of Alexandria.

Until recently our knowledge of the great paintings that decorated the interior walls of Greek temples and public **Painting** buildings was wholly reliant upon literary descriptions, which failed to convey any real sense of the technical quality of the originals. Recently, however, thanks partly to the discovery of the Macedonian tombs at Vergina, we have direct evidence of these murals.

Even so, when we talk about Greek painting, we tend to think of the humble medium of vase painting. Vase painting is a major source of information about Greek life. Especially popular subjects are drinking

Diagram to illustrate the position of sculpture on the Parthenon.

parties and visits to the tomb because most painted pottery was intended either to be used at a symposium or to be deposited in the grave. Other popular subjects include athletic activities and scenes taking place in the women's quarters. Earlier vases are decorated in the black-figure technique against a red background. Around 525 B.C., however, the process was reversed, and the background was painted in black, leaving the figure in red. Most scenes of daily life are rendered in red-figure.

The Politics of Greek Art   Though art was predominantly religious in function and though its subject matter was largely confined to the mythological, it was often used to make a political statement. When, for instance, in 447 B.C., the Athenians made the historic decision to rebuild the temples on the Acropolis destroyed by the Persians, they incorporated a number of barely disguised references to Athens' heroic struggle for freedom into the sculptures. The Parthenon metopes, for instance, which depict the battle between the Lapiths and the Centaurs, evoked the Persian Wars, since this involved a conflict between a higher order of civilization and a lower. It is possible, too, that the great frieze which ran around the outer wall of the *naos*, whose principal feature is a cavalcade of Athenian cavalry, is intended to depict the 192 Athenians who died at the battle of Marathon, here shown as the heroized dead.

Greek artists were constantly learning new techniques and addressing new problems. As a consequence, even in **Conclusions** the absence of an archaeological context that would enable us to date a given artifact with chronological exactitude, we are often able to situate it to within a single decade. Coupled with this inherent innovativeness, however, was an inherent conservatism. For instance, although the different orders of architecture underwent refinement over the centuries, the temple remained the preferred medium of architectural expression. Similarly, the human body served throughout Greek antiquity as the focus for all sculptural and pictorial endeavor.

The Greek world did not foster artistic movements in the modern sense of the term. Nor did artists utilize their skills to make a personal statement. At all periods of history their level of achievement was remarkably uniform. They have bequeathed to us remarkably few bad or even indifferent works of art. Even in their poorest productions, it is generally the taste rather than the technical accomplishment that is deficient. Clearly artists were intimately familiar with one another's work and saw themselves as participants in a collective enterprise. Not the least distinctive feature about Greek art is its acceptance of society's norms.

MYTHOLOGY

The side panel of my amiable cereal box seeks to enlighten me about the differences between what it calls "myth" on the one hand and "fact" on the other, in regard to the perennially fascinating subject of how to lose weight. Under the heading "myth" it identifies the widely upheld claim that carbohydrates are fattening, that I do not need to exercise, and that I can eat as much diet food as I want. "Myth" in the sense that it is applied here is synonymous with a fiction or falsehood that commands widespread assent but has no basis in fact. *Mythos*, from which our word "myth" is derived, however, carried no such negative connotation for the Greeks. Its basic meaning was "word," "speech," or "story." Even in the sense of "story," *mythos* did not signify or imply a fiction. On the contrary, it denoted an exemplary tale that revealed a fundamental truth, whether about the nature of the world, the deeds and activities of the gods and heroes, or the composition and evolution of Greek society.

The subject matter which the Greeks utilized for mythic treatment comprised all the events that had occurred from the beginning of the universe down to the aftermath of the Trojan War. This included the succession of divine dynasties that ultimately led to the current ruling dynasty of Olympian deities, the beginnings and evolution of human existence, the Trojan War itself, and the tales that took place in the so-called Age of Heroes.

Though myths have reached us primarily through literature, this was not how they were transmitted in antiquity.
On the contrary, they were the product of an oral culture,
a culture that passes down its lore by word of mouth from
one generation to the next. Though it is impossible to reach
back in time to discover a myth's origins, we need hardly doubt that
many of them are rooted in Greece's preliterate past. It was a past that
possessed no other means of preserving what needed to be preserved
except by word of mouth. Precisely because they were transmitted orally,
myths underwent considerable change in each retelling. Inevitably some
details were lost or modified, while others were invented or recast. What
has survived, in other words, is the result of a long evolutionary process
that took place over several centuries. It was a process that was organic
in the true sense of the word. Indeed it is hardly any exaggeration to
state that once a myth acquired a canonical or fixed form, it ceased to
retain its contemporary relevance for the teller and his audience.

The vitality of the mythic tradition can be aptly demonstrated by reference to the myth of Oedipus, the king of Thebes, who inadvertently
fulfills the prophecy of the Delphic Oracle by killing his father and marrying his mother. It is a story that provides a stern warning about the
terrifying power of coincidence. But in Sophokles' play *Oedipus the King*
it is much more than that. For when Oedipus discovers what he has
done, he is so appalled by his crimes that he blinds himself. This act of
self-mutilation, which is undertaken in response to his previous ignorance about his own identity, has a deeply symbolic meaning. Oedipus
might have hanged himself, as he does in another version of the story.
But it was central to Sophokles' interpretation that the king should go
on living after learning the tragic facts about his identity. In other words
he lives on with his understanding enlarged but darkened, and in the
full consciousness of his own unintended crimes. Sophokles thus infuses
the myth with his own personal vision of the human condition, for which
Oedipus is the quintessential symbol.

Myths were not therefore immutable artifacts written in stone. There
was never any official version of a myth, though some versions inevitably became more popular than others. This did not prevent different
versions from coexisting in different places and at different times—or
even at the same time. Such a state of affairs was probably the rule rather
than the exception. Though myths were the common property of all
Greeks, they often bore a distinctly localized character. Each city-state
disseminated its own versions and gave prominence to those myths that
celebrated its own local heroes and local deities.

Our primary source for the study of Greek mythology is Greek literature. The oldest surviving myths are to be found in the poems of Hesiod

and Homer. There is no evidence to suggest that Hesiod or Homer invented the myths they incorporate, however. Another important early source is an anonymous compilation of works called the *Homeric Hymns*, which provide us with charter myths that explain the establishment of cults in honor of the various Olympian deities. In addition, many of the best-known myths were dramatized by Athens' tragedians, who, as we saw earlier, for the most part set their plays in Greece's heroic past. The most comprehensive anthology is Apollodoros' *Library*, which was probably written in the late first or early second century A.D. It is the product of a period when myth had become foremost a subject of antiquarian interest. The visual arts, particularly vase painting and sculpture, also provide a useful source of information.

Most myths are preserved merely in part. The only one that receives exhaustive treatment in any surviving work is Jason's search for the golden fleece, as narrated in an epic poem entitled *Argonautika* by Apollonios of Rhodes. Even the events of the Trojan War have come down to us only in a piecemeal condition. The lengthiest and most detailed treatment is provided by Homer's *Iliad*; however, the action of this poem, which is limited to the final year of the war, covers only a minor incident, namely Achilles' temporary withdrawal from the battlefield as the result of an insult from his commander in chief. The poem does not refer directly either to the cause of the war or to its conclusion, nor does it contain a summary. So well-known was its course, however, that Homer's audience could be relied upon to put the quarrel between Achilles and Agamemnon in its context and see within the events covered by the poem a foreshadowing and anticipation of the destruction of the city of Troy.

The following is a list of the most important literary sources for the study of Greek mythology:

Homer, *Iliad*: The havoc that is caused among the Greeks and the Trojans as a result of Achilles' anger.

Homer, *Odyssey*: Odysseus' return to Ithaka and his reunion with his wife Penelope.

Hesiod, *Theogony*: How the present Olympian dynasty came to power.

Hesiod, *Works and Days*: Zeus as the upholder of justice and champion of the common people against the kings.

The Homeric Hymns: Stories about the early days of the gods and how they came to acquire their powers.

Aeschylus, *Agamemnon*: Agamemnon's murder at the hands of his wife Klytaimnestra and her lover Aegisthus.

Aeschylus, *Choêphoroi* or *Libation Bearers*: Orestes' invocation of the shade of his father Agamemnon to aid him in a revenge killing of his mother and her lover.

Aeschylus, *Eumenides* or *Friendly Ones*: Orestes' acquittal on the charge of matricide before an Athenian court.

Sophokles, *Oedipus the King*: Oedipus' discovery that he is guilty of murdering his father and marrying his mother.

Sophokles, *Antigone*: Antigone's defiant determination to give burial to her brother Polyneikes in violation of Kreon's edict.

Sophokles, *Oedipus at Colonus*: The elevation to heroic status of the blind and aged Oedipus.

Euripides, *Hippolytos*: Aphrodite's vengeance upon Hippolytos for his refusal to worship her.

Euripides, *Bacchai*: The dismemberment of Pentheus, king of Thebes, as a result of his opposition to the cult of Dionysos.

Aristophanes, *Frogs*: Dionysos as antihero—cowardly, licentious, untrustworthy, and incontinent—and his descent to Hades.

Apollonios of Rhodes, *Argonautika*: Jason's search for the golden fleece in the company of the Argonauts.

Ovid, *Metamorphoses*: A highly individualistic treatment of Greek and Roman myth loosely bound together by the theme of shapeshifting.

Apollodoros, *Library*: The most comprehensive collection of mythology to survive from antiquity.

Myths of Origin   Where does the world come from? Why is there so much evil in the world? Why do we give the least edible parts of an animal to the gods when we sacrifice? Why is the year divided into different seasons? Why are women so seductive? Why in the face of all the terrible things that happen in the world do we still continue to hope that things will improve? These and other perennial questions are just a few of the issues that myths of origin seek to address.

The primary source for the mythic account of the origin of the universe is Hesiod's *Theogony*. According to Hesiod, the primordial being was Chaos, a word which roughly translates as "gaping void." Next Earth, Tartaros (the lowest region of the underworld), and Desire came into existence. Chaos then engendered Darkness and Night, and Night by coupling with Darkness gave birth to Day. Whereas the book of Genesis ascribes the creative act to a divine being who exists outside his own creation, Hesiod proposed a model whereby the means of propagation emerged out of nothingness. In other words, it was the instinct for mating rather than a series of disconnected acts on the part of a divine will that caused the world to assume its present form.

The Trojan War represented the supreme military enterprise of all time. It was undertaken to avenge the honor of Agamemnon's brother Menelaos, king of Sparta. His wife Helen had been abducted by the Trojan prince Paris, who was the guest of Menelaos at the time. Contingents from all over the Greek world **The Trojan War** participated in the venture, which was placed under the command of Agamemnon, king of Mycenae. After a siege which lasted ten years, Troy was taken and destroyed.

The Trojan War, which elicited deeds of great courage on both sides, has all the makings of an epic in the modern sense of the word. It was, moreover, a just war, inasmuch as the Greeks were the injured party. Despite this, however, both in Homer's *Iliad* and in the numerous dramas that treat incidents from the war, the emphasis is predominantly upon the sufferings of innocent victims, the intransigence of the victors, and the divided loyalties of the gods. Thus, far from being a nationalistic myth that jingoistically trumpeted the achievements of the Greeks, it served as a terrible reminder of the futility and cruelty of war.

Scene illustrating the Trojan War: the goddess Athena and the Greek hero Diomedes. From *Homer* by Martin Thorpe (Bristol, U.K.: Bristol Classical Press, 1973). Reprinted by permission of Duckworth Publishers.

Deception, duplicity, and deceit all play a major part in the legends associated with the war. Book 10 of the *Iliad*, which is devoted to this theme, relates the capture of a Trojan scout named Dolon by Odysseus and Diomedes, who promise to spare Dolon's life if he will reveal the military disposition of the Trojan encampment. As soon as Dolon has fulfilled his side of the bargain, however, Diomedes decapitates him. He and Odysseus follow up this breach of faith by slaughtering the Thracian prince Rhesus and his companions in their sleep. The famous incident involving the wooden horse, the example par excellence of Greek duplicity, leads directly to the fall of Troy. The wooden horse contained a contingent of warriors, who descended from its hollow belly at night and opened the gates to admit the rest of the army. Though this incident lies outside the events of the *Iliad*, its central position within the tradition suggests that in the eyes of the

Greeks their victory over the Trojans came primarily from cunning. Since, moreover, the wooden horse was ostensibly a ritual offering to the gods in appeasement for crimes committed by the Greeks, the gods were implicated in the ruse.

Though the Homeric poems are among the greatest legacies of Greek culture, they demonstrate a strong influence of Near Eastern epic. A notable instance of borrowing involves the death of Achilles' dearest companion Patroklos in the *Iliad*. The description is based on the death of Gilgamesh's friend Enkidu in the *Epic of Gilgamesh*, whose origins can be traced back to the third millennium B.C.—two thousand years before Homer. The source of many Greek myths ultimately lies in the Near East.

The Heroes
Greek mythology is full of tales about heroes such as Achilles, Orestes, Oedipus, Perseus, Herakles, Jason, Odysseus, and Theseus, all of whom are of divine parentage or ancestry. Achilles was the son of the sea goddess Thetis, Herakles and Perseus were the sons of Zeus, and Theseus was the son of Poseidon. Heroes are distinguished by their physical prowess, their appetite for adventure, and their willingness to take on challenges that would overwhelm the average mortal. The greatest challenge of all was the descent to the underworld, where the hero encountered what might be described as a negation of the self.

The range of heroic challenge is illustrated by the diversity of labors performed by Herakles, the greatest hero of all. Six of his labors take place in or around Olympia in the northwest Peloponnese, four send him to the cardinal points of the compass, and the last two—bringing Kerberos up from Hades and fetching the golden apples from the Hesperides—require him to journey beyond the confines of mortality. In meeting such challenges, Herakles stands as a symbol of the indomitability of the human spirit.

The Greek hero was not merely an ancient version of the Lone Ranger, however. On the contrary, many of the myths connected with him emphasize the violent streak in human nature that is integral to man's lust for achievement. Many heroes, too, are less than heroic in their dealings with women. Herakles was repeatedly unfaithful to his wife Deianeira, whose death he inadvertently caused when she sought to revive his flagging affections. Theseus abandoned Ariadne on the island of Naxos after she had provided him with the means of killing the Minotaur, a creature half-human and half-bull, which fed on a diet of Athenian youths and maidens. Jason abandoned the sorceress Medea after she had assisted him in his theft of the golden fleece and had aided his escape by slaying her own brother Absyrtos.

Unlike his popular, much diluted modern descendant, the Greek hero was a morally complex individual who frequently failed to conduct himself honorably, yet whose courage and prowess, in the eyes of the Greeks, did not release him from the obligation to live as a morally responsible human being. The hero was, in other words, by no means a forerunner of the Christian saint. Nor was he primarily or predominantly a public benefactor. Though many heroic exploits did provide incidental beneficial consequences to mankind, this was by no means the only reason why they were undertaken. Although Herakles' killing of the Nemean lion and the Stymphalian birds rendered the Greek world a safer place, his journey to the Hesperides in search of the golden apples was of no benefit to mankind whatsoever. In many cases the principal motive for taking on the challenge seems to have been similar to that which inspires modern mountain climbers to risk their lives climbing Mount Everest: simply because it's there.

A number of myths explore the tensions, rivalries, and violence that lurk beneath the surface of family life as a result of Greek mythology's identification of the family as the major producer of neurosis and psychosis. The divine realm produced more than its fair share of dys-

The Archetypal Dysfunctional Family

functionality. Kronos castrated his father Ouranos and attempted to kill all his children. Zeus' loveless marriage to Hera produced only one offspring, Ares, the god of war.

On the human level, the archetypal dysfunctional household was that of Atreus. The cycle of evil that characterizes its fortunes over the course of several generations began with the seduction of Atreus' wife by his brother Thyestes. Atreus then took revenge on Thyestes by inviting him to a banquet at which he served to him the cooked limbs of his children. Thyestes subsequently exacted his revenge on Atreus by inciting Atreus' son to murder his own father. Atreus' other son Agamemnon, who sacrificed his daughter Iphigeneia in order to obtain a favorable wind to carry the Greek fleet to Troy, met his death at the hands of his wife and her lover. The pair was murdered in turn by Agamemnon's son Orestes in revenge for his father's death. Outlined simply thus, the myth of the house of Atreus strikes one as melodramatic and even absurd. In the hands of a great playwright like Aeschylus, however, it is transformed into a searching investigation of a very real human dilemma. That is because Aeschylus focuses almost exclusively upon the agonizing moral choice that Orestes faces by having to perpetrate the most abhorrent crime imaginable, namely matricide, in order to discharge the most sacred filial duty, which is that of avenging his father.

Women in Myth

At first sight Greek mythology seems to exhibit a strongly misogynistic strain. The chamber of horrors includes Klytaimnestra, who murders her husband Agamemnon on his return from Troy; Medea, who kills her children in order to avenge the infidelity of her husband Jason; the fifty daughters of Danaos, who, with one exception, all murder their bridegrooms on their wedding nights; and Phaidra, who charges her stepson Hippolytos of raping her after he has scornfully rebuffed her sexual overtures. Only a handful are worthy of admiration, particularly Penelope, who remained faithful to her absent husband Odysseus for twenty years, and Alkestis, who was so devoted to her husband Admetos that she volunteered to die in his place.

Simply enumerating myths about violent women merely reveals that the Greeks understood that women are capable of extreme violence. What is much more significant is that almost all these female acts of violence are perpetrated in response to extreme provocation on the part of husbands and lovers. Medea, for instance, who is one of the darkest figures in Greek mythology, betrayed everything that was dear to her— family, homeland, culture—to follow Jason back to Greece, only to be betrayed by him in turn when he found a more suitable wife to take her place. She is a woman who has lost all her identity.

In addition to women whose acts of violence provide an outlet for their frustrations and disappointments, there is also a group of witchlike creatures who direct their destructiveness to all and sundry. These include the Gorgon Medusa, whose terrifying gaze turned men to stone; the half-woman, half-dog monster Skylla, who seized sailors and devoured them alive; a reptilian monster called Lamia, who stole children from their parents; the Graiai or Grey Ones, women born old, who shared a single eye and a single tooth; the monstrous bird-women called the Harpies, who kidnaped humans; and finally the Furies, who punished the guilty for crimes committed within the family.

Plato's Use of Myth It is often stated that mythology lost its preeminence when Greek tragedy died at the end of the fifth century B.C. since, from this time onward, other ways of understanding human behavior came to the fore. In fact, however, myth continued to provide a vital means of interpreting the world even after the death of tragedy, not least in the philosophical works of Plato. In *Symposium*, for instance, the comic poet Aristophanes claims that human beings originally possessed four arms, four legs, and two heads. Being globular, they were able to propel themselves at high speed by using all eight limbs so that they moved "like tumblers performing cartwheels." They were so arrogant, however, that they attempted to scale Mount Olympos and attack the gods. By way of punishment Zeus bisected them from head to toe, thereby creating the human body in its present form. Aristophanes ends with a stern warning that if human beings misbehave in the future, they run the risk of being bisected yet again and having to hop about on one leg! Fanciful though this myth is, it nonetheless makes some important points about human identity. Since these globular beings came in three forms before they were bisected, namely male-male, female-female, and male-female, the myth provides us with an explanation as to why some people are attracted to members of the opposite sex and others to members of the same sex, since, in Aristophanes' words, we are all seeking our missing half.

The primary importance which Plato attached to myth, coupled with the degree to which he regarded it as an indispensable tool for attempting to make sense of the world, is reflected in the following comment which he puts into the mouth of Sokrates at the end of *Republic* (621b): "And so, Glaukos, the *mythos* was saved and did not perish, and, if we pay attention to it, it may save us."

Giants with a single eye in the center of their foreheads, hideous hags with the capacity to petrify those **Did the Greeks** who gazed upon them, monstrous snakes with numer- **Believe Their** ous heads which doubled in number if they were **Myths?** lopped off—did the Greeks actually believe this stuff? The question does not permit a simple answer. Even the ultrarationalistic historian Thukydides did not dismiss outright the monstrous Cyclopeans as purely imaginary. In his discussion of Sicily, where this fabulous race was thought to have once resided, he gives the following cautious pronouncement:

> The most ancient inhabitants are said to be the Cyclopes. . . . I cannot say who their relatives were nor where they came from or where they went. We have to content ourselves with what the poets said and with what anyone else knows. (6.21)

The Greek geographer Eratosthenes, however, who lived two centuries later than Thukydides, was openly dismissive. He is reported to have stated, "You will find the scene of Odysseus' wanderings when you find the cobbler who made the bag of winds in which Aeolos [king of the winds] deposited them" (in Strabo, *Geography* 1.2.15).

Though the Greeks in general did not question the veracity of their myths, from the fifth century B.C. onward some effort was made to try to explain away some of their more fanciful elements. One that came in for rationalization concerned the god Dionysos, who was conceived when Zeus impregnated his mother Semele in the form of a thunderbolt. Having at the same time incinerated Semele, Zeus rescued the embryo by sewing it into his thigh. In Euripides' *Bacchai*, however, the seer Teiresias claims that this myth is based on a verbal confusion. What Zeus really did was to make a replica of the god which he then "showed," rather than "sewed," to Hera. This laborious pun, which can be only approximately reproduced in English, demonstrates an attempt on the part of a rationalist to explain away an extravagant mythical claim, without denying its essential veracity.

Myths express the patterns that underlie human existence; **Conclusions** they do not, however, determine the consequences of those patterns. Rather they admit variants in line with the Greek belief in free will. Myths allowed the Greeks to live their lives freely, while laying down certain parameters within which repetitive cycles occur.

Myth played a central role as a teaching tool. In Book 9 of the *Iliad*, when Phoinix, the tutor of Achilles, is trying to persuade his erstwhile pupil to return to the battle and accept the gifts that Agamemnon has offered him in reconciliation, he tells the story of Meleager who refused to participate in battle and was ultimately compelled to return to the fray, foregoing the gifts that had previously been offered to him. This same fate, Phoinix suggests, awaits Achilles, if he remains obdurate and does not accept Agamemnon's gifts.

In general, Greek mythology presents an exceedingly menacing and troubled landscape. Though it does not entirely banish what is generous and noble in human nature, few myths have happy endings. And such happiness as does occur is either fleeting or purchased at the cost of much misery. Through myth we encounter the dark side of human life, from which many of us would perhaps prefer to avert our gaze. Yet myth also provides us with an incomparably rich language for coming to terms with that dark side.

Within the disunited and fractured world of Greece, mythology served as a powerful cultural unifier, by providing its people both with the sense of a shared past and the means of interpreting it. Nothing in the modern world performs a comparable function, and our society is poorer for the lack of it. Yet, in Plato's words, if we pay attention to it, it may yet save us.

8

The Impact of Ancient Greece on Modern Culture

Greece has always been the favorite destination of those who seek to revive both body and soul. Because for centuries Greece's sun, waters, mountains and air have helped to refresh the body. While its culture, festivals, and warmth of its people have purified the soul. . . . Discover the part of Greece that lives in you. . . . And meditate upon the possibilities.

—Greek National Tourist Organization

The school that I attended in the 1960s in north London produced a booklet in which all the pupils' names were arranged according to form. In pride of place on page one were those in Classical Sixth A. Although there were not many of us even in those days, in putting us at the "top" the school was making the point that nothing surpassed a classical education. My school was not alone in its prejudice for the Greeks and Romans, which it shared with many others of its kind throughout Europe. Its pupils today, however, are unlikely to be told that nothing equals a classical education or that the literature of the Greeks and the Romans is superior to that of any other civilization. Contemporary teachers of classics, whether in schools or universities, are the guardians of a type of knowledge that has moved to the margins of the curriculum. Some of them even hold the Greeks and Romans responsible for many of the problems that society faces today.

If this were all I could say about the current state of classical learning, there probably would be little point in reading this book. But while only a few—albeit a very dedicated few—submit themselves to the rigors of mastering the ancient languages, interest in the ancient world shows no signs of abating. The *Histories* of Herodotos has recently become a best-seller, thanks to references to his work in the prize-winning film *The English Patient*; the *Odyssey* of Homer is selling like hot cakes in the news-agents in John F. Kennedy Airport in response to a recent "blockbuster" television miniseries; and Disney's latest animated cartoon film is based on the exploits of Herakles. One of the most significant verse plays of recent years is Nobel prize-winner Derek Walcott's dramatization of the *Odyssey*. Reports of the death of the Classics are premature.

THE CONTINUING CLASSICAL TRADITION

We may not like it, but it is virtually impossible to shake off the influence of our classical past. It is evident in our way of thinking, in our concept of government and political theory, in our art, in our architecture, and in our poetry. In some branches of learning its influence remains paramount. In philosophy its legacy is overwhelming. In the writing of history we remain dependent on our classical antecedents, notably Herodotos and Thukydides, who established the proper business of a historian. We could even claim that with Herodotos came the birth of anthropology, since the criteria for cultural differences that he established—style of dress, eating habits, burial customs, language, religion, and so on—remain at the center of any anthropological definition of the "other."

Over the course of the past two hundred years, Greek words have been imported into the English language in vast quantities to describe new fields of inquiry and new scientific accomplishments. Modernity and the modern experience have been described and defined very largely by words of Greek origin. Examples include psychiatry, paranoia, schizophrenia, ophthalmology, euthanasia, pornography, cybernetics, cryogenics, eugenics, prosthetics, chemotherapy, orthodontics, pediatrics, pedagogy, and technology.

In art and architecture, too, what we call neo-classicism, so-named because it draws its inspiration from classical motifs and principles, is enjoying a revival. Neoclassicism was largely initiated by two Britons, the painter James Stuart and the architect Nicholas Revett, who visited Athens from 1751 to 1753 and produced detailed plans of the buildings on the Acropolis. These plans later served as the basis of design for many important buildings, including the British Museum. In the same era the German archaeologist J. J. Winckelmann classified Greek art according to his own subjective notion of style. He gave pride of place to what he called the "grand, elevated" style of Pheidias, the chief sculptor of the

Parthenon. Winckelmann's judgement, though no longer universally upheld, continues to dominate discussions of Greek aesthetics to this day.

The middle of the eighteenth century also saw the birth of the great
public museums, destined to become storehouses of the most prestigious
works of art from Greco-Roman antiquity. They continue to serve as a
palpable reminder to the public of the achievements of the classical
world. A particularly controversial episode in the scramble to secure
such treasures was the removal of the Parthenon's sculptures by Lord
Elgin, the British ambassador to Turkey, at the beginning of the nineteenth century. His cache included twelve statues belonging to the pediments, fifty-six slabs belonging to the frieze, and fifteen metopes. After
being initially rejected by the British Museum, they were eventually purchased and put on display in 1817. The legality of Lord Elgin's action,
which was conducted with the consent of the Ottoman rulers of Greece,
continues to be a matter of dispute between the British and Greek gov-
ernments.

The influence of Greece did not go only in one direction. When the
Greeks rebelled against the Ottoman Turks in 1821, enthusiastic Britons
like Lord Byron, who called themselves Philhellenes and who cherished
their classical roots, saw the struggle as a reenactment of the Persian
Wars:

> The mountains look on Marathon
> And Marathon looks on the sea:
> And musing there an hour alone,
> I dreamt that Greece might still be free. (*Don Juan* III.86)

It is hardly any exaggeration to claim that the modern Greek nation state
owed much to the Victorian image of classical Greece.

Postmodernism, the term used to describe the prevailing cultural climate, signifies in effect a return to and reworking of classicism, following
the rejection of the past, as exemplified by the preceding movement
known as modernism. One of the most important skyscrapers to be
erected in New York City in recent years is topped by a broken pediment
that is inspired by the designs of the eighteenth-century English furniture
maker Thomas Chippendale, who was himself inspired by the design of
a classical temple. The entrance to the new extension to the Tate Gallery
in London designed by Sir James Stirling is also based on a simplified
outline of a temple.

A more literal example of the influence of Greek architecture is the
reconstructed Parthenon in Nashville, Tennessee. Built of concrete and
gravel from the Potomac River, it is an exact copy of the original. In 1990
it acquired a forty-foot-high replica of the gold and ivory statue of
Athena by Pheidias, made out of concrete and fiberglass. As Umberto

Eco has said, "The post-modern reply to the modern consists of recognising that the past, since it cannot fully be destroyed, because its destruction leads to silence must be re-visited: but with irony, not innocently" (quoted in Taplin, *Greek Fire*, p. 25). In upstate New York I reside between towns called Ithaca and Ilion, and not much more than 26 miles from another town called Marathon.

Nor is the influence of Greek culture an exclusively Western phenomenon. Thanks to the conquests of Alexander the Great, Greek influence spread as far east as northern Afghanistan and the Indian subcontinent. Sculpture from Gandhara in northwest Pakistan, which laid the foundations for representations of the Buddha, was profoundly influenced by the canons of Greek sculpture.

THE CRADLE OF DEMOCRACY

And yet we should be careful not to go too far. It is all too easy—and tendentious—to claim an unbroken tradition from antiquity to the modern day. Consider the following editorial which appeared in a center-left Greek newspaper called *Ethnos* in the summer of 1983:

> In this land of ours, throughout the centuries, the foundations of democracy were firmly laid by people determined to establish the right of the majority to manage freely their thought and activity. For the first time in the fifth century B.C., democracy shone and the basic principles governing society were established. Those principles were equality of rights, equality of political rights, equality of speech, and freedom of speech. . . . These four basic principles which have remained unchanged throughout the centuries should govern today all democratic regimes.

Although the sentiments expressed in this passage are not in dispute, we might question the accuracy of the claims. To begin with, the fifth-century democracy to which the editor alludes but does not mention by name is obviously that of Athens. Athens, however, was just one of over a hundred city-states, the majority of which were ruled by oppressive oligarchies. It was not the case, therefore, that democracy "shone" throughout the Greek world. Far from it. As for "the right of the majority to manage freely their affairs"—well, that is only true if one omits the slaves, the metics, the women, and of course the children—well over half the population. We might even raise questions about the claim of freedom of speech, at least in the case of Sokrates, who was accused of corrupting the youth. Though we cannot know precisely what was meant by this obscure charge, it evidently referred primarily to his teachings.

There are other errors in the passage. The phrase "In this land of ours" refers, of course, to modern Greece. But modern Greece has been a nation-state only since 1833, and it is questionable, to say the least, whether the principles of democracy "remained unchanged throughout the centuries." For most of their history the people whom we call Greeks have been denied democracy; that is to say, through the period of the Macedonian empire (150 years), the Roman empire (500 years), the Byzantine empire (1,100 years), the Ottoman empire (400 years), the Greek monarchy (on and off about 100 years), the fascist dictatorship of General Metaxas (1936–1941), and the rule of the Colonels (1967–1974).

For more than a thousand years, democracy completely died out, not only in Greece, but throughout the whole of Europe. The roots of our modern democratic systems have much more to do with feudalism and the medieval republics which directly preceded them than they do with fifth-century B.C. Athens.

Problems of historical fact have not, however, deterred serious scholars from seeking to establish an unbroken democratic chain from antiquity to the present. In 1993 numerous celebrations were held in both America and Britain to mark the twenty-five-hundredth anniversary of the so-called "birth" of democracy—2,500 years, that is, since Kleisthenes carried out his reforms. These celebrations begged another important question besides that of continuity: whether the origins of a process as complex as democracy can legitimately be pinned down to a single year and to a single historical personage. Situating the birth of democracy in 507 B.C. is ignoring the fact that a democratic tendency had been present in Athenian society long before Kleisthenes came to power.

OUR SO-CALLED CLASSICAL ROOTS: THE CONTROVERSY OVER *BLACK ATHENA*

The study of classical antiquity is also in the forefront of our current concerns about racism, cultural imperialism, and the like. In 1987 Martin Bernal wrote a book called *Black Athena*, which investigated the origins of Greek culture. Bernal came to the conclusion that there had been a willful conspiracy of silence on the part of eighteenth- and nineteenth-century ancient historians, who ignored or, at any rate, minimized the contribution made to Greek culture by the African and Semitic races. He then attempted to demonstrate the contributions made by these races to the origins of Greek culture by appealing to etymology, mythology, and so on. Bernal's hypothesis that earlier generations of classical scholars underplayed the contribution made by the African and Semitic races has some merit, though his claim to be able to detect an "Aryan model of Greek culture" propounded by nineteenth-century scholars carries little weight. Nor is it true that contemporary scholars are reluctant to ignore the contribution of Egyptian and Near Eastern cultures to Greek culture, though they do not, for the most part, consider their contribution to have been overriding.

Even so, few classical scholars would concede that the African contribution was made by the black African races, and that is where the heart of the controversy lies. With the recent publication of Mary Lefkowitz's response to Bernal, entitled *Not out of Africa*, the debate has become so politicized that rational discourse between the two camps has become almost impossible. Yet, if it has achieved nothing else, it has at least demonstrated the continuing importance of classical antiquity.

Such is the enduring status of Greek culture in the West that cultural descent has come to be regarded almost as a precondition to cultural identity.

Glossary of Greek Terms

Greek terms that commonly exist in English are Anglicized.

acropolis citadel (literally "high city"); when capitalized, the citadel of Athens

agôgê Spartan public education system

agora market place, civic center; when capitalized, the market place of Athens

andrôn dining room (literally "men's quarters")

apella Spartan assembly

archon magistrate

asty urban center of a polis

Attica territory of the Athenian state

aulos wind instrument similar to the oboe

barathron pit into which condemned criminals were hurled to their death

barbarian non-Greek speaker, foreigner

boulê council

cella central room of a temple

centaur mythological creature half-human and half-horse

chitôn ankle-length linen garment worn by women

chôra territory owned by a polis

colony an independent foundation sent out by a mother-city

dêmos people, citizen body; deme or village

Dionysia festival in honor of Dionysos at which tragedies were performed

drachma silver coin equivalent to a day's pay in the late fifth century B.C.

ekklêsia legislative assembly consisting of the citizen body

ekphora the transporting of the body from the house to the place of burial

ephebe Athenian cadet

ephor one of five Spartan magistrates

ethnos racial group

eunomia "obedience to the law" (used of Spartan military discipline)

exômis poor man's garment worn over the shoulder

genos noble kin group

gerousia Spartan council of elders

gymnasium exercise ground

gynaikeion women's quarters

hêliaia law court or meeting of Athenian citizens to hear a legal case

helot state-owned Spartan slave

herm image of the god Hermes consisting of head and genitalia

hetaira courtesan (literally "female companion")

himation woollen cloak worn by both men and women

hippeis cavalry

hippodrome horse track

homoios Spartan peer or citizen

hoplite heavy-armed infantryman

hoplon round bronze shield carried by hoplites

Kerameikos cemetery in Athens

kithara stringed instrument resembling a modern guitar

klêros apportionment of land

klinê couch or bed

klismos chair

koinê Greek dialect that became universal in Hellenistic Period

kômos band of revelers

krypteia Spartan organization resembling a secret police

liturgy the subsidizing of important public programs by wealthy citizens or metics

metic resident alien

mina unit of currency worth 100 drachmas

obol coin worth one-sixth of a drachma

oikia, oikos household

orchêstra circular dancing floor

ostracism Athenian procedure by which a leading politician was sent into exile for ten years

ostrakon potsherd, broken piece of pottery; ballot for ostracism

paidagôgos　slave who accompanied a boy outside the home
paidotribês　athletic trainer
palaistra　wrestling school
pallakê　common-law wife
Panathenaia　the major Athenian festival in honor of Athena
pankration　combination of all-out boxing and wrestling
pediment　triangular gable surmounting a temple
peplos　ankle-length woollen garment worn by women
peristyle　colonnade surrounding a building or court on all four sides
phratria　subdivision of citizen body (literally "brotherhood")
phylê　tribe
polis　city-state
politês　citizen
prothesis　the laying out of the dead
prytany　executive committee of the Athenian state
sophist　itinerant teacher of rhetoric
stade　distance of about 210 yards
stadium　running track
symposium　drinking party
synhedrion　council of Greek city-states established by Philip II
syrinx　wind instrument consisting of a number of pipes bound together
syssition　Spartan dining club
thês　member of the lowest economic group; hired worker
trireme　three-banked warship
tropaion　trophy erected on the battlefield after a victory
tyrant　self-appointed ruler of a state

For Further Reading

TRANSLATIONS OF SELECTED GREEK TEXTS
(in alphabetical order of Greek authors)

Aeschylus: The Oresteia. Translated by R. Fagles. Introduction and notes by R. Fagles and W. B. Stanford. New York: Penguin Books and Viking Press, 1979.

Archestratus: The Life of Luxury. Translated with introduction and commentary by J. Wilkins and S. Hill. Devon, U.K.: Prospect Books, 1994.

Aristophanes' Acharnians. Translation, introduction, and notes by J. Henderson. Bristol, U.K.: Bristol Classical Press and Focus Publishing, 1992.

Aristophanes' Clouds. Translation, introduction, and notes by J. Henderson. Bristol, U.K.: Bristol Classical Press and Focus Publishing, 1993.

Aristophanes' Lysistrata. Translation, introduction, and notes by J. Henderson. Bristol, U.K.: Bristol Classical Press and Focus Publishing, 1988.

Aristotle, The Politics. Translation by T. A. Sinclair. Revised by T. J. Saunders. Harmondsworth, U.K.: Penguin Books, 1981.

Euripides' Bacchae. Translation, introduction, and notes by S. Esposito. Bristol, U.K.: Bristol Classical Press and Focus Publishing, 1997.

Euripides' Medea. Translation, introduction, and notes by A. Podlecki. Bristol, U.K.: Bristol Classical Press and Focus Publishing, 1991.

Herodotus: The Histories. Translated by A. de Sélincourt. Revised translation and notes by J. Marincola. New York: Penguin Books and Viking Press, 1996.

Hesiod: Works and Days and Theogony. Translated by S. Lombardo with introduction by R. Lamberton. Indianapolis: Hackett Publishing, 1993.

Hesiod's Theogony. Translation, introduction, and notes by R. Caldwell. Bristol, U.K.: Bristol Classical Press and Focus Publishing, 1987.

Hippocratic Writings. Translated by J. Chadwick and W. N. Mann. Edited with introduction by G. E. R. Lloyd. New York: Penguin Books and Viking Press, 1978.

The History: Herodotus. Translated by D. Grene. Chicago: University of Chicago Press, 1987.

Homer: The Iliad. Translated by R. Fagles. Introduction and notes by B. Knox. New York: Penguin Books and Viking Press, 1990.

Homer: The Odyssey. Translated by R. Fagles. Introduction and notes by B. Knox. New York: Penguin Books and Viking Press, 1996.

Homeric Hymns. Translation, introduction, and notes by A. Podlecki. Bristol, U.K.: Bristol Classical Press and Focus Publishing, 1991.

Homer's Odyssey: A Companion to the Translation of Richmond Lattimore. Introduction and notes by P. V. Jones. Carbondale: Southern Illinois University Press, 1988.

The Iliad of Homer. Translated by R. Lattimore. Chicago: University of Chicago Press, 1951.

The Landmark Thucydides: A Comprehensive Guide to the Peloponnesian War. Translated by R. Crawley. Edited by R. B. Strassler. Introduction by V. D. Hanson. New York: Free Press, 1996.

The Odyssey of Homer. Translated by R. Lattimore. New York: Harper and Row, 1967.

Plato: Complete Works. Edited by J. M. Cooper. Indianapolis: Hackett Publishing, 1993.

Plato's Symposium. Translation and introduction by A. Sharon. Bristol, U.K.: Bristol Classical Press and Focus Publishing, 1991.

Select Papyri vols. 1–2. Translated by A. S. Hunt and C. C. Edgar. London and New York: Loeb Classical Library, 1932.

Sophocles' Oedipus at Colonus. Translation, introduction, and notes by M. Blundell. Bristol, U.K.: Bristol Classical Press and Focus Publishing, 1991.

Sophocles: The Three Theban Plays. Translated by R. Fagles. Introduction by B. Knox. New York: Penguin Books and Viking Press, 1986.

Soranus' Gynaecology. Translated by O. Temkin. Baltimore, Md.: Johns Hopkins University Press, 1991.

Three Plays by Aristophanes: Staging Women. Translation, introduction, and notes by J. Henderson. New York: Routledge, 1996.

Thucydides: The Peloponnesian War. Translated by R. Warner. Introduction and notes by M. I. Finley. New York: Penguin Books and Viking Press, 1972.

ANTHOLOGIES OF TRANSLATIONS OF GREEK TEXTS

Greek Lyric: An Anthology in Translation. Translated with introduction by A. M. Miller. Indianapolis: Hackett Publishing, 1996.

Greek Lyric Poetry. Translated by W. Barnstone. New York: Schocken Books, 1972.

Greek Orations: 4th Century B.C. Translation with introduction by W. R. Connor. Prospect Heights, Ill.: Waveland Press, 1987.

The Murder of Herodes and Other Trials from the Athenian Law Courts. Translated with introduction by K. Freeman. Indianapolis: Hackett Publishing, 1994.

REFERENCE WORKS

Civilization of the Ancient Mediterranean. Edited by M. Grant and R. Kitzinger. 3 vols. New York: Charles Scribner's Sons, 1988.

The Oxford Classical Dictionary. Edited by S. Hornblower and A. J. Spawforth. 3d edition. Oxford: Oxford University Press, 1996.

The Penguin Dictionary of Ancient History. Edited by G. Speake. Harmondsworth, Middlesex, U.K.: Penguin Books, 1995.

GENERAL

Adcock, F. E. *The Greek and Macedonian Art of War*. Berkeley: University of California Press, 1967.

Amundsen, D. W. *Medicine, Society, and Faith in the Ancient and Medieval Worlds*. Baltimore, Md.: Johns Hopkins University Press, 1996.

Baldock, M. *Greek Tragedy: An Introduction*. Bristol, U.K.: Bristol Classical Press and Focus Publishing, 1989.

Baldry, H. C. *The Greek Tragic Theatre*. London: Chatto and Windus, 1978.

Barrow, R. *Athenian Democracy: The Triumph and the Folly*. Surrey, U.K.: Thomas Nelson, 1992.

———. *Greek and Roman Education*. Basingstoke, U.K.: Macmillan, 1976.

Beck, F. A. *Greek Education 450–350 BC*. London: Methuen, 1962.

Bernal, M. *Black Athena: The Afroasiatic Roots of Classical Civilization*. New Brunswick, N.J.: Rutgers University Press, 1987.

Bickerman, E. *Chronology of the Ancient World*. Revised ed. London: Thames and Hudson, 1980.

Biers, W. R. *The Archaeology of Greece*. 2d edition. Ithaca, N.Y.: Cornell University Press, 1996.

Boardman, J. *Greek Art*. Revised edition. London: Thames and Hudson, 1973.

———. *Greek Sculpture: The Classical Period*. London: Thames and Hudson, 1985.

Boardman, J., ed. *The Oxford History of Classical Art*. Oxford: Oxford University Press, 1997.

Boardman, J., J. Griffin, and O. Murray, eds. *The Oxford History of the Classical World*. Oxford: Oxford University Press, 1986.

Bonnefoy, Y., ed. *Greek and Egyptian Mythologies*. Translated by W. Doniger, et al. Chicago: University of Chicago Press, 1991.

Bremmer, J. *The Early Greek Concept of the Soul*. Princeton, N.J.: Princeton University Press, 1983.

Bronowski, J. *The Ascent of Man*. London: British Broadcasting Corporation, 1973.

Burford, A. *Land and Labor in the Greek World*. Baltimore, Md.: Johns Hopkins University Press, 1993.

Burkert, W. *Ancient Mystery Cults*. Cambridge, Mass.: Harvard University Press, 1987.

———. *Greek Religion*. Oxford: Basil Blackwell, 1985.

Buxton, R. *Imaginary Greece: The Contexts of Mythology*. Cambridge, U.K.: Cambridge University Press, 1994.

Cameron, A., and A. Kuhrt, eds. *Images of Women in Antiquity*. London: Croom Helm, 1983.

Camp, J. M. *The Athenian Agora: Excavations in the Heart of Classical Athens*. London: Thames and Hudson, 1986.

Cantarella, E. *Pandora's Daughters: The Role and Status of Women in Greek and Roman Antiquity*. Translated by M. Fant. Baltimore, Md.: Johns Hopkins University Press, 1987.

Carpenter, T. H. *Art and Myth in Ancient Greece*. London: Thames and Hudson, 1991.

Cartledge, P. *Aristophanes and His Theatre of the Absurd*. Bristol, U.K.: Bristol Classical Press and Focus Publishing, 1990.

———. *The Greeks*. Oxford: Oxford University Press, 1993.

Casson, L. *Ships and Seamanship in the Ancient World*. Princeton, N.J.: Princeton University Press, 1971.

———. *Travel in the Ancient World*. Baltimore, Md.: Johns Hopkins University Press, 1994.

Chadwick, J. *Linear B and Related Scripts*. London and Berkeley: British Museum Publications and University of California Press, 1987.

Clark, G. *Women in the Ancient World*. Oxford: Oxford University Press, 1989.

Cook, R. M. *Greek Art: Its Development, Character and Influence*. Harmondsworth, Middlesex, U.K.: Penguin Books, 1972.

Dalby, A., and S. Grainger. *The Classical Cookbook*. Getty Trust Publications. Oxford: Oxford University Press, 1996.

Dasen, V. *Dwarfs in Ancient Egypt and Greece*. Oxford: Oxford University Press, 1994.

Davies, J. K. *Democracy and Classical Greece*. London and Stanford, Calif.: Fontana and Stanford University Press, 1986.

Davies, N. *Europe: A History*. Oxford: Oxford University Press, 1996.

de Ste. Croix, G.E.M. *The Class Struggle in the Ancient Greek World*. London and Ithaca, N.Y.: Gerald Duckworth and Cornell University Press, 1988.

———. *The Origins of the Peloponnesian War*. London: Gerald Duckworth, 1972.

Dean-Jones, L. *Women's Bodies in Classical Greek Science*. Oxford: Oxford University Press, 1994.

Deighton, H. *A Day in the Life of Ancient Athens*. Bristol, U.K.: Bristol Classical Press and Focus Publishing, 1995.

Demand, N. *Birth, Death, and Motherhood in Classical Greece*. Baltimore, Md.: Johns Hopkins University Press, 1994.

———. *A History of Ancient Greece*. New York: McGraw-Hill, 1996.

Dodds, E. R. *The Greeks and the Irrational*. Berkeley: University of California Press, 1951.

Dover, K. J. *Greek Homosexuality*. London: Gerald Duckworth, 1978.

———. *Greek Popular Morality in the Time of Plato and Aristotle*. Oxford: Basil Blackwell, 1974.

———. *The Greeks*. Austin: University of Texas Press, 1961.

Drews, R. *The End of the Bronze Age: Changes in Warfare and the Catastrophe ca. 1200 BC*. Princeton, N.J.: Princeton University Press, 1996.

Ducrey, P. *Warfare in Ancient Greece*. Translated by J. Lloyd. New York: Schocken Books, 1986.

Dunmore, C. W. *Studies in Etymology*. Bristol, U.K.: Bristol Classical Press and Focus Publishing, 1993.

Easterling, P. E., and J. V. Muir. *Greek Religion and Society*. Cambridge, U.K.: Cambridge University Press, 1985.

Edelstein, L. *Ancient Medicine*. Revised edition. Baltimore, Md.: Johns Hopkins University Press, 1967.

Etienne, R., and F. Etienne. *The Search for Ancient Greece*. New York and London: Harry N. Abrams and Thames and Hudson, 1990.

Falkner, T. F., and J. de Luce, eds. *Old Age in Greek and Latin Literature*. Albany: State University of New York Press, 1989.

Fantham, E., H. P. Foley, N. B. Kampen, S. Pomeroy, and H. A. Shapiro. *Women in the Classical World: Image and Text*. Oxford: Oxford University Press, 1994.

Faraone, C. A., and D. Obbink, eds. *Magika Hiera: Ancient Greek Magic and Religion*. Oxford: Oxford University Press, 1991.

Ferguson, J. *Among the Gods: An Archaeological Exploration of Ancient Greek Religion*. London: Routledge, 1989.

———. *Morals and Values in Ancient Greece*. Bristol, U.K.: Bristol Classical Press and Focus Publishing, 1989.

Ferguson, J., and K. Chisholm. *Political and Social Life in the Great Age of Athens*. London: Ward Lock, 1978.

Finley, M. I. *The Ancient Economy*. London: Chatto and Windus, 1973.

———. *The Ancient Greeks*. New York: Penguin Books and Viking Press, 1963.

———. *Ancient Slavery and Modern Ideology*. London: Chatto and Windus, 1980.

———. *Early Greece: The Bronze and Archaic Ages*. London: Chatto and Windus, 1970.

———. *The Legacy of Greece: A New Appraisal*. Oxford: Oxford University Press, 1981.

———. *The Olympic Games: The First Thousand Years*. London: Chatto and Windus, 1976.

———. *The World of Odysseus*. 2d revised edition. Harmondsworth, Middlesex, U.K.: Penguin Books, 1978.

Fisher, N.R.E. *Slavery in Classical Greece*. Bristol, U.K.: Bristol Classical Press and Focus Publishing, 1993.

———. *Social Values in Classical Athens*. London: J. M. Dent and Sons, 1976.

Forrest, W. G. *A History of Sparta*. London: Gerald Duckworth, 1968.

Fox, R. L. *Alexander the Great*. London: Futura Publications, 1975.

Frost, F. J. *Greek Society*. 5th edition. Boston: Houghton Mifflin, 1997.

Gagarin, M. *Early Greek Law*. Berkeley: University of California Press, 1989.

Gantz, T. *Early Greek Myth: A Guide to Literary and Artistic Sources*. Baltimore, Md.: Johns Hopkins University Press, 1993.

Gardiner, E. N. *Athletics of the Ancient World*. Reprint of 1930 edition. Chicago: Ares Publishers, 1978.

———. *Greek Athletic Sports and Festivals*. London: Macmillan, 1970.

Garlan, Y. *Slavery in Ancient Greece*. Translated by J. Lloyd. Ithaca, N.Y.: Cornell University Press, 1982.

———. *War in the Ancient World: A Social History*. London: Chatto and Windus, 1975.

Garland, R.S.J. _The Eye of the Beholder: Deformity and Disability in the Graeco-Roman World_. London and Ithaca, N.Y.: Gerald Duckworth and Cornell University Press, 1995.

————. _The Greek Way of Death_. London and Ithaca, N.Y.: Gerald Duckworth and Cornell University Press, 1985.

————. _The Greek Way of Life: From Conception to Old Age_. London and Ithaca, N.Y.: Gerald Duckworth and Cornell University Press, 1990.

————. _The Piraeus: From the Fifth to the First Century BC_. London and Ithaca, N.Y.: Gerald Duckworth and Cornell University Press, 1987.

————. _Religion and the Greeks_. Bristol, U.K.: Bristol Classical Press and Focus Publishing, 1994.

Garnsey, P. _Famine and Food Supply in the Graeco-Roman World_. Cambridge, U.K.: Cambridge University Press, 1988.

Garnsey, P., C. R. Whittaker, and K. Hopkins. _Trade in the Ancient Economy_. London: Chatto and Windus, 1983.

Glotz, G. _Ancient Greece at Work_. Translated by M. R. Dobie. New York: W. W. Norton, 1927.

Godwin, J. _Mystery Religions in the Ancient World_. London: Thames and Hudson, 1981.

Golden, M. _Children and Childhood in Classical Athens_. Baltimore, Md.: Johns Hopkins University Press, 1990.

Graf, F. _Greek Mythology: An Introduction_. Translated by T. Marier. Baltimore, Md.: Johns Hopkins University Press, 1993.

Green, J. R. _Theatre in Ancient Greek Society_. New York: Routledge, 1996.

Green, P. _Alexander to Actium_. Berkeley: University of California Press, 1990.

————. _The Greco-Persian Wars_. Berkeley: University of California Press, 1996.

Grimal, P. _Dictionary of Classical Mythology_. Translated by A. R. Maxwell-Hyslop. Harmondsworth, Middlesex, U.K.: Penguin Books, 1990.

Grmek, M. D. _Diseases in the Ancient World_. Translated by M. Muellner and L. Muellner. Baltimore, Md.: Johns Hopkins University Press, 1989.

Halperin, D. M., J. J. Winkler, and F. I. Zeitlin. _Before Sexuality: The Construction of Erotic Experience in the Greek World_. Princeton, N.J.: Princeton University Press, 1990.

Hammond, N.G.L. _A History of Greece to 322 BC_. 3d edition. Oxford: Oxford University Press, 1986.

Hanson, V. D., and J. Keegan. _The Western Way of War: Infantry Battle in Classical Greece_. Oxford: Oxford University Press, 1990.

Harris, H. A. _Greek Athletes and Athletics_. London: Hutchinson, 1964.

————. _Sport in Greece and Rome_. London: Thames and Hudson, 1972.

Harris, S. L., and G. Platzner. _Classical Mythology: Images and Insights_. Mountain View, Calif.: Mayfield Publishing, 1995.

Harris, W. V. _Ancient Literacy_. Cambridge, Mass.: Harvard University Press, 1989.

Harrison, A.R.W. _The Law of Athens: Family and Property_. Oxford: Clarendon Press, 1968.

Hartong, F. _The Mirror of Herodotus_. Berkeley: University of California Press, 1988.

Hasebroek, J. _Trade and Politics in Ancient Greece_. London: G. Bell, 1933.

Hawley, R., and B. Levick. _Women in Antiquity_. London: Routledge, 1995.

Higgins, R. _Greek and Roman Jewellery_. London: Methuen, 1980.

Highet, G. *The Classical Tradition: Greek and Roman Influences on Western Literature.* Oxford: Oxford University Press, 1949.

Hope, T. *Costumes of the Greeks and Romans.* New York: Dover, 1962.

Hopper, R. J. *Trade and Industry in Ancient Greece.* London: Thames and Hudson, 1979.

Hornblower, S. *The Greek World 479–323 BC.* London: Methuen, 1983.

Hughes, J. D. *Environmental Problems of the Ancient Greeks and Romans.* Baltimore, Md.: Johns Hopkins University Press, 1996.

Jenkins, G. K. *Ancient Greek Coins.* 2nd revised ed. 1990.

Jenkins, I., and S. Bird. *An Athenian Childhood.* London: British Museum Publications, 1982.

———. *Greek Dress.* Greek and Roman Daily Life Series no. 3. London: British Museum Education Service, n.d.

———. *Greek Music.* Greek and Roman Daily Life Series no. 4. London: British Museum Education Service, n.d.

Just, R. *Women in Athenian Law and Life.* London: n.p., 1981.

Kagan, D. *The Outbreak of the Peloponnesian War.* Ithaca, N.Y.: Cornell University Press, 1969.

———. *The Peace of Nicias and the Sicilian Expedition.* Ithaca, N.Y.: Cornell University Press, 1981.

Kebric, R. B. *Greek People.* 2d edition. Mountain View, Calif.: Mayfield Publishing, 1997.

Kirkwood, G. M. *A Short Guide to Classical Mythology.* Reprint of 1959 edition. Wauconda, Ill.: Bolchazy-Carducci Publishers, 1995.

Klein, A. *Child Life in Greek Art.* New York: Columbia University Press, 1932.

Knox, B. *Essays Ancient and Modern.* Baltimore, Md.: Johns Hopkins University Press, 1990.

Kraay, C. M. *Archaic and Classical Greek Coins.* Berkeley: University of California Press, 1976.

Kurtz, D. C., and J. Boardman. *Greek Burial Customs.* London: Thames and Hudson, 1971.

Lacey, W. K. *The Family in Ancient Greece.* London: Thames and Hudson, 1968.

Lawrence, A. W. *Greek Architecture.* 5th edition. Revised by R. A. Tomlinson. New Haven, Conn.: Yale University Press, 1996.

Lefkowitz, M. *Not out of Africa: How Afrocentrism Became an Excuse to Teach Myth as History.* New York: HarperCollins, 1996.

———. *Women in Greek Myth.* London: Gerald Duckworth, 1986.

Lefkowitz, M. R., and M. B. Fant. *Women's Life in Greece and Rome: A Source Book in Translation.* London and Baltimore, Md.: Gerald Duckworth and Johns Hopkins University Press, 1992.

Lefkowitz, M., and G. M. Rogers. *Black Athena Revisited.* Chapel Hill: University of North Carolina Press, 1996.

Levi, P. *Atlas of the Greek World.* New York: Facts on File (Equinox Books), 1995.

Lissarrague, F. *The Aesthetics of the Greek Banquet.* Princeton, N.J.: Princeton University Press, 1991.

Luck, G. *Arcana Mundi: Magic and the Occult in the Greek and Roman Worlds.* Baltimore, Md.: Johns Hopkins University Press, 1985.

MacDowell, D. M. *The Law in Classical Athens*. London: Thames and Hudson, 1978.

———. *Spartan Law*. Scottish Classical Studies no. 1. Edinburgh: Edinburgh University Press, 1986.

Marrou, H. I. *A History of Education in Antiquity*. London: Sheed and Ward, 1956.

Martin, T. R. *Ancient Greece: From Prehistoric to Hellenistic Times*. New Haven, Conn.: Yale University Press, 1996.

McAuslan, I., and P. Walcot. *Women in Antiquity*. Oxford: Oxford University Press, 1996.

Meiggs, R. *The Athenian Empire*. Oxford: Oxford University Press, 1979.

Meijer, F., and O. van Nijf. *Trade, Transport and Society in the Ancient World: A Sourcebook*. London: Routledge, 1992.

Melas, E. *Temples and Sanctuaries of Ancient Greece*. Translated by F. M. Brownjohn. London: Thames and Hudson, 1973.

Mikalson, J. *Athenian Popular Religion*. Chapel Hill: University of North Carolina Press, 1983.

Morris, I. *Death-Ritual and Social Structure in Classical Antiquity*. Cambridge, U.K.: Cambridge University Press, 1992.

Mossé, C. *The Ancient World at Work*. New York: W. W. Norton, 1969.

Murray, O. *Early Greece*. 2d edition. Cambridge, Mass.: Harvard University Press, 1993.

Murray, O., ed. *Sympotica: A Symposium on the Symposium*. Oxford: Oxford University Press, 1990.

Ober, J. *The Athenian Revolution: Essays on Ancient Greek Democracy and Political Theory*. Chicago: University of Chicago Press, 1997.

Olivová, V. *Sports and Games in the Ancient World*. London: Orbis, 1984.

Ormerod, H. A. *Piracy in the Ancient World*. Liverpool, U.K.: University of Liverpool Press, 1924.

Parke, H. W. *The Festivals of the Athenians*. London: Thames and Hudson, 1977.

———. *Greek Oracles*. London: Hutchinson University Library, 1967.

Parker, R. *Athenian Religion: A History*. Oxford: Clarendon Press, 1996.

———. *Miasma: Pollution and Purification in Early Greek Religion*. Oxford: Clarendon Press, 1983.

Peradotto, J., and M. Levine, eds. *Women in the Ancient World*. The Arethusa Papers 1984. Albany: State University of New York Press, 1984.

Pickard-Cambridge, A. *The Dramatic Festivals of Athens*. Revised by J. Gould and D. M. Lewis. Oxford: Oxford Clarendon Press, 1968.

Poliakoff, M. B. *Combat Sports in the Ancient World: Competition, Violence, and Culture*. New Haven, Conn.: Yale University Press, 1987.

Pollitt, J. J. *Art and Experience in Classical Greece*. Cambridge, U.K.: Cambridge University Press, 1972.

Pomeroy, S. *Families in Classical and Hellenistic Greece*. Oxford: Oxford University Press, 1997.

Richter, G. *The Furniture of the Greeks, Etruscans and Romans*. London: Phaidon Press, 1966.

Rider, B. C. *The Greek House: Its History and Development from the Neolithic to the Hellenistic Age*. Cambridge, U.K.: Cambridge University Press, 1965.

Robertson, D. S. *A Handbook of Greek and Roman Architecture.* 2d edition. Cambridge, U.K.: Cambridge University Press, 1945.

Robertson, M. *A Shorter History of Greek Art.* Cambridge, U.K.: Cambridge University Press, 1981.

Rohde, E. *Psyche: The Cult of Souls and Belief in Immortality among the Ancient Greeks.* Translated from 8th edition by W. B. Hillis. Chicago: Ares Publishers, 1987.

Roisman, J. *Alexander the Great: Ancient and Modern Perspectives.* Lexington, Mass.: D. C. Heath, 1995.

Sage, M. *Warfare in Ancient Greece: A Sourcebook.* New York: Routledge, 1996.

Sealey, R. *A History of the Greek City States, 700–388 BC.* Berkeley: University of California Press, 1976.

Sharwood Smith, J. *Greece and the Persians.* Bristol, U.K.: Bristol Classical Press and Focus Publishing, 1989.

Simon, E. *Festivals of Attica.* Madison: University of Wisconsin Press, 1983.

Slater, W. J. *Dining in a Classical Context.* Ann Arbor: University of Michigan Press, 1992.

Smith, J. A. *Athens under the Tyrants.* Bristol, U.K.: Bristol Classical Press and Focus Publishing, 1989.

Smith, R.R.R. *Hellenistic Sculpture: A Handbook.* London: Thames and Hudson, 1991.

Snodgrass, A. *Archaic Greece: The Age of Experiment.* London: J. M. Dent and Sons, 1980.

———. *Arms and Armour of the Greeks.* London and Ithaca, N.Y.: Thames and Hudson and Cornell University Press, 1967.

Sourvinou-Inwood, C. *"Reading" Greek Death: To the End of the Classical Period.* Oxford: Oxford University Press, 1995.

Soyer, A. *The Pantropheon or a History of Food and Its Preparation in Ancient Times.* Boston: Ticknor, Reed, and Fields, 1983.

Starr, C. G. *The Ancient Greeks.* Oxford: Oxford University Press, 1971.

———. *The Influence of Sea Power on Ancient History.* Oxford: Oxford University Press, 1988.

Stewart, A. *Greek Sculpture: An Exploration.* New Haven, Conn.: Yale University Press, 1990.

Stone, I. F. *The Trial of Socrates.* New York: Anchor Books, 1989.

Strassler, R. B. *The Landmark Thucydides: A Comprehensive Guide to the Peloponnesian War.* New York: Free Press, 1996.

Strauss, B. S. *Fathers and Sons in Athens.* Princeton, N.J.: Princeton University Press, 1993.

Swaddling, J. *The Ancient Olympic Games.* London: British Museum Publications, 1980.

Sweet, W. E. *Sport and Recreation in Ancient Greece: A Sourcebook with Translations.* Oxford: Oxford University Press, 1987.

Taplin, O. *Greek Fire.* London: Jonathan Cape, 1989.

———. *Greek Tragedy in Action.* London: Methuen, 1978.

Todd, S. C. *Athens and Sparta.* Bristol, U.K.: Bristol Classical Press and Focus Publishing, 1996.

———. *The Shape of Athenian Law.* Oxford: Clarendon Press, 1995.

Tomlinson, R. A. *Greek Architecture*. Bristol, U.K.: Bristol Classical Press and Focus Publishing, 1989.

Travlos, J. N. *A Pictorial Dictionary of Athens*. London: Thames and Hudson, 1971.

Tsigakou, F.-M. *The Rediscovery of Greece: Travellers and Painters of the Romantic Era*. New York and London: Caratzas and Thames and Hudson, 1981.

Vermeule, E. *Aspects of Death in Early Greek Art and Poetry*. Berkeley: University of California Press, 1979.

———. *Greece in the Bronze Age*. Chicago: University of Chicago Press, 1972.

Vernant, J.-P., ed. *The Greeks*. Chicago: University of Chicago Press, 1995.

Walbank, F. W. *The Hellenistic World*. London and Stanford, Calif.: Fontana and Stanford University Press, 1981.

Wardle, K., and D. Wardle. *Mycenaean Greece*. Bristol and Newburyport, U.K.: Bristol Classical Press and Focus Publishing, 1997.

West, M. L. *Ancient Greek Music*. Oxford: Clarendon Press, 1993.

Whitehead, D. *The Demes of Attica: 508/7–ca. 250 BC: A Political and Social Study*. Princeton, N.J.: Princeton University Press, 1986.

Wilkins, J., D. Harvey., and M. Dobson. *Food in Antiquity*. Exeter, U.K.: University of Exeter Press, 1995.

Wilkinson, L. P. *Classical Attitudes to Modern Issues*. London: William Kimber, 1978.

Williams, D., and J. Ogden. *Greek Gold: Jewellery of the Classical World*. New York: Abrams, 1994.

Woodford, S. *An Introduction to Greek Art*. London: Gerald Duckworth, 1986.

———. *The Trojan War in Ancient Art*. London: Gerald Duckworth, 1993.

Wycherley, R. E. *How the Greeks Built Cities*. 2d edition. London: Macmillan, 1962.

———. *The Stones of Athens*. Princeton, N.J.: Princeton University Press, 1978.

Zaidman, L. S., and P. Schmitt Pantel. *Religion in the Ancient Greek City*. Translated by P. Cartledge. Cambridge, U.K.: Cambridge University Press, 1992.

NOVELS

Among the most celebrated novels about Ancient Greece are those by M. Renault. They include *The Last of the Wine* (1956), *The Mask of Apollo* (1966), *The King Must Die* (1958), *The Bull from the Sea* (1962), *The Nature of Alexander* (1975), and *The Persian Boy* (1972).

MAGAZINES

A magazine called *Omnibus*, produced by the Joint Association of Classical Teachers, 31–34 Gordon Square, London WC1H OPY, intended primarily for high schools, contains many very useful articles on classical themes. Somewhat more sophisticated, but intended for the general reader, is a magazine called *History Today* (London), which occasionally includes articles on the ancient world.

VIDEOS

There are numerous videos now available about the Greek world. *Homer's Odyssey, The Greeks, The Athenian Trireme, Staging Classical Tragedy, The Role of*

Theatre in Ancient Greece, Applying the Lessons of Ancient Greece, and *In the Path of the Gods* are all published by Films for the Humanities and Sciences, P.O. Box 2053, Princeton, New Jersey 08543–2053 (tel. 1–800–257–5126; fax 609–275–3767). *Joseph Campbell and the Power of Myth* is a six-part PBS program series published by Doubleday (tel. 1–800–223–6834).

CD ROMS

Centaur Systems Ltd., 407 N. Brearly Street, Madison, Wisconsin 53703–1603 (tel. 1–800-CENTAUR; fax 608–255–6949) distributes a number of CD ROMs about classical Greece including *Olympia: 2800 Years of Athletic Games, Parthenon,* and *Grammar: Drills for Greek Students.* Perseus 2.0: Interactive Sources and Studies on Ancient Greece for Macintosh ® Computers. Editor in chief, G. Crane. Yale University Press, New Haven, Connecticut.

Index

About the Author

ROBERT GARLAND is the Roy D. and Margaret B. Professor of Classics at Colgate University. He is the author of a number of books on the ancient world, including *The Greek Way of Death* (1985), *The Piraeus* (1987), *The Greek Way of Life* (1990), *Religion and the Greeks* (1994), and *The Eye of the Beholder: Deformity and Disability in the Graeco-Roman World* (1995).